Dear Rick,

I hope that no one else has bought you this on the occassion of your move to Bangladesh. There appears to be a bit of a dearth of literature on the subject! Maybe you could write one?!

Anyhow, hope both this book & the experience are FANTASTIC. Look forward to seeing you very soon!

All the very best & thanks again for your kind hosting.

Lots of love Jane Tonbinon xxx

EXPATRIATE

Games

662 days in Bangladesh

by

Mark Trenowden

THE DERWENT PRESS

Derbyshire, England

www.derwentpress.com

Expatriate Games - 662 days in Bangladesh

© 1999 Mark Trenowden

All Rights Reserved

ISBN 1-84667-001-2

Cover art and book design by:
Pam Marin-Kingsley
www.far-angel.com

Published in 2005 by
The Derwent Press
Derbyshire, England
www.derwentpress.com

For Brenda, Teddy and India

acknowledgements

I wish to acknowledge my gratitude to Ian Trenowden for his advice and the following people for their support and contributions:

In England:

Brens, Teddy, India Jane, Mummy, Papa, Barrie, Dianne, Marcus, Riaz, Bridget, David, Elsie and Burlyboy.

In Bangladesh:

Feroz, Masum, Selim and poor Mr Momin (deceased) 'Abracadabra bin galle galle'

In India:

Peter, Sue, Aysha, Callum and Ethan

prologue

On the 26th May 2005 Javed Omar and Nafees Iqbal entered the Long Room of the Marylebone Cricket Club. The Marylebone Cricket Club (or MCC) is the home of the game, the international headquarters and custodian of the game's laws. For any cricketer, amateur or professional, this institution is the cricketing world's equivalent of Mecca. Imagine then the feelings of these two young men as they were ushered into this revered place by their team manager on this the first morning of their nation's first test match in England. A daunting scenario for a pair whose bellies doubtless contained their fair share of butterflies. A virtually silent welcome by the somewhat mature membership of MCC, broken by the squeak of pimpled soles on linoleum and the gentle sigh of the hinges of the door through which they entered closing behind them, and finally a somewhat restrained but polite ripple of applause from the men in red and yellow striped ties. However, shadowing them was a man who has seen much as a soldier, businessman and pillar of his country's sporting establishment. Sometime soldier, sometime international boxing referee, sometime proprietor of Dhaka's Security and Pest Control Company, Colonel Abdul Latif, Manager of the Bangladeshi Cricket Team. Here at this precise moment as a reassuring presence for the two young batsmen and a nice fatherly touch of his to accompany them on their traumatic entrance.

As fate would have it, on this morning I was propping up one of the Long Room's walls adjacent to one of the large windows that give a panoramic view of the playing area. From the door through which the Bangladeshi batsmen entered I might have been the first person that their eyes met with, had their heads not been securely helmeted and bowed with concentration. Colonel Latif, however, was not so distracted by his charges' predicament and as he surveyed the scene his eyes locked onto mine. An uncertain look of 'Don't I know that man over there in this land where I know no one?' gave way to one of mild astonishment before his features settled into a beaming smile.

'Mr Mark!' he boomed forgetting his young charges. With that he strode over and met me with as intimate an embrace as any man has ever given another. There was a momentary pause as he stood back to take in the moment of this remarkable meeting and then once again I was pressed to his chest so fondly that the aroma of garlic from a previous meal that hitherto presumably only Mrs Latif was aware of met my nostrils.

I have no record of how this scene was greeted by the membership of MCC, but I can only imagine that it met with a certain degree of consternation and a collective raising of greying eyebrows at this demonstrative and seemingly mistimed display of affection.

Having exchanged pleasantries, snapshots of children and promises to keep in touch, Colonel Latif's mobile rang calling him to whatever task the Team Manager was obliged to perform at this stage of the proceedings. As he left me, I gazed out on the luxurious expanse of London's most lovingly tended turf and reflected on the events of ten years ago when I had first made Latif's acquaintance in Dhaka, the capital of Bangladesh. My wife and I had met him and a host of other extraordinary, charming and wonderful characters on an adventure that we had embarked on with little knowledge of the country, an uneasy feeling about what we would encounter and certainly not the slightest notion of how things would pan out.

chapter one

The full impact of just what we were embarking on still hadn't struck me. As someone with a chronic, intense and increasingly desperate fear of flying, all I could think about was that I was about to subject myself to my worst nightmare.

The weeks prior to boarding our flight to Bombay had been jam-packed full of departure-related details: the letting of property, the packing and sealing of our material lives in a 20ft container already dispatched to our new home and, of course, my fear-of-flying course. The initial disbelief with which our friends greeted the news of our chosen destination was small beer compared to the reaction the fear-of-flying course prompted.  My Canadian wife, Brenda, then fiancée, fired with the doubtless good sense of having been brought up to confront one's fears, had enlisted me on our National Airlines Fear of Flying course. So with the goal of returning in one piece, clutching a certificate proclaiming that I was a reformed frightened flyer, I was bundled off to Heathrow and its environs. Doubtless a touchy, feely session of counselling on a one-to-one basis—followed by a quick run-down on how the wings are bolted on and a short practical demonstration—would cure me for life.

One hundred and eighty of us arrived at the Skyline Hotel—all of us, it can only be assumed, had been similarly misinformed. A hundred and eighty adults, each us bearing the sort of petrified look that Edvard Munch might have been proud of, shuffled into a conference room, resigned to the fact that in all likelihood this was their last day on earth. My initial horror-tinged reaction of incredulity to this unlikely scenario was similar to those who later heard the story: 'They put 180 people who were scared of flying on the same plane— now that I would have liked to have seen!'

As a prelude to this, for two hours we were lectured, kidded and assured that it was a miracle that aircraft ever remained on a runway even when stationary, let alone crash, so easy is it for them to become and remain airborne. This was followed by a session conducted by a psychologist who endeavoured to pigeonhole each and every one of us. Those who had never flown, those who had flown and who'd had a bad experience, and those who had flown and just didn't get on with it—which was my particular niche. This final group are apparently the really difficult ones to cure and since my views on flying hadn't changed one jot for all the calming words of our lecturers, I had to agree.

The analysis complete, a short drive took us to the airport—all of us, that is, except for one gentleman who never made it to the bus and was last seen jogging into the middle distance on his way to the car park. This was the second time the poor devil hadn't even made it on to the bus, a stewardess assured me with a sad shake of the head. For all my own doubts I *had* made it on to the bus and indeed was fortified by the problems others endured. Grown men in the departure lounge gazing into space in abject terror. A tiny white-haired old lady who, seemingly unruffled, was explaining to a fellow passenger that having never flown before she thought it a wise precaution to have a test run before embarking on that feat of endurance: a flight to the Antipodes. I took some solace from the fact that an oily youth clad from head to toe in black leather was able to weep openly whilst clutching an older woman and wailing an inaudible 'Muuummm.'

The pilots were charming and reassuring—solid, reliable types, acting as surrogate fathers to an extended brood. I had retreated behind a newspaper when one of them interrupted my attempt to pretend I wasn't there, and asked if I was all right. Any slight feelings of well-being that the pilot may have begun to engender in me were quickly dissipated by a rather raucous woman who broke into our conversation to point out—charitably enough, I suppose—that I was displaying all the signs the psychologist had described in that morning's session and 'Sorry for interrupting, but could the Captain assure her that there wouldn't be a bomb on board!'

With all that behind me, the course in the bag, the certificate clip framed and packed in the shipment, here I was ensconced in business class feeling decidedly self-conscious and wishing that I looked more the part. It was the young lady to my left who was the jetty businessperson and—if the truth be known I, an unemployed wine merchant, was only in the rarefied World of Club thanks to her. The adventure we were embarking on had seemed a gamble worth taking, an excellent opportunity for Brenda to improve her status and experience. An opportunity to save a wad of cash and, if all went according to our notional plan, a chance for me to find employment and broaden my own hitherto rather closeted experience of the London Fine Wine Trade. A national newspaper had found our situation of sufficient interest to produce a small article on Brenda. 'Going to work overseas' was the gist of the report, which was supplemented a couple of weeks later by my side of the story. A couple of column inches on 'Giving up gainful employment to follow your partner to the middle of nowhere', gleaned from a horribly misquoted telephone interview given down a crackling line from the sub-continent.

That I had survived to give this interview was largely due to the various precautions I had undertaken to ensure our safe passage: my ritual entry to the aircraft, giving the fuselage a surreptitious, reassuring pat as I crossed its threshold. The extra lift my vice-like grip had imparted through the armrests of my seat until the trauma of take-off had passed and the paraphernalia of business class had distracted me sufficiently. Some eight hours later the after-effects of my other precaution, that of drinking sufficient alcohol to render me unconscious, lent a sense of unreality to our predicament as we made our final approach to our destination. The adrenaline rush of the last agonising feet of our descent and the euphoria that filled me as my bottom sensed tarmac beneath the wheels helped bring me back to my senses. It was 1 June 1995 and the view through the aircraft window was India.

The last time I had set foot in Asia I had been a student. For twelve weeks I had backpacked round South-East Asia, setting off with a meagre sum lent to me by an aged aunt, and the comfort of a return ticket to sustain me. At the age of twenty, for me this was a big adventure and Asia a new and extraordinary experience. Any misgivings I might have had about my remote location were mitigated by the fact that as long as I made it back to Bangkok on September the whatever-it-was, then I would be home. Bigger, better, stronger, brimming with new knowledge and wisdom. Whether I had softened with age, I found that on arriving in India I had adopted a different mindset, one hitherto unexplored. The assault on the senses of the protracted drive into downtown Bombay crammed into a Hindustan Ambassador in pre-monsoon heat, however fascinating the plethora of sights, sounds and smells might be, stirred only one reaction in me. 'My God, this is where we are going to live for the next two years ... and this is the relatively cosmopolitan bit of the sub continent compared to what is to come'. Without wishing to do my sub-continental chums any injustice, it must be said that Bombay is pretty daunting to the uninitiated and even now, having gained a certain amount of Indian sub-continental street smartness, it can be a struggle.

This was not, however, our final destination. The stop in Bombay was our initiation and would serve two purposes: first, Brenda had been hired to help set up a branch office of an international investment bank from scratch, and our short stay in Bombay would provide Brenda with an opportunity to observe the fully functioning Bombay office; secondly it would provide us both with a chance to acclimatise physically, mentally and culturally. Having said this, we were hardly thrown in at the deep end and the prospect of two weeks at the Taj Mahal Hotel was an agreeable one.

Eager to find a friendly face, we lost no time in contacting a friend of a friend of Brenda's whose number we had managed to scavenge in London. This single lifeline put us in touch with an English girl, Cordelia, who by a bizarre twist of fate I had known in my early wine-trade years. She too was staying at the Taj and, as a resident of some sixteen months, she had become so much a part of the furniture that she was at liberty to use the hotel's kitchen as her own. The dampness behind our ears seemed exacerbated by her seasoning and when on our first evening we ventured out with her to a local fish restaurant, this 5ft 4inch woman was indeed a Titan in our eyes. Firmly putting all our trust in her, we hailed a taxi and sped off into the Bombay night.

One cannot visit a place like India without doing a little groundwork first. There are many well-observed, lyrical and erudite pieces on this complicated place. Much as I would love to have been swanning around gleaning information for a collection of poems entitled 'Mother India' or writing notes for a passable sequel to A Passage to India, this was survival training. The group of self-assured and blooded expats we encountered at the Sealion Seafood Restaurant were physical proof that it could be done and I hoped that soon it would be us on the other side of the table who would be ministering to the hopes and fears of baby expats.

'What sort of kit allowance have they given you?' my godfather, a retired personnel manager who had dispatched countless fresh-faced types to Africa, had enquired at a farewell lunch. I had had to admit that we had been given no such allowance, revealing the attitude of gay abandon that we had applied to the monetary side of things. In the end, even with this warning, we had set off with nothing more than a few hundred dollars and Brenda's American Express card. Unwittingly, however, a far more dangerous seed had been sown by our conversation. Dangerous, that is, for that strange breed of man that loves to shop and particularly so for one who will happily shop for anything, knows where to get it and how much for. I needed kit. Unfortunately, given the contents of my meagre bank account, my office in Knightsbridge was rather too well placed for the acquisition of 'kit' and soon I was the proud owner of all those things any self-respecting Englishman would need overseas. A cotton suit, cotton trousers, cotton everything, cool sunglasses, Panama hat, stout brogues, sensible shorts, amusing swimming trunks and shiny new cricket bat.

This assorted collection of possessions meant that I had a view, however jaundiced, of just what being an expat was going to be like. That first evening accompanied by Cordelia and assorted cronies sipping beer from silver tankards being ministered to by a bevy of waiters, we weren't a million miles from the picture in my mind's eye. It had been an enjoyable evening and we will always be grateful to Cordelia for the kindness she showed us, but couples are wont to analyse an evening, and the hypothesis we reached was that expats were pretty stuffy, and baby ones definitely not cool.

Day one, of course, is a fairly early stage to write everyone off and given time we too would become comfortable with our environment. Brenda's first day in the Bombay office added a new dimension to our status. Here were people who had to be nice to us or at least take an interest. This is not doing a disservice to anyone we met but when you're given a brief to meet so and so, show them around and take them out to dinner, then whether the person you look after has two heads or not, you have a certain obligation. Brenda's opposite number in the Bombay office was a girl of Eastern European descent named "Kasia", who had undoubtedly read the 1925 pamphlet on "How to Conduct Oneself in Foreign Parts" (if such a tome existed) and did so with relish. Kasia was a great help to Brenda in finding her feet in the company and, by virtue of an invitation to dinner, was to give us our first glimpse of how one might set up home overseas.

Real estate in Bombay is right up there in the world stakes for expensive square footage both in the commercial and residential sectors. It is a sobering thought that many Bombayans travel for two hours to and two hours from work. As such, Kasia's apartment next to the Taj and overlooking the Gateway to India in downtown Colaba was prime residential property. She was quite justly proud of her desirable residence and had been at pains to decorate it with a view to the past. For the wide-eyed expat babes, this was how we had envisaged our life overseas, but the story behind the serene scene was not so glamorous. The apartment had been stripped of years of old paint, wiring repaired, floor scraped and so on. Large numbers of small Indian gentlemen had camped overnight while the process of painstakingly sanding the doors inch-by-inch had been completed. This sort of project is not for the faint-hearted and the success of the whole transformation owed much to Kasia's eye for detail, patience and ultimately the deep pockets of her employer.

7

Dinner was served on the roof terrace by a small and unsmiling home help who was under no misapprehension of just who was the boss. We had known from the outset that we would need to acquire home help, but here it was in reality and you had to admit that it made entertaining a joy. It was a therapeutic evening as we sat overlooking the Arabia Sea, talking about London, drinking wine and later whisky. Our hostess disappeared into the apartment to put on some music, announcing loudly that her CD player had adopted sub-continental tendencies, working occasionally and not necessarily to the best of its ability. No apology was made for the selection of music—and perhaps it was rather over the top—but just at that moment in India, drink in hand, in the warm humid air, listening to the strains of Julie Andrews and *The Sound of Music*, life was good.

The two weeks in Bombay were over all too soon. In retrospect, with Brenda at work all day, I didn't make the most of our stay.

Frankly, India was all rather difficult.

Taxi-taking for me had become a major trauma. One was either buffeted about the sharp and bruising interior of these small black and yellow vehicles or accosted at traffic lights by beggars who at close quarters would brandish deformities in the face of unsuspecting new arrivals. My distrust of this mode of transport was further heightened by a trip made to Mahatma Gandhi's house when a metallic clunk announced the parting of the offside front wheel from its mounting. I had stepped unscathed from the listing vehicle and paid my driver, who announced with a cheery wave, that he would be back to take me home should I require it—an optimist indeed.

Despite the fact that no ergonomic expert was ever consulted on the design of these vehicles, taxi fares are extremely reasonable in Bombay, the average being 10–14 rupees (which translated then to around 25p). In my view the charges were sufficiently low that when overcharged I took the view that the man behind the wheel earned a lot less than me and as such I wouldn't begrudge him his ten or fifteen rupees over the odds. When I admitted to this in an unguarded moment to an acquaintance, I was left in no uncertain terms that this was not the way to conduct oneself. Overpaying was neither good for the driver nor for the rest of the paying public. I felt a traitor to everyone's cause and as a result whenever possible took to the streets on foot. Walking in Bombay pre-monsoon is not for the faint-hearted. Forget the grime and pollution—the heat is overpowering and any stops I made would demonstrate just how much my exertion was taking out of me. When I stopped at the Bombay Yacht Club to enquire about overseas membership, I should have been conferred a life membership on the spot—if gushing gallons of perspiration on to the secretary's desk was the qualification.

We would see India and Bombay again and in a more favourable light. For the meantime we were glad to head on to Hong Kong where Brenda would consult with various luminaries at her company's head office, prior to setting off for our final destination.

chapter two

Nine pieces of luggage is an awful lot for two people to lug around. With the bulk of our possessions floating about on the sea somewhere, we had tried to pack for every eventuality. For Brenda, this meant that we had to take a portable CD player, for me my cricket bat. The CD player turned out to be a very wise choice and slightly less controversial than the bat. In fact, as we departed for Hong Kong I was swiftly parted from it by an airline official who advised me that it was classified as a dangerous weapon and

that I would be reunited with it on landing. This turn of events at least gave me something other than the flight to worry about, although for anything to blot out a descent into Kai Tak airport, it would have to be something of even greater magnitude than the confiscation of my pride and joy.

However, positioning fingers in ears and screwing eyes tight shut can do a lot to aid the wary air traveller and, although this hadn't been suggested on the course, I had used it to good effect in the past. As we approached Hong Kong, the close proximity of the buildings to our metal tube was something for the pilot and the other passengers to worry about. I would never see them, in fact I was a few thousand miles away, as a hypnotherapist had suggested, walking out to bat. Taking guard from Jonesy (our umpire), with the reassuring feeling that at this stage of the game and with him marshalling the proceedings it would have to be the most comprehensible LBW ever bowled, for me to leave the wicket in that manner. No, my problem at the moment was: would my repertoire of shots be as varied as those executed in the pavilion against imagined wonderfully wayward bowling, or would it be one of those days when the well-intentioned defensive prod inexplicably became a cross-batted hoick?

Nope! no good, I would have to have a peek out of the window on our final approach.

With a couple of years still to go, propaganda regarding the handover of the colony to China was in evidence and everyone had a view. Brenda and I, however, were more preoccupied with surviving the stomach cramps and other attendant stomach-associated spectaculars that we had acquired in India. We sought out a doctor, whose prescribed treatment to take an exotic combination of pills and starve ourselves left us in a quandary. This being Hong Kong, where the varied international cuisine at every turn had provided us with the opportunity to go culinarily crazy before our departure, eating was not negotiable. The pills would have to suffice.

With our mind firmly in Asian mode, it was strange to be in Hong Kong with the tribes of white faces and British street signs that we had left behind just a couple of weeks before. It was all faintly reassuring. Like country mice visiting the city we were blinded by all Hong Kong had to offer and despite the fact that it was currently enjoying the status of being one of the most expensive places on earth to live in, frugality was not an option. We were the condemned. It was a case of four days of last blast prior to our departure and an opportunity for Brenda to exorcise the ghosts of having spent a year in Hong Kong as an intern with a big corporation eking out a living on a subsistence wage. There would be no skimping second time around.

The torrential downpour which greeted our departure could only make leaving easier. My initial fears that heavy rain might for some reason render jumbo jets immobile dissipated when the shocking news was broken to me that in fact we were taking two flights with a pit-stop, so to speak, at Bangkok. This was not good. One more take-off, one more landing, more hanging around. To be fair, Brenda had kept this information from me until the last moment to minimise the ordeal. While I wandered about the terminal with 'turmoil' writ large on my visage, Brenda was dealing with more pressing matters, namely that our luggage was over the limit and that the airline was demanding that we pay through the nose for the privilege of transporting it. Stopping just short of fisticuffs, Brenda remonstrated vehemently with an official from the airline. Good sense might have dictated that since we had passed unchallenged up to this point Brenda's argument was justified. As a long-suffering British subject, I meekly accept these annoyances and would rather be parted from my cash than make a fuss. However, my service-orientated Canadian companion would have nothing of it and after a very messy, not to mention loud, scene we eventually capitulated and set off for the departure lounge some 70 dollars poorer, Brenda spitting nails and resolving to get even, some day.

The announcement that 'We will be landing in about twenty minutes', I always receive with a certain amount of suspicion. Firstly twenty minutes is a very long time when you're frightened and it's invariably during these twenty minutes that the pilot puts the aircraft through all its most tortuous manoeuvres: the steep bank, the application of the air brakes and the undulating sensation of the descent, which to those of us with a nervous disposition feels more like being in a car on a steep hill without a brake pedal.

This particular aspect of this particular flight was made all the more interesting by the fact that there seemed to be very little or no land on which to set down our plane. Just small rural, residential circles of land isolated by muddy water, which are doubtless of great geographical and anthropological interest but not a lot of use to the pilot of a 747. On subsequent flights the landscape would be less alien, and we would be able to pick out areas of the city, the diplomatic area and even our apartment block. For now I was observing what I could see of Dhaka, the capital of Bangladesh, our new home, with deep suspicion. My reverie was broken by a rush of greenery appearing in the window and *blump* we were down on the far edge of the runway, the reverse thrust of the engine bringing us up sharply before we ploughed into a collection of antiquated aircraft and architecture mouldering in the outlying reaches of the airfield. It seemed unlikely that any of this equipment was still functional until we taxied round to face the main terminal building and a similarly decrepit line of hangars housing aircraft of the national airline came into view. With the prospect of some day having to fly out from this field, I viewed with some trepidation the dirty white, propeller-driven aircraft and the spindly, grimy men tinkering with them.

It can only be assumed that the architect who designed the terminal in Dhaka had only straight edges in his box of templates, such is the geometry of that building. It is however the most distinctive feature of the airport, leading one to conclude that a book entitled *Buildings of Distinction within the Airport Confines* would be a very short one indeed. Nevertheless our first impression as we descended the stairs into the immigration hall was that everything was fairly orderly, if rather spartan.

We were both already armed with visas, having undertaken the lengthy, problematic process in London which had required detailed qualification of just who our sponsors were to be in Dhaka. On the ground in Bangladesh a gentleman called 'Azizur Rahman' was hard at work fighting our corner. Liasing with the London authorities by fax and telephone, explaining just what it was Brenda was going to do and just why I was going too, why we had different names and why I needed a business visa when I had no job. The kinds of questions that would have solicited the kinds of answers from us that would have lost something in translation and slowed the process further. Finally after a number of visits to the Bangladeshi High Commission in London SW7, we had been presented with the precious documents and both decided that to query the fact that our £14 visas had cost us £30 was probably not a good idea.

Speaking of which, anyone seeking a glimpse of office life in Bangladesh should pop into the High Commission in London. A marvellous time capsule, circa 1950, sustained by piles of paper processed on typewriters. As well as an initiation into Bangladeshi bureaucracy, the High Commission had also given me an opportunity to sample the local media and I read the *Bangladesh Observer*, published in Dhaka, with interest and a certain amount of eyebrow raising. 'Hue and cry' in the streets, 'marauding mastans', 'the scurrilous activities of dacoits' and the shooting of a businessman while travelling to work on a rickshaw. . . and this was just the front page. One knows now that these things happen and if you are the unfortunate soul caught up in some such incident, then that—as my Muslim friends would say—is because 'God wills it.'

There is violence on the streets of New York, and I for one was convinced when I visited that city that a murder was being committed behind every window of those massive, dark and brooding apartment blocks. But, of course, it is the sensational that sells newspapers and as news of our plans to live in Bangladesh had filtered through to friends and relations the overriding reaction was one that had been fostered by isolated reporting. How could we possibly go to an impoverished Third World country with nothing but floods and cyclones to recommend it? How could their perception be anything else? 'It was a sunny day in Bangladesh yesterday and everyone just went about their own business' somehow doesn't make such good copy.

The news reports and general consensus were all rather academic now that we were on Bangladeshi soil and through immigration, waiting for our luggage while, to borrow Wilfred Owen's expression, a man 'sewn short at elbow' or in this case knee, walked the conveyor belt. This unfortunate fellow with truncated legs stuffed into surgical leather booties had all the qualifications for the job as he was able to clear the opening from conveyor to carousel without ducking. The macabre scene made me smile and one could sense the diminutive baggage-handler played to the crowd, up-ending suitcases and parcels with a flourish.

Our bags appeared one by one, and as we waited, a disembodied voice announced all those things that we were not permitted to bring into the country. All those things that one was most likely to secrete about one's person: 'gold bar', 'refrigerator', 'microwave oven' and so forth. Despite the authorities' caution, any of these things, had one large-enough pocket or bags, could have been brought into the country quite easily as the X-ray machine that might detect illicit imports was unattended. The guard who had deserted his post had secreted his rifle inside it while he nipped off for prayers or lunch, leaving the crisp image of the fire-arm displayed on the monitor for all to see.

One always has to suffer those irritating people who say 'Well of course when I was there . . . blah, blah, blah,' but when we were there . . . the free-for-all outside the airport terminal really was mayhem. Hordes of men with gleaming sweaty faces and a thousand grasping, bony arms stretched towards us, each endeavouring to lay a hand on our belongings while armed security guards failing to police the situation did little more than look hostile at us. This, I am glad to say, has been sorted out to a degree these days, which is no bad thing. It is no exaggeration to say that most people arrive with a fairly negative outlook about the country; and to be mobbed within half an hour of stepping off the plane doesn't go down too well.

We were jostled mercilessly by the crowd and as I sized up our luggage with a view to which piece would make the best weapon, a neatly turned out gentleman of about fifty came to our rescue.

'Mark, Brenda, I am Feroz,' he called above the mêlée. Feroz was a name that we had already come across. He had been involved in the smoothing out of officials with regard to our visas and I assumed him to be one of the mythical Azizur Rahman's flunkies. Whoever he was he was friendly and as far as I was concerned he had excellent timing, if not the largest car in the world. A small, white Mazda was summoned and we set about the impossible task of getting everything into its crammed interior.

After a stunt that would undoubtedly have earned us Blue Peter badges, nine pieces of luggage and four people squeezed into the car and we set off for central Dhaka. Despite having sat down heavily on the handle of it, Feroz seemed pleased that I was toting a cricket bat, and it served as a good icebreaker.

'There is plenty of cricket here and you can play for my club. You will love my club, Mark. So like an English club and it will be very good for business and meeting people. Perhaps you would like to stay in one of its guest houses instead of living in the hotel. I can arrange it!'

Making plans for future jolly times with Feroz at his rather male-dominated-sounding club was all very well, but the exclusion of Brenda from our conversation seemed a mite unjust as, after all, we were only there because of her job. Steering the conversation round to the subject of Brenda's new role, it was clear that Feroz's involvement ran deeper than that of social convenor. Whatever sidelines he had going in his involvement with Azizur Rahman or with Bangladeshi immigration, we were able to discover that he was, in fact, working for Brenda's new company, where his role would be pivotal.

The two-lane airport road we were haring down, courtesy of Rohim the driver, was flanked by ditches, beyond which swathes of rust orange soil lay before being broken up by bright green tropical foliage. *Where would this club be?* I wondered to myself. Beyond these bushes perhaps, and my mind cast up images of the Bombay Gymkhana with its low-lying club-house looking out over manicured playing fields. Waiters in starched uniform taking orders for our first drink of the evening. Yes, I could see it now: I'd be sending out to Bates the hatters for a solar topee by the end of the week.

Looking back now, this is my abiding memory of that journey. Feroz was our one and only friend in this country and so hard at work were we in cultivating his friendship, that before we knew it we had arrived at the Lalbagh Hotel.

chapter three

A man with a neatly trimmed and waxed moustache and piercing blue eyes, presided over by the duty manager, stood each of us in turn against a wall to take our picture. Having classified us as long-stay guests, the Management would need photographs of us to circulate among the staff. This would ensure that we had their best service at all times.

Perhaps this should have set alarm bells ringing that the hotel staff actually made a distinction, but I think it fair to say that at that moment neither Brenda nor I were firing on all cylinders. Blame it on sensory, cultural, emotional—you name it— overload. At this point we just needed Feroz's number and to be left to our own devices.

After three weeks of squeezing items out of, and back into, overstuffed bags the prospect of a lengthy stay in one place and a chance to unpack everything completely was something of a relief. We were already looking forward to being reunited with our shipment and a chance to establish some sort of order in our new life. However, a check on the whereabouts of our container could wait until morning, and since it was not expected to arrive for at least another ten weeks, it was hardly a pressing matter. With any luck the Bangladeshi counterparts of the removal firm we had used would be fairly competent, although it was unlikely that any organisation could match the ruthless efficiency with which our home was dismantled.

The packers we had used were impressive men, so impressive in fact that we had twice had to get them to unpack from the container suitcases that we were taking with us. A friend who dropped by to say goodbye, inadvertently put her Filofax down for a minute, which was sufficient time for it to be wrapped in tissue paper and stowed along with everything else in the house. We discovered it was missing just as the tailgate of the pantechnicon was raised and bolted shut. At least we knew where it was and where it would be in due course.

Our room on the glorious seventh floor, second only to the eighth floor (we were assured), was situated at the back of the hotel. This all-important location ensured that we delicate, long-stay guests wouldn't be disturbed by traffic noise. The fact that the back of the hotel overlooked, and was downwind of, one of the city's largest slums was incidental. Slum is one of those words that makes me shudder. It can hardly be a career decision that leads one to becoming a slum dweller and although the word 'slum' does have a sort of onomatopoeic ring to it, it degrades the people housed in 'make-do' dwellings. In Bangladesh such living, shocking as it may be, is the norm for many people. As such, the locals are very matter of fact about it. I would no doubt learn.

We had already encountered slum dwelling in Bombay, but never before had we had a grandstand view of one and I found it mesmerising. With the monsoon rain, some huts had been half submerged; others completely isolated. Groups of small children paddled homemade rafts up to and around these constructions. Tiny children. The sort that if left playing alone in the street at home one would seriously have to question the sanity of their parents. Not so here. In fact one parent, as I watched, handed a small child a sharp-looking instrument with which to pare the bark of some sugar cane. One is always going to apply one's own values to these seemingly alien situations, but whatever my reaction, and no matter how often I might wince inwardly at the sights and sounds of Dhaka, I wasn't going to change them. That said, when towards the end of the afternoon we ventured out to the swimming pool, our highly tuned Western nostrils detected just how close we were to this makeshift residential area, rendering our disposition towards our new neighbours slightly less charitable.

It is a strange feeling when, in a town where nobody knows you, the telephone in your hotel room rings. It happened to me in Rome at a tender age in an inexpensive *pensione*. Then the call was even more alarming as the telephone appeared to be from another decade and almost certainly defunct.

'Who on earth?' I enquired of Brenda.

Who quickly brought me to my senses. Of course, Feroz. But we were wrong.

'Hello, is Mala Arune available please?' enquired a male North American voice.

Mala Arune was the mastermind behind our whole adventure. Brenda and I had met her in New York earlier in the year, an informal interview for Brenda and an orientation for me. As a foreign-educated Bangladeshi, Mala would be the hub of the office in Dhaka, not only as Managing Director but as an ideal representation of East meeting West.

'No I'm afraid Ms Arune isn't due in Dhaka for a couple of days.'

'So, may I ask who I'm speaking to?' asked the North American male.

As is my wont, I rambled off into an apology for not being the person he wanted, acutely aware that this must be business, and that I was very poorly qualified to field his questions.

'Well, not to worry, I'm David Baird, the Canadian High Commissioner, and I was just calling to invite Mala to a dinner I'm hosting this evening.'

Ah, here was common ground at last.

'How extraordinary!' I blurted out. 'My wife is Canadian. How fitting that you should be the first person we've made contact with.'

Pleasantries exchanged, it was decided that—as new arrivals in Dhaka and as Mala's sole representatives—we should come to dinner instead.

'The hotel will know where the residence is. See you at eight.'

In the country a matter of hours and we had secured our first invitation already.

We were still revelling in our good fortune when the concierge, in response to our request, apologetically reported that all the hotel cars were busy and that he would do his best to find a taxi, but that such things were not freely available in Dhaka. Available or not, after a number of calls and spirited negotiations on our behalf, we were led out of the hotel lobby to wait for our ride. A blood-red saloon car miraculously appeared from out of the Dhaka night and the driver having been carefully briefed, we were sent blindly on our way.

Our journey had clashed with what appeared to be rush hour and as we were transported through the city, shadowy vehicles and pedestrians pressed us from all sides. Frenzied but ineffectual horn tooting was all about us and continued unabated until we broke free of the built-up area and passed into less densely populated suburbs. This was uncharted ground for our driver and it soon became apparent that, despite the instructions of the hotel doorman, he was none too sure of himself when it came to locating residences of High Commissioners.

After a number of stops, barked enquiries to passers-by, and their heavily gesticulated responses, our comfort level decreased as the surface on which we were travelling deteriorated. Either we were nearing our destination or hopelessly lost. Tentatively we turned into an unlit, unmade road and a uniformed guard stepped from the shadows. Down came the driver's window again and fortunately this time the response that his enquiry solicited was positive. Unbidden the guard opened the car door and we stepped out, following the direction of his gesture through a gate and into the back garden of the residence of the Canadian High Commissioner in Dhaka.

Despite our unorthodox entry we were greeted warmly by a member of staff who escorted us round to the front garden and into the residence through a screened porch. We were ushered into an amber glowing, crowded room of guests and as our eyes grew accustomed to the light and it was obvious from a cursory glance around the room that as expats went, we were fairly young ones. We were greatly relieved to find that the Bairds' daughter and her boyfriend were at the party, home from university for the summer vacation, which helped to redress the balance on the age scale. As chance would have it, Brenda and the boyfriend had the same university in common and while they exchanged stories I ran a cursory eye over my surroundings. The Bairds, if the contents of their home were anything to go by, were by no means on their first posting. Evidence of African and Aboriginal purchases were displayed. Did one, I wondered, have to wait until you had long departed those shores before you owned up to being taken in by the local salesmen? As one might buy a T-shirt in Bali and wait until you are at the opposite point on the globe before wearing it. The been-there, seen-it, done-it factor.

The announcement that the buffet dinner was being served broke up our cosiness, and our established perches had been taken by the time we returned from making a wary selection of the fare on offer, forcing us to broaden our exposure to the other guests. The alcohol flowed freely, which made this ordeal slightly less traumatic and, with inhibitions suitably relaxed, there followed a number of disjointed and awkward sallies into forced convivial conversation. For all our best efforts these overtures seemed to be rebuffed by those inhabitants of the rather grand quarter of Dhaka we had stumbled upon.

After one particularly difficult monologue with a Swiss woman with a face like a tight shoe, I found myself talking to the freely perspiring editor of Dhaka's financial daily. A short, heavy man with a splendid Bobby Charlton-style hairdo neatly plastered to the top of his head. He was certainly good value and had plenty to say on a wealth of topics, but with a focus mainly on just what a damn fine job he did. Brenda joined us, which lent a significantly more learned tone to the conversation, but with less than a day on the clock in our new surroundings we were in a position to pontificate about nothing. When the conversation did turn to us we established the fact that we had no idea where we were geographically in relation to our hotel and that we were at the mercy of local transport, should we find any. Much to our invisible jubilation this parting shot had the desired effect and solicited a lift home.

During the course of the evening a great production had been made of the presentation of business cards and I accepted them all graciously. The sooner we were in a position to take part in this indigenous convention then the greater our credibility. I pocketed all the cards carefully but there were few people I would recognise again. That said, within days of this initial encounter whilst on a tour of the golf course with Feroz we had stumbled across many of these select individuals who not surprisingly made up the 'Golf Club Committee.' They had peered snootily down their noses at us as we clattered into their veneer-panelled inner sanctum, but not a glimmer of recognition had we received from any of them. So this impromptu invitation was as dizzy as the expatriate social heights would get for us, it could only be downhill from here on in. Of this unapproachable collection only two people left us with abiding memories. The High Commissioner's secretary had made a big impression by dint of being the only person slurring extravagantly and the US Ambassador who displayed a fine grasp of diplomatic relations and ignored our introduction. Of course as a mere Joe on the street at home the rubbing of shoulders with ambassadors was hardly a daily event, but it seemed unnecessary as, after all, we were for the most part foreigners in a social setting overseas. The whole evening had been a bit of a struggle but, let's hope, character-building stuff. It had been a kind thought to ask us and we were genuinely pleased to have made some sort of social contact so quickly and in a family, albeit rather formal, setting. The Bairds seemed fairly friendly natives and as we left the residence I noted the Canadian Flags on the gateman's uniform, a tangible link with the world that we had left behind, which I found faintly reassuring.

As we waited for the car, I realised this was the first time we had really been out of doors in Dhaka since our arrival seven hours earlier that day. With the exception of our transfer at the airport, our life so far in Bangladesh had been entirely air-conditioned. The monsoon had abated leaving everything warm, damp and, with the absence of street lighting, pitch-black. The car's headlights lit up our party as it pulled up at the side of the road. After a small round of musical chairs we were all safely installed, Brenda and I squashed in the back of the car with the editor's voluminous wife as we set off for the hotel.

chapter four

I have always been an enormous fidget and find the idea of sitting around sunbathing all day torture. The countdown to Brenda's having to knuckle down to her job for real was well and truly underway and Mala's arrival was imminent. Fair enough that Brenda should relax a bit: after all, she had been hard at work for just about all the time we had been away. The hotel no longer held any secrets for me and with no transport we were pretty well stranded. Having settled Brenda by the pool and downwind of our slum-dwelling neighbours, I decided to go walkabout to see just what our new home had to offer.

We had struggled to find any information on Bangladesh. P.J. O'Rourke's no holds barred account of the country, *Just Enough of Me, Way Too Much of You*, was our sole point of reference. His brutal insight into what we could expect to find in Bangladesh had led us to conclude in the occasional dark hour of uncertainty prior to our departure that to be embarking on such an adventure we must be completely mad. As a supplement to the 'tell it like it is' approach, a trip to Stanford's, the centre of the known universe in terms of maps and travel books in London's Covent Garden, yielded a less entertaining albeit less controversial volume. Much to my distrust, it was by the same people who had blighted a previous trip to Asia with a similar publication which had offered the same sort of guidance one's friends do when handing out directions for weddings. Imploring you to follow signs to your destination, but omitting to point out that there is no sign at the roundabout with three exits you encounter when just spitting distance from the function. Having studied the book before leaving the UK, we had found that the section 'Sights and sounds and happening type things in Dhaka' had been slender to the point of being non-existent. But, hell, I could make my own mind up.

Both entrance and exit to the hotel were manned at all times by languid, Lee-Enfield toting, security guards. Despite the obvious antiquity of these weapons one had to ask oneself: were these guns loaded and under what circumstances would they be used in anger? If it came down to these chaps being the thin blue line then indeed all would be lost. Whatever their effectiveness as a defence force, they saluted me in a friendly manner as I left my cosseted environment behind and passed through the hotel gates.

Bombay had taken the pinkness out of my skin, but I was still quite obviously a whitey and my appearance did not go unnoticed. Street hawkers, small children, and even a gentleman carrying a pole bedecked with assorted sizes of flags, vied for my attention. Still within sprinting distance of the hotel, I resisted the temptation to put off my exploring for another day and pressed on. The hawkers I could handle—one either smokes or not, eats pan or not, wants a cup of milky tea and assorted intestinal guests or not. Small children that hang on to and will not let go are a different matter. Akin to having one's leg molested by a small dog in a social setting. One wants to give the irritant a firm boot up the backside, but social conventions will not allow. These poor kids were permadirty, repeatedly grabbing at my hands and arms, and I'm ashamed to admit that it did cross my mind that there might be some cross-pollination of my body with certain inhabitants of their own. As the urge to strike out welled, a slim figure in an orange sari came to my rescue with a cry of 'Jowww!'

'I am Indian, sir,' announced my saviour as my tormentors scuttled away. I was none the wiser, but delighted to make her acquaintance and with that she stepped from the raised pavement into the busy road motioning for me to follow. Having safely reached the other side, my companion made to leave me with a salaam and a splendid display of straight but discoloured teeth, some ten Bangladeshi taka (fifteen pence) richer.

The traffic in Dhaka is crazy and assorted and it is the variation in modes of transport that is its downfall. The lowliest form of transport is the bicycle rickshaw, an ill-conceived design that is unwieldy and uncomfortable yet proliferates in the streets of the capital. It's basically an ancient and sturdy tricycle with a hazardously angled double seat mounted over the rear wheels. On a par with these one might group the flat bed, hand-pulled telegaries, an 18ft-long bamboo construction with a pair of wheels at the pivotal point and powered only by two human horses. Progress of these often horribly overloaded vehicles is understandably slow, but all too often they are inclined to impose their own top speed on the rest of the traffic, although to overload any vehicle is a trait that comes naturally to Bangladeshis and a rickshaw heaving past with up to four people and maybe even a motorcycle is not an uncommon sight. Various nondescript cars throng the gaps and from time to time a precursor of a London Routemaster bus cuts a sedate swathe through the mêlée.

Traffic-dodging is a matter of confidence. There is no reason why it should be any more difficult in one country than another. In Dhaka, having negotiated the manpower and some of the horsepower there is the two-stroke. Wave after wave of Bajaj baby taxis. Three-wheeled, two-stroke, minute milk floats that house a driver and up to a whole family of Bangladeshis. Just when you think there is a gap in the traffic one of these will whisk up the inside of all the other road users in a blue cloud. Fortunately they plug all the holes so well that eventually the whole lot comes to a standstill, giving new arrivals a chance to be led to safety, picking a path through the bumpers, assorted sharp protruding pieces and fumes.

Having made this intrepid excursion from the hotel, nothing on the surrounding horizon really had any obvious cultural, artistic, historic or architectural appeal. I was pleased to see, however, that on a patch of waste ground to my right an animated and impromptu cricket match was in progress, which had neither an upper or lower age limit. The boundary was dotted with lean-to homes of plastic sheeting and sacking and small huddles of black goats, tied by string to posts. As I walked beside the game watching, a gangly youth collected himself to launch a sickeningly quick delivery at an unsuspecting eight-year-old with nothing more than a well used bat for protection. As it happened, the goats on the boundary were in more peril as the ball was well wide of both bat and outstretched arms of the jumble of fielders behind the wicket.

If at this point I could have had an out-of-body experience to give me an aerial view of my whereabouts I would have seen that I was on a large pear-shaped plot of land surrounded by nothing but traffic. Sadly, I was oblivious to this and completed a circuit no more the wiser of what pearls Dhaka had to offer. Now at least I knew that there was life outside the hotel and a fair collection of roads to explore when and if we ever we became mobile.

Feroz had called in my absence and invited us to join him at the Dhaka Club for dinner that evening. This would give us a change of scene and a break from the hotel, but the prospect of uncharted gastronomic waters was cause for concern. Despite the kind invitation, when later that evening Brenda and I had been standing in the hotel foyer for forty-five minutes past the appointed time and we had started to mutter 'Where the hell is he?'—we were not feeling so kindly disposed towards him. The moment he eventually walked through the door, his jet black hair immaculate as before, we were relieved to see him and genuinely pleased to see a friendly face.

The entwined letters DCL, Dhaka Club Limited, decorated the columns that described the entrance and, as we drove between them, two rather bedraggled, uniformed characters flicked a salute. The scenery on our short drive from the hotel had been completely urban, scarred and decaying to boot. There had been no sudden diversions off-road leading us to a tranquil, tree-hidden setting wherein lay the Dhaka Club. We had tried to conjure mental images of Dhaka prior to our arrival. We had driven these streets in our imagination a thousand times, but never had we visited the wasteland that we found in reality. With the benefit of hindsight we should have demanded a *recce* of the place prior to accepting our posting. Instead we had spoken to a couple of people from the company who had flown in and out to conduct business, and the picture they had painted did not match the reality. However, the visit to the Dhaka Club was only our second major outing in Dhaka and as such perhaps our expectations were a little too high.

In 1911 the then British Lieutenant Governor of East Bengal, Lancelot Hare, had dedicated the building as a retreat for administrators of the Raj. The intervening years had apparently not been kind to the building. Although first impressions can be misleading, the Dhaka Club appeared to be little more than a low-lying concrete bunker with the cosmetic addition of plaster columns to lend it an air of elegance. Hopefully our predecessors had seen to it that it had things to recommend it. As a consolation, it was clear that Feroz was excited that we were there and as he signed us in he explained to the gentleman on duty that I would soon be joining the club. Brenda flashed a glance at me and I did my best to give her as eloquent a response.

We followed Feroz down a series of institutional corridors before reaching a heavy, dark wooden door panelled with glass, through which we could make out a dimly lit bar. Leading the way Feroz directed us to a corner of the bar and we installed ourselves at a smoked-glass circular table. It was apparent that the Members Bar had suffered at the hands of an interior designer who had paid a fleeting visit to the West in about 1972. As we eased back into the vinyl upholstery, a round of Heinekens arrived. Brenda was conscious of the fact that she was the only woman in the place, but Feroz assured her that plenty of ladies attended the club, particularly on 'Housey' evenings. Perhaps this should have raised alarm bells: a right rollicking good time in downtown Dhaka meant an evening of up-market bingo? Surely not. We did not press our host on this subject and Feroz had nothing to add, preferring to sit back and smoke while taking in the room. Just when it appeared that this was going to be the most uncomfortable evening of our lives, a steward appeared. Dressed in a starched tunic with brass buttons and wearing a pillbox hat sporting the legend *Dhaka Club Ltd*, he escorted a tall individual with luxuriant hair and a pipe to our table.

Feroz greeted our guest in Bengali and spent some time in conversation before acknowledging our presence.

'This is Anwar Hosain,' he announced.

Still struggling with what to me were alien names I was sure we had already met several Mr Hussains, Hosains, Husains? Nonplussed, I took the proffered card that declared the fact that Anwar was the proprietor of at least five establishments and shook his hand. Anwar had joined us, not in his guise as manufacturer of umbrellas, sadly, but due to his intimate involvement with the local stock exchange. This was business

I supposed, and resolved to pass the evening as First Lady.

Not so the boys, who directed all conversation to me, which I in turn deflected to Brenda, who I think was rather taken aback by her usurping partner. Up until now the fact that we were now living in a Muslim country had not really crossed our minds. It had registered in our preliminary research of Bangladesh and Brenda had adapted her business wardrobe accordingly. Other than that, neither of us had given much thought to just how this regime would affect our daily lives. This evening was to give Brenda an inkling of what she was up against. However charming Feroz and Anwar were outwardly, she was no equal, whatever her qualifications.

There was, however, one department in which they showed no bias and the beer continued to flow despite our protestations. By the time we were shown into the dining room we were all a little the worse for wear. Anwar had obviously decided to make a night of it and had switched to whisky. The effects of intoxication were for him, therefore, more profound.

The dining room was brightly lit and sparsely decorated. Groups of diners sat at round, white-clothed tables ministered to by ageing waiters sporting the pillbox hats. The Dhaka Club had, I venture, seen better days and our chef for the evening, I think, probably came under that same heading. We were offered an assortment of dubious-looking dishes, each greeted by an 'ooh' or an 'ahh' by our hosts. In this situation there is nothing one can do other than eat everything that is put in front of you, whatever the cost. When everything looks as though it is laden with a dose of amoebic dysentery, how can one be selective? The head of the much-vaunted *Hilsa* fish was touted about by Feroz before being plonked on Brenda's plate. This was apparently a great honour, but I knew now what it was like to be in George Orwell's room 101— yes, 'Do it to Brenda, Do it to Brenda!'

chapter five

While we had been whooping it up at the Dhaka Club, Mala had arrived in Dhaka. I was now on my own as Brenda would have to concentrate all her energies on her job. I would no doubt survive, we had been in each others' pockets now for getting on for a month and a break would do us good. Besides I had plenty of things to be getting on with and it was time I galvanised myself into some sort of action.

An old college friend of mine was the son of a career diplomat and, as luck would have it, he had spent some time working at the British High Commission in Dhaka. The gist of the advice we had received from this well-qualified source regarding life in Bangladesh was to find a home and get settled as soon as possible. The geographic location of our possessions would dictate when this point of equilibrium would be reached. It was also suggested that we seek out and join one of the various expatriate clubs in Dhaka. Joining one of these was of paramount importance for both recreational and educational purposes. Being a joint nationality pairing we were laughing, as we had a choice of two. And if all this wasn't enough—and if we had the time, the inclination and were willing to part with the cash—we could also join the golf club.

Following this advice, the first item on the agenda to address was to secure membership of the club to which I held best claim. A local receptionist fielded my call to the British High Commission and I was put on hold while the official who doubled as social secretary came to the telephone.

'Hello,' said a cold female voice.

'Hello, my name is Mark Trenowden and I am a British national who has just arrived in Dhaka,' I ventured.

'Yes?' came the not too constructive reply.

'As a newcomer to Dhaka I wondered whether there was anyone at the High Commission who could give me any information concerning residential accommodation in the city or whether there is a pamphlet on orientation in Dhaka,' I asked.

'We provide none of those services, I'm afraid,' replied Her Majesty's representative.

I decided that if I filled this person in on my circumstances, tugged on the heartstrings a bit perhaps, then she couldn't help but crack.

'My partner is working here and I'm as yet unemployed. As you can imagine, the whole place appears a bit alien at the moment, but I believe that there is a British Club that I might join.'

'I'm afraid that the British High Commission Club is reserved for British High Commission staff or British nationals representing British companies in Bangladesh.'

'Yes, but surely if I have no other contact in Dhaka, who else should I approach?' I was getting desperate.

'Look, do you realise how many British people there are in Dhaka? . . . Thousands. As such we cannot cater to individual cases, goodbye.'

Bloody British, I thought, and gave the Canadians a try.

The response was the same.

Whatever the rules, it seemed blatantly clear to me that all that needed to be applied to this situation was a tiny bit of common sense. Stuck overseas, thousands of miles from anywhere, should it not be a case of mucking in together, of making the best of things, of just getting along, damn it?

With or without the help of the combined governments of Britain and Canada, we would need to find somewhere to live. Feroz had arranged for his office manager, Ismail, to take me on a tour of suitable neighbourhoods. With the trusty Rohim at the wheel, we drove in a hitherto unexplored direction – or so I thought until we passed a sign announcing the residence of the Canadian High Commissioner. We were in the residential area of Gulshan and it was a relief to be there.

As a capital city Dhaka has plenty of bad things to offer: it is poorly planned and, although expanding rapidly due to an influx of people from the countryside, is still relatively backward. The upside of this is that there are parts of Dhaka that, whilst still being classed as areas of the city, are really quite rural in their aspect. Gulshan is one such area and consists basically of a large elongated 'H' of roads with a roundabout at each of the points where the crossbar meets the uprights. These are the celebrated Development Improvement Trust or DIT-1 and DIT-2 circles. Once you have mastered these two points, you are nearly a local. Within the boundaries of the 'H' lies a network of roads laid out in a grid. These are all imaginatively named 'Road 1, 2, 3' and so on, so as long as you have the address, a map and have mastered the two DITs, then you are well on your way.

Gulshan, for all its greenery and relative tranquillity, has been laid to waste by the same architects who have done so for the more commercial parts of the city. All the buildings are concrete blocks of some shape or form and these are in various states of repair. Any aspirations we had had to set up a colonial-style *mon repos* would have to be sidelined. By now the romance was lost from the whole project, my main concern being to find something that we could actually live in, that had a half-decent kitchen and bathroom – and loos that functioned.

Bangladesh boasts only one established retail chain that provides something approaching the customer-service experience one might expect in more developed countries. Although this can be annoying when trying to locate everyday necessities, it is a positive joy for activities involving other service industries such as house-hunting. With nothing approaching an estate agent, potential landlords adopt a more basic marketing tool, the hand-painted 'To Let' sign pinned to the outside of the vacant property. Prospective lessees just cruise the streets looking for these signs and when a suitable one is found a honking of the car horn normally solicits the attentions of the resident key-holder.

Our friend Rohim at the wheel had up until now been pretty undemonstrative. He had greeted both Brenda and myself in a friendly way when ushering us into cars and had always responded to our goodbyes with a smile and a wave. The energy with which he announced our arrival at a whitewashed concrete wall bearing a sign with the magic words revealed a hitherto undisclosed passion beneath his passive demeanour. In the way that the driver of the latest Vauxhall Astra Equipe Sportif GTX honks you in London traffic if you hesitate the split second the light goes green, Rohim was back on the horn when his first attempt drew no notice. This time the scraping of a white-painted metal gate being lifted on its hinges and opened suggested that there was life beyond the wall.

Beyond the gate we found a small concrete drive, bounded on one side by a postage stamp of coarse grass and some pleasingly tropical-looking foliage. The house itself looked as though it had been empty for some time, but even the lived-in ones had this air. Rectangular openings which had housed air-conditioning units and which had been plugged with the sides of packing cases did not contribute to the general sense of a well-maintained dwelling. These were merely cosmetic details, however, and once inside the house I was pleasantly surprised at the space available and the general condition of the place. The house was about twenty years old and a mixture of red brick, white-painted concrete, grey tiles and orangey-brown wood, a combination that might be described as drab at the best of times. Ismail pronounced it an excellent house and I decided not to hurt his feelings and point out that the whole place smelled of damp carpet.

For him, this was becoming a fascinating day out; an opportunity to see how and where the other half lived. No doubt the three bedrooms, living room cum dining room and assorted bathrooms appeared palatial, and a kitchen that had running water and a cooker – riches beyond avarice. To the more critical Western eye the house, in truth, was rather tired and one got the impression that living there it would require regular and extensive maintenance. Nevertheless, not wanting to hurt his feelings, I continued to show interest and mounted a small concrete staircase to the left of the kitchen. At the top of these stairs a three-foot-high door lead out on to the roof and a small construction which I supposed contained a water tank. The door was locked but peering between the wall and the red corrugated-iron roof, I could make out a small four-foot-square room.

'Ah, Ismail, we have got some storage space up here,' I exclaimed.

'No, sir,' he replied. 'This is where your cook will live.'

Although not ideal, the house was liveable and that was heartening. We continued our search up and down the back roads of Gulshan and for most of the time we seemed to be the only car on the dusty tracks. Occasionally we would come across a rickshaw *wallah* idling down the middle of the road, rocking on the balls of his feet in an upright stance, letting his weight turn the pedals. Rohim was not so sensitive to this pastoral activity and would toot the offender to the side of the road so that we might pass. The housing we encountered seemed to fall into three main categories. Houses similar to the one that we had visited, white blocks of new apartments and sprawling white-stuccoed dwellings that housed the Dhaka elite.

When I bought my first flat in London the prospect of not having a garden was unthinkable. Caged like an animal in London with nowhere to go but the street was an unimaginable prospect. I definitely needed my own back door. A suitable property was selected - and yes indeed there was a garden - but did I use it? No. Now here there was a jolly good reason not to have a garden. The dust factor and the creepy-crawly factor had to be taken into account. Our ex-Dhaka resident contact had said of the wild life that the number of animals that in Britain reach a reasonable size, say a dog or a cat, are very small in Dhaka. Whereas creatures that we are quite used to being on the small size back home, say a mouse or a spider, are enormous great monsters in Dhaka. One should cut off their access. I was all in favour of that and when we came upon a five-storey white block nestling on the banks of Lake Gulshan, I was the first one out of the car.

I had a sense of déjà vu about the apartment on the fifth floor. Ismail confirmed that his office had faxed me the floor plan and that we were currently standing in the property of the local Police Commissioner. My colleagues had greeted the floor plan that had spilled from the fax machine into my Knightsbridge office with delight. The fact that the apartment had four lavatories either had something to do with the unreliability of the local apparatus or indicated that we would be needing to utilise more than one at any one time. Of course at the time I had laughed too, but after our brief stopover in Bombay the second option looked the most likely. True to the plan, all these conveniences were in place and the whole flat finished to a relatively high standard. In a city that had a reputation for things going wrong, starting off in a brand, spanking new apartment seemed a wise precaution and now I had a benchmark by which all others could be judged.

There is a temptation when one finds something that will do to ease off. Somehow, elements of a solution that might at first have been deemed to have fallen short of the demands of key criteria can be reasoned out or justified. I was definitely close to this point with the lakeside flat and was pretty gung-ho in my billing of it to Brenda. She, as a more measured and wiser soul than I, would give the place the once-over but didn't necessarily want to take the first place that looked as though it would do. This wisdom had last manifested itself in Marks & Spencer one Saturday afternoon. Then I had been a distracted man. Though she tried to encourage me with 'You'll be thanking me six months from now,' and 'The cricket team will still be there when you get back,' as she stockpiled the pesto and olive and caper pasta surprise, I could only think about the fact that I was missing one of my last opportunities to do battle with the lads on the cricket fields of Kent.

Acutely aware that we couldn't keep dragging Imail away from his office, Brenda had accepted on my behalf the services of a young Bangladeshi businessman who knew all about the available real estate in Dhaka. With Raybans no doubt riveted to his ears, Faisal had collected me in his brand new Toyota Corona. It is a tricky one when you take an instant dislike to someone who is doing you a favour, but not to put to fine a point on it, he was full of it. Yeah, he'd been there, seen it, done it, passed it, slept with it: this boy was a god. This was my encounter with that diabolical being, the young, overseas-educated, rich Bangladeshi. Having said that, here he was doing a complete stranger a favour, so could he be all that bad?

Our first stop was the apartment overlooking Gulshan Lake. Of course, I didn't have the heart to say that I had seen it already, so I expressed delight and amazement at all the built-in mod cons and positive disbelief at the number of WCs.

'This is excellent, Faisal, no, no really nice,' I said apologetically. 'I'm just a bit wary about the large drop into the dining room.'

The main living space was split-level, with each half being accessed by five or six three-foot wide stone steps to one side. The alternative access was to fall four feet from concrete to concrete. It was a justifiable worry.

'Sure, we can go find somewhere else but all the apartments are built by the same company so they are basically all the same.' Faisal didn't seem all that game.

Across Gulshan Lake lay the promised land of Baridhara, an overflow from Gulshan and site of the magnificent 'Red Fort'. The red fort was not, as one might have hoped, the remnants of a Mughal Emperor's luxurious dwelling, but a massive fortification designed to keep the locals out and the Americans in: the American Embassy. I was rather surprised that Faisal hadn't rushed me straight over there as he was doing a passable impersonation of some American good ol' boy and doubtless his alma mater was on those fair shores. The British had taken the American lead and had raised the Union Jack within spitting distance of the Star and Stripes, but in a rather more subdued way. Faisal dutifully pointed out the BHC and I looked as enthusiastic as possible while inwardly wailing and gnashing my teeth. One had to hand it to them: the Brits had done a nice job and I noted that the gates were guarded by slightly long in the tooth *Gurkhas*, supplemented by a small band of elderly locals, each topped with a navy and red forage cap to denote their allegiance.

Baridhara was to all intents and purposes a building site and, despite the fact that one was under the impression that everything Faisal said had to be taken with a largish pinch of salt, he was fairly accurate on the layout of the other newly constructed apartment buildings. They fell into two categories: a peculiar narrow design that would dictate a living-in-a-corridor type of existence and the unfinished variety. The unfinished variety was in fact in high demand as they were housing all the workers on site which seemed to comprise whole families. Small children laboriously sanding enormous lengths of banister and the ladies humping vast quantities of wet concrete in dishes, balanced on their heads. These damsels in saris sometimes carried their loads up seven or eight flights of stairs. One couldn't help thinking that the gentleman who had handled that particular piece of delegating needed a good shake to bring him back to his senses. Presumably the dads did muck in at some stage, but the majority of the ones we encountered were on extended fag and cha breaks.

A look at the shipping news section of the daily newspaper still failed to divulge the exact whereabouts of the good ship *Bangla Moni*, to which our shipment had been consigned. The half-finished apartment, therefore, presented an option. Faisal thought this a rather unreliable ploy and said that he had another flat to show me before I made a decision. I've always prided myself on a reasonable sense of direction and although we had done a certain amount of to-ing and fro-ing I was aware that we had crossed back over the water and as such we must be back in Gulshan. The turn off the main drag we were heading down did disorientate me slightly and I was surprised to find that the water was once again on our right side.

By the startled looks of a group of impromptu launderers jumping up and down in a bathroomless bath I wasn't the only surprised party in the district. Faisal pressed on as he squeezed his precious Corona between a six foot wall and a small hut, which suggested only one thing to me: that we must be lost. But no, here was a building after all—and one it seemed to me that was remarkably familiar. When one has been in a country for a period which it is still possible to count in hours (if you can be bothered to do so), you don't expect to come across familiar buildings in the middle of the bush.

I had been here before.

This was the *third* time I had been here.

'This is where the Police Commissioner's apartment is,' I said knowledgeably.

For a moment I was sure I saw Faisal's eyes blink in disbelief behind his sunglasses.

'Oh! Do you know my uncle?'

chapter six

I had now been pretty idle for a month. With a couple of weeks on the clock in Bangladesh, cabin fever had set in. Brenda was already pretty busy, although breakfasts were as yet unaffected. Making a point of starting the day when she did was no doubt good for my soul, but it did make the days interminably long.

Totally reliant on other people for transport, I was very much a prisoner of the hotel and the hotel seemed bloody small. With a definite language barrier, the local transport was not an option and, if my guidebook and the local hotel staff  were anything to go by, there wasn't any-where to go anyway. I resolved to buy a gun.

That evening at dinner Brenda bought news that Mala had something she wanted to talk to me about the following day. Now, far be it from me to point out the errors of a large corporation, but on paper the Bangladesh business plan had been fairly hastily cobbled together. We had got wind of the project towards the end of February and it was still only May when we finally left London. The whole project had moved on apace and the odd thing was going to slip through the net. The nuts and bolts of the plan were to send out a team of well-qualified expatriates to establish a presence, hire and train up a team of local staff and then somewhere down the line these 'know-alls' from overseas would exit stage left leaving a completely local office. Of the expatriate staff Brenda and Mala were to be the first people on the ground who, with the help of Azizur Rahman, would spend three months getting licences and laying the groundwork before the second wave, who were due in September, arrived.

I can sit back smugly now and say that there seemed to be a slight gap, but even as a desperate man wracking my brains for something to do, it hadn't occurred to me. Assuming all the licences were collected and approvals given, the office would need, well, an office. Furniture, computers, photocopiers, cars, all of those office-type things. Ah, a gap. It was a brainwave and in the nick of time too: enter the new office manager. I'd love to think that I was the ideal man for the job but the phrase 'right time, right place' does come to mind. There would be other spouses accompanying their loved ones who would go through the same initiation process as me and I had been truly fortunate to extricate myself from that gloomy situation so painlessly.

The interview has never been my forte. I like to put it down to an enormous truthful streak but as five-minute sessions go, my five-minute session with Mala was pretty successful. Yesterday I had been a glorified beach-bum, kicking about the hotel pool, breaking up my day by lovingly fingering the Cadbury's selection in the hotel shop. Today I was a man with a mission and a title, and boy what a title: Chief Administrative Officer. How long a business card would I need for that? In the wine trade I had always been part of a small team and had always sensed that the grass might be greener on the side of the big corporation. All those friends in the cosy world of BUPA and pensions, pooh-poohing the advantages of being a corporate animal and positively cooing at the thought of a small business. In reality a small business is a hassle, an elaborate balancing act of bank manager, landlord and suppliers, while the customers are a mere side issue.

Sod's Law declares that all burglar alarms will develop a fault at five to six on a Friday evening and that the alarm maintenance company will be apologetic but not speedy in the handling of your request. In the world of the corporate employee such minor annoyances affect someone else. Doubtless most people aren't aware that there is an alarm in their office at all. In such organisations does the company director find his whole weekend's plan decimated by the fact that the delivery driver has shortened the van by a foot against some inanimate object and that the said van is in fact your car? I don't think so. This was a different world, with talk of a contract, of compensation, whatever that was, and as we had not been incorporated in Bangladesh, I would be employed by the Hong Kong office. It was heady stuff.

Feroz was waiting for us in the lobby of the hotel. I was being pressed into action rather sooner and in a more overt manner than I had imagined for one so new and clueless. We were off to the Board of Investment, an institution established for accelerating private investment in Bangladesh and our first meeting regarding work permits for the expatriate staff. Feroz had worked the oracle on getting us extended business visas, myself included, but if we were going to do this thing properly then work permits were pretty crucial. We were enjoying a lull in the monsoon and the air conditioning was putting in a fair amount of overtime to cope with five of us jammed into the car as we approached the commercial area of the city. No amount of sunlight was going to jolly up our destination: the glorious Board of Investment, sited in the none too decorous building, *Shilpa Bhaban*, a gloomy, tired facility, as featureless as the other concrete blocks that proliferate around Dhaka. What one might term the Dhaka 'functional style' or 'rectilinear all-purpose edifices', a catchy phrase dreamt up by some Sixties madman.

Two small lifts faced us as we entered the building and a small, hopeful-looking crowd had gathered beside them. Circumnavigating the lifts and having climbed the stairs to the second floor, I was transported to London SW7 and the Bangladesh High Commission in Queen's Gate. There was an overpowering sense that there had been busier days in the life of this building and that the furniture and fittings had at one time been more resplendent. At the end of a corridor a door bearing an illegible Bengali inscription was opened and we were shown into an office with a threadbare deep red carpet, a smell of mildew and a gleaming Sony television set of gigantic proportions. A man with a fair complexion the colour of weathered pigskin seated behind a large desk motioned for us to sit while he continued an animated tête-à-tête with another gentleman. I felt rather uneasy at bursting into someone else's meeting, but both parties seemed unconcerned by our presence and continued their conversation, which seemed to be of a most intimate nature, if the close proximity of their chairs was anything to go by.

I was ushered into the middle chair of three facing our host, and Brenda and Mala took up flanking positions. Feroz was literally taking a back seat on this one and a glance over my shoulder found him sunk into an aged sofa at the back of the room. Bengali was still a mystery to me, so I surveyed the desk in front of me while the men continued their conversation. The glass-topped desk had a grimy, oily patina and it was hard to imagine that it had ever been new. The same could be said of all the furniture and I was amused to note that between my legs the intricately woven cane seat of my chair was in actual fact a substance not dissimilar to fuse wire.

The desk itself displayed evidence of periods of activity and periods of complete slothfulness. At one end a number of beige cardboard files bursting with paperwork and neatly fastened with string were stacked, while the central area of the desk was definitely the least populated area I had yet seen in Dhaka. A clear expanse of glass was peppered only with a well-used ashtray, remnants of morning tea and a two-tone Perspex pen-holder. When we had let our home in London an inventory was carried out for our tenants. The happy-go-lucky-sounding *Looby Lou Inventories* had then painstakingly investigated the most intimate parts of our dwelling, describing with evident disgust every blemish and mark on each item. Messrs *Looby Lou* would have had a field day with this desk:

- one desk (executive)—soiled, glass cracked and discoloured
- ashtray—well used and soiled
- perspex two-tone pen-holder—missing pen, tasteless, crappy item, gift?

Our host swung his chair towards us and cast a wary look upon us. I felt distinctly uneasy, armed as I was with zero information and aware that it was I who was under closest scrutiny. As perspiration bubbled out of my shirt collar, Mala eased into a well-oiled routine outlining in English the finer points of our mission in layman's terms.

'Ahhhh yesssss,' our host responded, now hopefully considerably better informed, as indeed was I.

'And Mr Rahman?' He cast a look over to Feroz.

'Mr Azizur Rahman is our Senior Adviser and has been helping us with introductions within the Ministries,' replied Mala.

This was real news to me, Azizur Rahman and Feroz were one and the same. The widespread use of nicknames being one aspect of local convention that had so far passed me by.

It was no wonder I had found the odd conversation hard to follow. The Director greeted this information with a furrowed brow. After a pause, his countenance brightened as he addressed me again.

'My wife—his wife—thinks that it would be a very good idea for me to become involved with an organisation such as yours.'

This was a horribly tricky one, countered neatly by Mala who pointed out that as yet we had no office but that in the months to come such an arrangement might be of mutual benefit. This was a complete lie, but for the meantime it sidestepped the problem and ensured that he would be on our side.

And with that, tea arrived. The drinking of tea is an important cultural activity, an important bonding rite. I surveyed my small cup of strong milky tea with suspicion, knowing that what I was doing was for the cause, but might well provide a one-way ticket to the smallest room in our hotel room. As a child I had enjoyed hair-bristlingly sweet tea, but here the combination of sweet and tannin was startling, leaving you well and truly caffeined up and with a slight twitch in one eye. This shock to our systems aside, our first meeting had been quite successful. We left our friend Tajul Islam, who had seen fit to proffer his card during tea, to the rest of his day of frenzied chatting and telly watching.

The fourth floor of the Board of Investment to which we had been directed was considerably less splendid than the executive floor had been. A distinct waft of urine wrinkled our noses as we passed an open door to the staff comfort station, a door-framed, unvisitable black hole in the corridor. The entire floor was encased in chestnut-brown-coloured wood panelling and partitioned off in the same, topped with yellowing glass. Behind one of these partitions lay our destination, the inner sanctum that was Abdul Malek's office. A rough approximation of the layout of the office downstairs but about quarter the size. The overall impression was of a tiny room full to bursting with furniture. The same three chairs in front of the desk and a crimson vinyl sofa for Feroz against the back wall.

Malek rose as we entered and offered his hand to me. Restricted by the limited amount of space, he had to push his chair back from behind his desk—he could only manage a crouching stance but it was a courteous gesture. My overwhelming impression was that Malek was the spitting image of a friend of mine, Trevor. Of course Trevor would have to be wearing an excellent false beard and small white crochet scull cap but the likeness was there. I liked this man.

Feroz from his station behind us filled him in on the events of the morning and the three of us sat in silence with fixed smiles. Life on the fourth floor was a good deal hotter than downstairs and the antiquated solitary fan in the ceiling was doing a valiant job, but in vain. My beautiful navy blue suit, which in Piccadilly had seemed ideally suited to such situations, obviously had not been field-tested. Brenda was visibly feeling the heat too as the sharp points of wet hair by her ears testified. I felt within, however, that this was precisely what the whole experience was all about. Sweating it out in the local environment against insuperable odds—and why? To extend our stay officially, to part with money to do so, just so that we could legally continue to endure such hardships. However, Malek was not insensible to our discomfort and just when it seemed that we could take no more, three small chipped cups of tea arrived.

Tea, that great leveller, seemed to have a common effect on the officialdom of this organisation. As we all sipped, Malek spoke.

'In order to carry out my responsibilities more efficiently I really need to go on a computer course in Canada.'

Jolly good, I thought, until his eyes met mine,

'Do you think your company can me send me on such a course?'

I winced inwardly; they were all after baksheesh. Unwittingly he had, however, played right into our hands as the 'Canada' part gave Brenda an excuse to ramble off at a tangent on the considerable merit of the Canadian Higher Education system. Soon our man was rhapsodising about his own *alma mater*, the University of Manchester, curiously enough the same as his look-alike Trevor's.

The relief to be back in the car was considerable, although the car had been sitting in bright sunlight for a couple of hours and the heat inside it was intense. Amusing as the scene at the Board of Investment was in retrospect, these people carried considerable powers and for an office being built on the foundations of expatriate staff it was of considerable importance not to put these people out. I would have to pay regular visits to Malek and his friends. A daunting prospect for me and one of considerable amusement to my fellow passengers.

chapter seven

We had unwittingly stumbled upon a rather harsh regime. The Muslim six-day work week had taken us aback and our close proximity to our 'office', room 732 along the corridor from our own 729, meant that work breaks were few and far between. With the rental of a hotel car at a premium, and otherwise still reliant on Feroz for transport, our one day off a week was passing us by. The acceptance of the whole 'Bangladesh Job' had been a fairly civilised arrangement and it was now becoming apparent that the wide-eyed  benevolence with which we had accepted the word of our employers was not only naïve but misplaced. Brenda's credit card was starting to show signs of weakness and the hotel was now asking that we settle our account on a weekly basis. A local bank account for the company depended on the granting of a number of licences and would definitely take time.

The acquisition of a car was of paramount importance as far as we were concerned but, having nothing with which to pay for one other than good will, it was a tricky proposition. Our first local hire had signed on the dotted line at about the same time as I had joined the company and, although a quiet, unassuming young man, Schezade was highly connected. Although well qualified, with a degree from the States in an appropriate discipline, there was little doubt that he had been brought on board to exploit his contacts and to my eternal shame I was first in the queue.

'Mr Haque is a very good friend of my father'
were the magic words I wanted to hear and one Saturday morning the two of us set off for his emporium,
Haq's Bay. Our aim, come hell or high water, was to
procure a motor vehicle of some description.

Someone once said to me: never judge a person by
their car. My parents at the time had a rather ghastly
aged red Cortina and I found myself agreeing with
this saying wholeheartedly. What would I have given
to have lived in Dhaka then. As vehicles go, Dhaka is
a largely classless place. There are of course exceptions, but for the average punter when it comes to car
selection you have one choice. It's white, at least five
years old and of Japanese extraction. Dhaka is the
home of the white Toyota Corolla and half a mile or
so of one of the main roads into the commercial area
of the city is flanked on both sides by unlikely sounding purveyors of motor cars: showrooms called Real
Motors, Hong Kong Automobiles and Kleen Car Systems, all presenting three or four slightly dated, white
Japanese cars. These boys were not in the league of Mr
Haque, whose turquoise and yellow painted 'Bay',
topped by an enormous satellite dish, took up a site
that would have comfortably housed four of these
smaller dealers.

I felt quite comfortable at Haq's Bay. In a former
life with a delivery van that was constantly undergoing some sort of surgery I had spent a number of af-
ternoons at Ron's Garage in Peckham, South London.
The familiar smell of oil and rubber transported me
back home. Mr Haque inhabited a modest office at the
back of the showroom which belied the impression
created by the razzmatazz of the glitzy exterior. I was
shown into his inner sanctum by a number of earnest
salesmen and was greeted by the proprietor. Mr Haque
himself appeared to be a very respectable gentleman
with neatly parted hair, watery eyes and a toothy
smile. A thick scar ran through his left eyebrow giving
his face a slightly lopsided look.

Schezade was obviously well known to this man and when greeting him I was interested and impressed with the deference that youth showed to age. The ritual cha was produced and we all sat down to discuss my needs, both current and future, and my impecunious state. With the proposed size of the office Mr Haque was onto a pretty good thing and it was soon agreed that I could have a car immediately and settle up as and when the funds arrived. The understanding was that Mr Haque would get the first opportunity to quote on future purchases. A deal was struck and I was soon climbing in and out of a number of likely looking Corollas, trying to look knowledgeable, checking the mileage and, well, just checking the mileage as I know little or nothing about cars.

Hamid, a very charming and dapper salesman, attended to my every need and assured me that although none of the cars had been test-driven on arriving in the country, any teething problems with 'de veercul' would be ironed out. So after a respectable amount of time spent looking, and with the assurance of Schezade that it was a good one, I finally plumped for a nice enough looking car, with a Bengali registration number that meant nothing to me but which I was informed read Dhaka Metro 1617. Rob, the driver, was designated to take the car and me to the hotel and, waving to Schezade and Hamid left on the forecourt, we departed. At last I was mobile.

Of course, in Dhaka with the vagaries of its traffic system, a driver is as important as the car itself and on reaching the hotel, through a mixture of pidgin English and driving gestures, I think I managed to ask Rob if he knew of a driver. With the promise of 'night time, coming' my chauffeur bade me farewell and I went off to look for Brenda to tell her my news. Her delight was obvious and we both rushed to the car park to give our car a closer look. Feroz presumably had arrived in the meantime, for we found Rohim, his driver, warily eyeing the wheels of our car. On closer inspection it was obvious that the wheel hubs had been touched up with silver spray and for a fleeting second the word 'duped' sprung to mind. Well, maybe, I was the new kid on the block and perhaps I had been taken for a ride, but the fact remained we now had our own transport.

The telephone in the room rang and Rob announced his presence. I went down and met him in the lobby. His demeanour suggested a delight in being in the hotel but a sense of being out of place at the same time. The slim character lurking just behind him seemed to be feeling even more self-conscious and I did my best to appear friendly to put him at his ease. This was Masum, my prospective driver, and I was jolly glad to see him. An unofficial driving test would have to be sat so that I might satisfy myself that Masum was a capable driver and so we all trooped to the car park and took up our various stations. Then disaster—Masum had never driven an automatic car. The fact that the car was automatic was news to me and the thought that I had got so close to finding a suitable driver only to be thwarted rather distressing.

'Eck Minit, Eck Minit!' urged Rob. I decided it was best to leave them to their own devices and signalled with both hands held up with the fingers outstretched that I would give them some time to get to grips with the automatic transmission and went back into the hotel.

Returning to the car park, we took up our positions again and Masum eased us out of the parking space. Rob, it seemed, had made a good fist of 'How to drive an automatic car in ten minutes' and Masum to my delight seemed cautious and able. If we could cure him of appearing to look out of the windscreen through the gap between wheel and dashboard then he would be fine. A short drive around the hotel environs proved good enough for me and it was decided that he should start work the following day for a two-week trial period.

Ironically, having secured a car and driver, it was days before we really needed to use him. It was a given that he should be around during the day and trips to the business area of Motijheel were becoming more frequent. More often than not, though, Feroz would be in attendance and Masum would spend a long boring day sitting in the car park. Brenda had done some more investigating on the club front and a member of the Canadian High Commission staff suggested that we go to the open night at the Canadian Club on the following Thursday evening. Prior to this momentous development in our affairs Feroz had been a godsend, not only in providing a car but in easing us into the business community both professionally and socially. We had spent numerous evenings in the company of local businessmen who had been both friendly and generous. Up until now, however, everything had centred around work and we really needed a break.

Business dinners were fraught with difficulties. Brenda struggled as they were nearly always all male or, if not, certainly male-dominated. I struggled because it was expected that I eat ten times my own body weight in food at each meal which often incapacitated me through sheer volume or through some little local nasty that made its way into my digestive system. Brenda struggled because whisky, despite the fact that Bangladesh is 'dry,' was normally the only alcoholic beverage on offer. I struggled because all the topics of business conversation were directed to me and we both struggled when so much whisky had been consumed that our hosts lapsed into giggling, Bangla-punctuated fits. There was no doubt that we needed a diversion, a glimpse of a culture that we recognised and an opportunity to let off a bit of steam.

The Canadian Club lies adjacent to the High Commissioner's residence so it was well-charted ground for us. As most of our travelling to the residential and diplomatic quarter of Gulshan had been under cover of darkness we were still struggling to orientate ourselves, recognising small areas and slowly linking one to another. One particular part of the route took us over a small causeway, a mid point between the urban city and the more rural swanky part of town. Here the effects of the monsoon were in evidence, with electricity pylons marooned by flood waters and small impromptu dwellings encroaching on to what might be termed the pavement. Their occupants had relocated from the now inundated colonised common land that bordered the road. Presumably this was an oft-repeated pattern of events and one either marvelled at the inhabitants' dignified resignation to their predicament or wondered why they didn't set up shop elsewhere. The only beneficiaries of this sad state of affairs were those proud owners of traditional flat bottomed boats who did steady trade at this time of year, plucking their fares from distant hillocks of dry land and depositing them at the roadside with a wash of displaced water that made one think wistfully of things like the wellington boots stowed in our shipment.

For a city with not a lot of charm, Dhaka's saving grace is the element of rural life. Once over the causeway, concrete gives way to lush vegetation partly concealing small developments of grass-roofed huts. Pats of dung dry on the road and small ladies squat, relentlessly bashing green coconuts, splitting the fibres for fuel. The profusion of trees and corrugated roof visible from behind the whitewashed wall sporting a cipher describing Canada's imperious roots might lead the casual observer to believe that a similarly pastoral tableau lay within. Instead, one's initial impression on stepping through the metal door set in the wall was of order. A large square of lawn of neatly trimmed broad-bladed grass, which gave way to a small paved area in front of a long white bungalow topped with a bright-red corrugated-iron roof. Lights from the building suggested that this was the hub of the evening's activities and three fit-looking young Bangladeshi boys, clad as if for tennis and sitting beside what we later discovered to be a squash court, confirmed this with various nods, shrugs and gesticulations.

The Bluenose Room, had it been on a pivot, would have been very lopsided. The majority of those present were at the bar to the right of the room whilst the chairs and tables, arranged to accommodate small groups of socialising Canadian types at the other end of the room, were being given a wide berth. Brenda felt at home right away as the tall ship *The Bluenose* has strong ties to her home town Halifax in Nova Scotia, while I felt instantly uncomfortable: a Brit now doubly away from home on Canadian soil in Bangladesh. The Canadians, however, are a friendly bunch and I needn't have worried. In fact we found them to be so friendly that in forthcoming months when we wanted a quiet day we would avoid the Canadian Club and so miss out on the barrage of 'Hullows' and 'How ya doin's.

Joanne, who had met Brenda at the High Commissioner's residence, recognised us and came to our rescue. It was obvious that she was having a pretty 'happy' hour and delighted in unsteadily filling out a chit on the bar and getting us drinks. It was the first time I had met a Quebecois and I found myself marvelling at the magnificent impersonation of a French national that this so-called Canadian was doing.

'Have you been posted overseas before?' was a question that I asked only once that evening since the response it solicited left me squirming at our greenness. Compared to the five postings she had racked up I was an embryo in expat terms. The more we circulated, the more this realisation was compounded. For many of these people working overseas was a complete way of life rather than a couple of lines of interest on your CV or a topic of conversation at dinner. It was also apparent that Brenda and I were somewhat unusual in as much as we represented the filthy, manipulative, money-grabbing private sector while the hat rack in the corner of the room was stacked high with the halos of those representing aid agencies and development programmes.

Brenda and I regrouped for a confab and discussed the merits of the alcohol supply. Yes, we were in a Muslim country but cocooned in the hotel we were still blissfully unaware of just how difficult life was going to be on the appropriation of booze front when left to our own devices. We had already had a couple of warnings that as yet had failed to register. One evening Feroz, as a special treat, had produced an aged bottle of red wine, a feat that by all accounts had tested his powers of ingenuity to the limit. All this effort had produced a sad specimen, which, in the vernacular of the wine trade, would have been deemed 'filthy.' While our own efforts, which so far had only amounted to a request at the hotel, had solicited a dubious-looking *Liebfraumilch* with a price tag of $40. Things were not so dire in the Canadian Club, however. Here they were well stocked and if our eyes weren't deceiving us there were bottles of reasonable Australian white and Californian red wines.

'Is it possible to buy a whole bottle of wine?' I asked Babul, the name-tagged barman.

'Oh yes, sir!'

'Excellent! So is it possible to take wine out of the club?'

'Oh no, sir!' Babul declared with a shocked expression.

This was not such good news and I reported my findings to Brenda. 'Darn' I think was the predominant word used in the conversation and there was much theatrical punching of hands into palms. The rain had started again with a vengeance and so sneaking a bottle outside on the pretext of drinking it there was going to be a pretty flimsy excuse. Still, we had to give it a whirl.

Giving the stickler for club rules Babul a wide berth, I directed my request to the more docile-looking waiter, Siddique, who was situated at the other end of the bar. A bottle was selected and a laborious transaction ensued which involved purchasing a Canadian Club Visitor's Card marked into units of the local currency which were then scratched out in ink until the appropriate funds had been deducted. My prize secured, I caught Brenda's eye and having met her at the door we stepped into the torrential downpour.

Running as fast as we could, we splashed our way to the gate and arrived back at the car wet, breathless and laughing, thus waking Masum who was stretched out on the reclined drivers seat. The warmth of the evening, the damp both inside and outside the car and the air conditioning produced an impenetrable mist on the inside of the windows. Despite the appalling visibility Masum pulled an extravagant U-turn and sped off in the direction of the hotel.

In the darkness I examined our bottle, emitting a small cry as I did so that startled Brenda.

'What is it?' she asked.

Soaked by the rain it had not occurred to me that the liquid running between my fingers was anything other than rain water until my retired wine merchant's nose sensed a vinous bouquet shortly followed by the horrific discovery of a substantial loss of our prized Californian red.

'The little bugger's kept the cork!'

chapter eight

'It is very important that you fill these forms in and submit each one with three attested photographs of yourself as soon as possible,' advised Feroz.

It seemed a simple enough request at the time, although I had done a certain amount of eyebrow-raising when handed twenty-four telephone line application forms, the amount deemed necessary to fulfil all our business and domestic requirements. The prospect of sitting in a photograph booth, even if there had been one, for eighteen strips of photos seemed ridiculous. Nevertheless, I did as I was told and carefully inscribed all  sorts of unlikely snippets of family history that had no bearing on whether or not my company should be awarded a telephone line.

Locally produced stationery in this region can have changed little this century. Foolscap is the standard paper size and thin fawn blotting paper is the appearance. This is the sort of paper that snags a nib and punctures under a ballpoint pen. Printed in a mixture of languages with an apparatus that produces a quality of lettering akin to something a child might produce by cutting a potato in half and using it as a stencil. Surely even Hercules would have balked at such a labour as the one with which I had been presented. However, with a job title in which the operative word was 'administrative', I reasoned that I should take such tasks in my stride and when I had finished I had an impressive sheaf of paper.

To complete the task, the photographer who had taken our mug shots on our arrival was located with the help of the hotel staff. A suitably sombre portrait was taken and delivery of the finished prints promised for the following day, which would enable me to complete the task of having the wad of photographs attested at the British High Commission without delay.

I was well suited to my role, which to a large extent consisted of a glorified shopping binge on a major scale. At present I was shopping for an architect to kit out an empty floor of office space that had been acquired by Mala. She had been seduced into parting with a substantial rent for space in what was being billed as the most state-of-the-art structure in Dhaka.

Various meetings during the course of my time in Dhaka provided information to the contrary. The tut-tutting of a structural engineer flown in from Singapore to give the building the once-over for another company gave me particular cause for concern, particularly since by the time I met him we had been resident in the building for the best part of a year.

I had had my knuckles rapped, after a meeting with the building's owner and flunkies, for inadvertently insulting the architect when I enquired about why he had neglected to put in a fire escape. The owner himself displayed the best demonstration of faith in the building's construction. Brenda was later to encounter him leading a charge of people fleeing down the stairs of the building after an earth tremor had shaken the place to its foundations.

All those architects I spoke to regarding the refurbishment of the space poured scorn on the design, but one had to wonder how many of them had had designs for a construction on the site turned down. As far as our contract was concerned, I had narrowed my selection to four possible contractors and spent a considerable amount of time being driven around the city by them in order to inspect, ah and ooh over and evaluate fully functioning examples of their work.

Iqbal Hussain was my favourite of these, but from an early stage it was clear he was never going to make it to the finishing post. He was a charming man with wire wool hair and a beard to match, which framed an orangey-red-stained mouth and teeth from the betyl. Driving me to distraction with his time-keeping, he would collect me from the hotel and drive me to some far-flung corner of the city. Together we visited offices that were a throwback to the fifties, offices that were a throwback to the seventies, offices under construction, offices in use, even floors exposed to the elements fifteen storeys up that one day would be offices. Full points for effort but in the words of Eurovision, finished article: 'Nul points'.

The selection procedure was largely a process of elimination rather than being based on any particular merit displayed by one architect over another. One fell by the wayside for an exemplary display of lack of interest, which left two frontrunners. The first of these was a glamorous and assertive lady who had been responsible for a number of key developments in the city. With a similarly assertive bossette who didn't always know what she wanted but wanted it 'now', the fireworks between the two of them might be spectacular. The second option, the acknowledged gurus of Dhaka interior design, did have a proven track record and Architect Habib, a gentle soul, had been extremely prompt for all our meetings, which was an unusual trait as it was an acknowledged national pastime to be at least twenty minutes late for any meeting. So, arming both parties with similar briefs, I awaited their quotations.

The photographer had proved himself pretty much a man of his word in only being a day late. Steeling myself, I took the proffered neat packet of passport-sized photographs and set off for the British High Commission. The BHC up until now was a place to which I had only made terse telephone calls. The ill feeling caused by the intransigence of the staff had been tempered by the well-being I felt whenever I had driven past the rust-red iron gates and caught a glimpse of the Union Jack fluttering on an immaculate white flag pole in the courtyard. Now I was at these gates emptying suit pockets, being probed with a metal detector and cross-examined by two local members of staff. Although this was no doubt necessary, I was not in the best humour as I walked the length of the red-brick building to the front door. The whole place had an air of familiarity which stemmed from the fact that a great deal of the fixtures and fittings had started their lives in Blighty, travelled some 5000 miles, only to find themselves pitted against the elements in Dhaka.

It was too much to hope that the surly attitude of my countrymen had not permeated the ranks of the local staff and the lady on reception had taken a keen interest in this aspect of her job. As I sat waiting for the summoned luminary who would attest my photographs, steam I felt sure must be seeping from my ears.

'Of course, you don't need attested photographs for a telephone application, you know.'

Oh great, now you're full of advice, I thought.

'Well, the form clearly states that the applicant's likeness should be attested and the telephones are rather important to us,' I said apologetically.

'I'm not sure that this is a service that we provide. I'll have to check.'

God, I hate the English. More waiting.

'That will be twenty-one pounds, but we close at noon so we can't do it today.'

There comes a time when you realise that if you really need some officious twit to comply with your wishes you just have to back down and thank them profusely for being so accommodating. The vehemence with which I whacked shut the back door of the car rocked the whole vehicle and gave Masum quite a start. Assuming his hunched posture over the wheel he drove me back to the hotel.

The architect selection procedure had been simplified considerably. My headstrong, interior designer lady friend had been so affronted by the news that her skills were being weighed up against those of a competitor that she had pulled out of the race, leaving Habib and the boys of Charuta the victors by default. It was a classic case of the threat of loss of face being all, and it suited my purpose. Time was of the essence: two rooms had at first been fine as our temporary office, but now, with all manner of comings and goings, life was becoming increasingly difficult. With one room almost constantly in use for meetings, all other activities were being co-ordinated from two trestle tables in the other. As such the sooner we could press on with the final design for the office and get the work started the better. Habib and the proprietor of Charuta, Mr Shifti, were summoned to the hotel for a summit on the finer points of office layout.

Until now I had had little direct interaction with Mala. In her own words she was a 'mover and shaker' and therefore the less contact she had with mere mortals like me the better. I felt comfortable overseeing the office design and construction. With a degree in Fine Art I have always considered that I have a reasonable eye for design and here was the first opportunity in my working life to utilise it. Comfortable, that is, until I encountered the steely will of Mala and her vision of a fully functioning Western-style office, fabricated from the sort of materials we were least likely to find in Bangladesh. This wasn't interior design, this was empire-building. Given the free reign of establishing an office which she was to preside over, it had to be the biggest and best Dhaka had ever seen or was ever likely to see. The Bangladeshi Taka signs must have been flashing in Mr Shifti's eyes, but he gave little away as he politely listened to and considered Mala's rantings and broad sweeps of pencil annotating Habib's technical rendering of the office space.

'The materials you describe will have to be imported from Singapore.'

'Do you know how long that is likely to take?' I asked nervously, envisaging the room next door with heaps of paper everywhere and arms and legs poking out of doors and windows as our numbers swelled.

'Perhaps we should look at what is available in Bangladesh. We are, after all, a local office and it might be an idea to reflect some of the local culture in our design' I ventured.

It was an ill-conceived idea—it just sort of popped out—but the rebuff I received could not have been more stinging or ferocious in its delivery. Lip-trembling fury was what I encountered as I looked over to Mala. How could I dare to suggest that this glorious edifice, being erected to the glory of the great and good Mala Arune be constructed in anything less than finest Singaporean Formica? In retrospect it was a huge gaffe. I must have taken leave of my senses to suggest that Chittagong teak could in any way be a substitute for the finest the man-made world had to offer. I am nothing if not a fast learner and I decided that taking a back seat on this one might well be the best course of action.

It had been a long old day by the time Messrs Charuta had left and Mala repaired to her room for a session of her 'important calls'—a euphemism Brenda and I suggested for television watching and cake eating. All this time Brenda was hard at work next door putting together an initial report giving an overview of the local political situation.

'I've a job for you,: she said, handing me a piece of paper. 'Rewrite that!'

Schezade had written a daily report on the local goings-on to dispatch to other offices in our corporate group. His style owed not a little to the entertaining and colourful prose to be found in the daily newspapers. In fact he had lifted whole paragraphs detailing 'mishaps', that old chestnut 'hue and cry' and 'marchers hurling brickbats'. It was all good stuff, but what on earth *was* a brickbat?

Having disseminated our work to all corners of the globe with the help of the hotel business centre, we wearily repaired to our makeshift home. Room 729 never felt better and I searched the TV channels on the off-chance of finding 'Kricket—with a K!', a hopelessly amateur Indian game show, hosted by an entertaining fellow named Mr Keith, in which two teams captained by ex-Indian players pitted their cricketing skills against one another. Low-key to say the least, but all good clean fun and I had become its number one fan.

The telephone rang.

'Yes, okay we'll be down in ten minutes . . . no really, that's fine,' Brenda put the telephone down. 'Mala wants us to have dinner with her and a man from the World Bank.'

As a fairly hirsute chap, after a hard day I can be sporting sufficient growth of beard to rival both Desperate Dan and Fred Flintstone. I would have to shave if we were going out. Muttering under my breath at our misfortune, I locked myself in the bathroom.

'I have to use the bathroom before we go,' called Brenda through the door, knocking as she did so and adding, 'What is it with you and your fixation about locking the door?'

The door handle was the variety that had a small locking knob in the centre which when depressed locks and when twisted pops out again. I twisted but there was no pop. I twisted and pulled, still no joy.

Having dealt with a round of 'You're kidding,' 'Look we're in a hurry,' and 'Quit fooling around,' Brenda finally called housekeeping.

Assorted banging and voices announced the arrival of my rescuers, accompanied by the dulcet tones of Mala who, alerted to my predicament, had arrived to stick her oar in. As the bangs continued, I sat on the lavatory and used the telephone, no doubt positioned for just such an eventuality, and called my mother.

'Guess where I am at moment.' There was a pause while my mother thought for a moment.

'Stuck in a lavatory!' came the considered reply

She knows me well, I thought.

Sounds of drilling and gouging continued and the door handle was definitely a lot less secure than it had been. Not wishing to miss out on the drama of the situation I wrote 'H-E-L-P' in eyebrow pencil on a length of toilet paper and posted it under the door. Mala, with her American sense of humour, failed to see the funny side of this and urged the work parties to try harder. The drilling subsided and was replaced by the sound of several small bodies hurling themselves at the door. With success imminent, I stepped into the bath and drew the shower curtain for protection as, with a cry of 'thar she blows' (or the local equivalent), the small party of odd-job men burst into the bathroom.

A touching scene greeted me as I emerged, a hero, from the wreckage, stepping over assorted tools and chunks of rough-hewn wood. For there not only was my wife and my boss, but also a representative of the World Bank.

chapter nine

TIB was an acronym that we were becoming more and more accustomed to hearing. 'This is Bangladesh' could describe all manner of minor irritations encountered on a regular basis: the fact that the hotel staff might break down the door to your bathroom and leave it for days hanging askew; clothing returned from laundry having been rendered several sizes too small; long periods of waiting for people who failed to show and then seemingly disappeared from the face of the earth; and of course the daily frustration of making a telephone call.

Telephone-related problems were fast becoming the dominant feature of our day and took three main forms. First there was the struggle to get through to any given number. This might take anything up to ten attempts even when only calling the other side of the city. The next problem was communication breakdown. A typical conversation would go:

'Hello . . . is that 854888?'
'Hullow?'
'Yes, hello is that 854888?'
'Hullow. Yait five four treeple yait.'
'Ah good. Could I speak to Mr Islam?'
'Hullow?'
'Yes, yes, hello! Is Monirul Islam there please?'
'Hullow, Yait five four treeple yait.'
'Oh God.'

Finally and perhaps the most bizarre, there was the call made to us from a mystery caller—or more accurately a call made by some underling on behalf of their employer on account of the time that might be spent in getting a connection:

'Hullow?'
'Hello, Trenowden speaking.'
'Meester Mork Trenowden.'
'Yes.'
'Yait one four siks siks seven?'
'Yesss.'
'Please hold!'

Pause.

'Hullow?'
'Yes, hello.'
'Who is this?'
'Look, you called me!'

Doubtless, however, all this would soon be behind us. I had finally got my attested photographs and passed these on to Feroz, together with my limp heap of completed telephone line application forms. The processing of telephone applications was a mysterious thing for which one might seek out the services of a 'fixer'. These shadowy-sounding figures, for a fee, could be called upon to handle the less official aspects of getting a line and ensure that any delays in acquiring a connection be kept to a minimum. Such intrigue was well out of my depth and in this sort of situation I relied implicitly on Feroz and had great faith in him.

For the most part things were under control. We had learnt from an early stage not to say things were going well as that state of affairs could reverse itself within minutes. When the newspapers started to report the passage of our vessel, the *Bangla Moni*, we greeted the news with tempered excitement. Intelligence gleaned from our shipping agents suggested that our shipment would reach the port of Chittagong in a week's time. This was heartening news, although the tales of woe that various 'old hands' had delighted in telling us about the efficiency of the port had made us wary of taking any estimated times of arrival as gospel. At least we could now start thinking more positively about setting up our home.

Having resisted the temptation to take the Police Commissioner's apartment, we had opted for an apartment in a block on the other side of Gulshan Lake. Purists would say that this is sanitised living overseas and I would be the first to throw my hands up and admit that we were hardly roughing it. Our plan by now had reverted to damage limitation, the glorious expat lifestyle of yesteryear we had envisaged was not to be—any glimpses of that had been left back in Bombay. No, in this spartan land we were going to be as comfortable and feel as safe as possible. Even if that meant there was an enormous red block full of US marines at the end of the road, then so be it.

The apartment we had singled out was on the fourth floor of a brand new block and of those we saw had a nice balance of layout, fittings and location. The timing of our arrival had not coincided with the annual change in Dhaka expatriate personnel and being the first of our own batch of staff, we had had the pick of all the available real estate in our price range. Our only real problem in securing a lease on the property had been in trying to track down the owner from the list of telephone numbers displayed on the 'To Let' sign. 'Two years', the lease we eventually signed had said. It was hard to believe and rather sobering to see it in black and white. I tried to picture myself on 14 July 1997 locking the door for the last time, but it was beyond my imagination.

The apartment gave us a new destination and a project for days off. Curtains would have to be measured up and ordered; air-conditioning units would need to be bought and installed; we would need a fridge, an oven and of course we would need that all important item for the small room adjacent to the kitchen: a cook. The small room was very small indeed and both Brenda and I felt pretty barbarous about committing a human being to its confines, a featureless room of 6ft by 4ft and a small bathroom with a shower and a hole-in-the-ground lavatory. Living 'in' needn't be compulsory, we decided, so we would leave it up to whoever our little friend might be, although the prospect of sharing our home with a complete stranger didn't exactly fill either of us with glee.

We had struck a rich vein at the Canadian Club one evening when talking to a girl called Sue who was into her fourth year in Bangladesh. She and her husband Peter had lived out at Mymensing some twenty-five kilometres outside Dhaka for a year before setting up home in Dhaka. I had met people who had clocked up six months, even a year, in Dhaka and each time thought to myself—I wish I were you. I wish I had that time under my belt and could speak with authority on how to survive this town. Awestruck maybe I was at the four-year landmark, but nope I didn't want to be her.

Of course, what you don't know about Dhaka if you have spent that sort of time there is not worth a mention and Sue could tell you just about anything you wanted to know. One might have guessed that the Americans already had things pretty well sewn up in that department and we were advised to get hold of a copy of the *American Women's Club Handbook*, which was the local expat bible. This to me covered topics as diverse as where to get yoghurt, who the German butcher was and how to join Alcoholics Anonymous. This last item we weren't too interested in, although it did cross our minds that we should go for a session to find out where all the ex-alcoholics had got their booze from. Drink was definitely going to be a problem and not even Sue could help us here. Duty-free warehouses existed, but without a passbook issued to the privileged few they were no-go areas. Perhaps we could work on Feroz. In the meantime Suvasta House, home of the American Women's Club, was definitely a good starting point and if we timed our visit correctly we could visit the servants registry held there once a week.

Suvasta House turned out to be just around the corner from us in Baridhara and one hardly had to look for the sign to know which building it was. Opposite the gates a group of hopeful 'servants' had gathered and no doubt they were eyeing us as warily as we were them. Inside the building a well-padded, blonde American lady explained to us how the registry worked and we were given the low-down on suitable prospective staff. *Ayahs*, *malis*, *chokidars*, bearers, cooks, drivers were all available, or alternatively there were those individuals who had been cross-pollinated and could fulfil a dual role. It was decided that what we really needed was a 'cook/bearer', who would minister to our every need from cleaning through ironing to cooking. I rather liked the sound of a bearer and inspected the cards laid out on the table for our ideal match.

'This man has worked overseas as a cook and has some English,' said the woman, leaning over the table, her roots betraying her true hair colour.

We liked the picture well enough and the man was summoned.

John Cruze was ushered into the room and stood before us, his eyes focused on two bare, leathery feet. He was well turned out in a yellow shirt and matching trousers which had seen some service but were newly laundered and if one had to make a snap judgement on a first impression, he looked the part. Rather taller than the average Bangladeshi, with a full head of hair and ubiquitous moustache, he was a not unimpressive character.

All these things one remembers now, but at the time my attention was focused on a horizontal scar through the middle of his nose. Did we have a fighter on our hands, an extremely clumsy person or just a likeable rogue? Who could say? For all our questions we were entering a lottery and only time would tell. Contact details were taken and we were given the telephone number of a local clergyman who would vouch for his good character. As a Christian, John would struggle to find employment with a local household but it was fine by us. We would be in touch.

With a home to furnish, we had long wanted to visit the antique shops at DIT 2 market. In a land almost totally devoid of outlets for retail therapy, the market from a distance is a sight for sore eyes. We had passed the site comprising three sides of a square of buildings on two levels many times. At night the whole place had appeared very intriguing, the dim lighting of the shops giving the whole facade a golden glow in the darkness. But now up close it was rather disappointing, the shops on the ground floor a strange mix of general stores, ironmongers, pharmacies and leather-goods shops. The first floor, however, was considerably more exciting and housed both antique shops and small art galleries, each manned by dubious-looking characters entreating us to come and sample their wares. We were easy prey and the shops full to the gills with curios and ageing furniture just too exciting.

Stopping to watch a man reweaving the cane back of a chair, we were nabbed by a shopkeeper hovering in a doorway.

'You like kar-rrr-pit, lovely kar-rrr-pit,' he ventured.

'Carpet no need,' I replied lapsing into the local vernacular, a hand raised in half greeting half submission. 'Chair need.'

'Plenty chair have, you come . . . come!'

We had to start somewhere and followed the man into his shop. As we entered, a small boy turned on lights and a ceiling fan, creating a suitable environment for delicate foreign shoppers to pick through the packed shelves. Small metal ornaments, old plates, bowls, watches, medals, coins and just about every small item salvageable from a ship, from soap dishes to portholes, were stacked in abundance. The whole scene was surveyed by a splendid marble bust of Queen Victoria, her eyeballs painted black atop a stone plinth. She was rather marvellous but we balked at the price of two *lakh taka*. We were still struggling to get our minds around *lakhs* and *crores* (some mental arithmetic produced a figure of something over 3,000 pounds). She was nice, but not that nice.

Something more in our price range was a couple of planters chairs stacked one on top of the other at the back of the shop and a great performance was made of disentangling these so that we could have a closer look. Both the chairs were a tiny bit the worse for wear and had been patched up in places, but with new cane seats they were serviceable and with an eye on the future they would be great souvenirs. Price negotiations were entered into. Some haggling, followed by feigned disinterest and then a theatrical stomping off into the middle distance from which we were grudgingly recalled, did the trick and both parties were satisfied at fifty pounds each.

With a promise to return, we set off from the market at a sedate pace, one of the seats precariously balanced in the boot while I held it open by means of an excellent piece of Heath Robinson improvisation with string and an open window. Our major obstacle overcome—a right-hand U-turn on to Gulshan Avenue—we approached the DIT 2 roundabout. Brenda and I were still not too adept with our direction-giving and a sudden request to go right (*dandig*) when there was only a possible left (*bandig*) threw Masum into confusion. We ground to a halt in the middle of the roundabout as Brenda and I both apologised profusely, which had the undesired effect of making Masum turn to face us, instead of keeping his eyes on the road.

'No, no, Masum, *bandig, bandig,*' Brenda blurted neatly concluding that '*dandig*' (with a 'd') had been the wrong way and *bandig* (with a 'b') was in fact correct. One had to admire Masum's composure under pressure. Despite the fact that we were heading backed-up traffic which was now engaged in heavy-duty honking of horns and ringing of bells we threaded our way off the roundabout and pulled in at the side of the road.

Our unscheduled diversion was on account of a prominent sign posted above a shop and declaring 'Video Connection', a recommendation from the crucial *American Women's Club Handbook*. Brenda had spotted it as we hit the roundabout and, despite the hazardous nature of the manoeuvre required to get us there, it was a destination that was high on our list of priorities. We left an unruffled Masum to guard our unstable cargo while we nipped inside to see what were the terms of membership and whether we could hire a video for the evening.

The air conditioning of the hotel was very welcome after our busy day running around and once more back in our room Brenda called the desk to ask if we could borrow a video recorder.

'Yes, certainly madam, we will send it right up to you, keep it as long as you like' was the gist of the conversation recounted to me by a disbelieving Brenda. It had been the first time that we had encountered anything approaching compliant service from the organisation. One normally got the impression that the hotel was a well-oiled machine that functioned efficiently just so long as the guests didn't get in the way.

A knock on the door proclaimed the arrival of housekeeping complete with video player. Although the gentleman concerned offered to set up the VCR, having witnessed the hamfisted efforts of housekeeping already I had a feeling that it would be simpler to install the player in my own time. No sooner had we said goodbye to this visitor than the doorbell rang again. This time it was a porter from the front desk bearing a bottle of wine. 'Aha!' we thought, an apology for the bathroom episode. But in actual fact it had been left for us by Peter and Sue, our Canadian friends.

It was a very kind gesture, particularly since they would have had to come all the way over to the hotel from Gulshan, a considerable dogleg that no one in their right mind would consider on a day off. We were both touched, but cringed inwardly at the amount of whinging we must have done about our alcohol-free status. However, such guilt dissipates quickly when there is a pizza to be ordered and the corkscrew on your Swiss army knife to be located. We were well tooled up for a truly vegetative evening.

chapter ten

I made a mental note to try and return to the office I was sitting in later on in the sporting year. By that time soccer would have given way to cricket and the centre spot of the National Stadium would be a faded mark on the synthetic wicket. From the north-facing windows we had a direct view down the half-way line of the National Stadium, which in my view marked this down as prime real estate. Feroz and I were at Panters Building at the invitation of a Mr Doti. It had been apparent for some time that the hotel 'office' had reached the end of its useful life. Not only had we grown out of it some time ago, but the cost of keeping it up was extortionate. Feroz in his own inimitable way had been  sounding out various options and Mr Doti, who, amongst other things, was Mala's uncle, had suggested we drop by to take a look at some available space in his office.

In classic local style our host failed to show at the appointed time, leaving us at the mercy of his partner who entertained us from behind a large desk situated at the end of the room. This man was something of a celebrity amongst the business community, having risen from obscurity to his now rarefied position. This it seemed gave him a licence to pontificate on numerous topics illustrating all his most salient points with swift abstract doodles on a pad of A4 paper. From time to time he would turn the pad to us so that we might admire his artistry before twisting it back to his face him and his poised pen. The clattering arrival of Doti through a side door saved us from further punishment and Feroz and I both rose to greet him. I was surprised that Feroz hadn't briefed me on the fact that Doti was recovering from a stroke which had seemingly left him paralysed down the one side.

'So sorry to keep you, it takes me such a long time to get dressed in the morning,' he said with a lopsided smile and I felt a pang of guilt for inwardly cursing this man's time keeping, while I shook the proffered left hand.

Feroz and Doti were obviously old friends and they lapsed into easy conversation in which I could take no part. I had tried to learn a bit of Bangla, but seemed to have little aptitude for it. I had found a charming teacher called Dolly who would come to the hotel for an hour once a week. The lessons comprised an hour of me repeating parrot-fashion the given sentence for the day. By the end of each session I could normally say one or two phrases quite fluently. Such as, *Kuleetake dak* ('Call the coolie') or *Likhte kashta hay* ('It's a cyclone') which one could argue, living in Bangladesh, was a pretty useful phrase to have. The problem with Dolly's method was that by the end of each session I had no idea which word in the sentence corresponded to its English equivalent. This not only hampered my ability to remember any new word, but also made putting all ones vocabulary into sentences an unlikely event. Outside 'class' all public notices were either labelled in English or Bengali, never in phonetic Bengali for students of the Dolly school, so one was never likely to pick up the odd word that way. If I did ever manage to trip over one of my few lines in a suitable situation then it was either assumed that as a foreigner I must be speaking my mother tongue or that with my lack of expertise in local intonation I had just said something vaguely insulting. The one area in which I had experienced some success was in my recognition of Bengali numbers: I had learnt the numerals from 1-9 and would practice my new found skill by reading out the number plates of cars which Brenda loyally thought a good party piece.

Bengali is, however, a very ancient language and as time has marched on it has become increasingly difficult to accommodate 'Twentieth Century Speak' in Bengali alone. The upside of this, for someone like me, is that one would occasionally get the gist of local conversation through the corruption of the mother tongue with English. 'Blah, blah, blah, computer, blah, blah, blah, fax machine, blah, blah, blah, telephone connection'.

'Blah, blah, blah, show him' acknowledged my presence whilst still excluding me from the conversation. It did at least result in some action as our hosts rose to their feet and motioned that I lead the party through a door in the back left-hand corner of the office behind the desk. As the days passed, I was becoming increasingly immune to the dank smell of mildewed carpet that met us as we entered the room. At least I assumed carpet to be the origin of the smell, but with no light source it was difficult to be sure. A knowledgeable hand felt its way down a wall for the light switch and fluorescent lights flickered into life. I was presented with a dismal scene of neglect, which I did my best to enthuse about. Whatever happened it would only be a temporary measure, but with no natural light at all we were going to have to perform something pretty miraculous to jolly up these surroundings. Feroz joined me in inspecting the proposed centre of operations and opened a second door into the room, which proved to afford us an extremely convenient route into Mr Doti's Accounts Department.

'You will see that once I have put in some new carpet and we have painted the walls it will be a fine office. You can buy some chairs and tables and can use one of the telephone lines at my desk,' chipped in Doti's partner.

'That is a very kind offer, but really there's no need,' I countered eager not to put them out too much.

'No Mark, let them do it,' came a voice through the amber gloom. Feroz had spoken and I wouldn't question him.

Back at the hotel a pow-wow was held to establish the merits of setting up shop at Panters Building. That we had to move had already been decided, but was this the right place? On the positive side we would save a substantial amount of cash. We would have to buy various bits and pieces, but these would all eventually find a home in the office proper. For Brenda and me personally, the prospect of relocating our place of work further than two doors away from our residence was a big draw. Fighting our way through traffic to and from the office would take the best part of half an hour each way, but with a fairly limited list of time-passing options this would be a welcome diversion. Mala definitely had her reservations, the main unspoken ones being that she wouldn't be able to disappear back to her room for protracted 'high level' telephone calls and there would be no room service.

'So, it is just the one room... so we will have to share a phone line... our confidentiality... no windows at all ... no ladies room!'

'Mala,' Feroz broke in, 'I want to speak to you.'

On cue Brenda and I left the room leaving them to their mysterious tête-à-tête. Behind the adjoining door I greedily called room service to stock up on tea and fruit cake, a small vice I had been driven to by hotel living. It having been delivered, I was musing on just how the chef managed to get all the currants to sink to the bottom of the cake with such monotonous regularity when we were summoned back into join them.

'Feroz has explained to me that due to the political sympathies of Mr Doti's partner, it is not advisable for us to be seen forming a close liaison with him. Instead Feroz has kindly offered that we use part of his office until the architects have completed ours,' Mala announced.

As I left the room with the unsavoury prospect of having to make a 'thanks, but no thanks' courtesy call to Doti, the logic of why Feroz hadn't made his offer slightly earlier in the proceedings escaped me.

Later that evening Feroz called and invited Brenda and me to join him, his wife and some of their friends for dinner. However well-intentioned the offer, having made it back to our room the prospect of having to drag ourselves back out again was not a happy one. We had sent Masum home for the evening, so the long-suffering Rohim had been dispatched to the hotel to pick us up and take us the short distance to Banani. This area, bounded on one side by the airport road and a thin river on the other, was chosen some twenty years ago as THE place to be for wealthy local families. This trend has been superseded somewhat by the development of Gulshan, but die-hards and contemporaries of Feroz's generation have stayed where they were, seemingly oblivious to the fact that any glory had long since faded.

A shrill blast on a whistle greeted us as Rohim turned off the main drag into a side street. A huddle of small tea shops with oil lamps illuminating their proprietors ran the length of what appeared to be an unmade road to nowhere. Coming to a halt, the car doors were whipped open by khaki-clad guards and feeling rather disorientated we stepped out into the darkness. The building we found ourselves at the foot of was imposing, although as we suspiciously made our way into the gloomy lobby it was obvious that it fell into the faded glory category.

'Restaurant twelve floor,' the guard informed us and we were thankful that the small row of lights above the lift doors proclaimed that it was in working order. I enjoy a good lift ride about as much as blasting down a runway at 100 miles an hour and so I was relieved to finally arrive at our destination: 'The Sky Room'.

Feroz and the rest of his party were already seated when we arrived and I didn't need to look at Brenda to realise that she would already be analysing the seating arrangements. A definite male-female bias to each end of the table would mean a tortuous evening for her and for me, since doubtless I would be sucked to the male and 'business' end of the proceedings. Our fears, however, turned out to be unfounded. This was a social evening, a gathering of Feroz and his wife's friends. As introductions were made we warmed to the smiling faces of these people who seem to be delighted to make our acquaintance. This was the first time we had met Feroz's wife, Barbi. A very glamorous, bejewelled lady with a pear-shaped face and olive skin.

'Ah, Mark and Brenda, at last I can meet you!' she beamed. proffering a fine and slightly inclined hand to each of us in turn.

Other introductions were made to the entire party, which including us comprised four couples. Much to our relief, we were directed to seats in the middle of the rectangular table facing one another.

'Now Mark, this gentleman has been very interested to meet you,' said Feroz, directing my attention to the man seated at the head of the table. 'This is Colonel Latif, he is a very sporty man and is very interested in cricket!'

Latif, as his title suggested, was an ex-military man and in retirement he had maintained a fastidiousness about his appearance, no doubt drilled into him through years of military service. His hair, plastered to his head in a black shiny slab, was immaculate and a barrel chest suggested that despite being over fifty he was still physically fit. Softly spoken, with kind eyes, it was hard to imagine Latif actually being tough. However, as the evening wore on and the whisky flowed, tales of his military and sporting prowess showed that he was brave to the point of recklessness, hallowed in local sporting circles and above all, in the nicest possible way, absolutely barking mad.

'Five o'clock in the morning I take exercise, this is very beneficial,' Latif assured us. An exchanged glance at my partner confirmed that this couldn't possibly be true. 'Then meditation, or writing or reading before I take food.' A man of many accomplishments and all before breakfast. 'Once I was a fit and strong young man, but now...' he said ruefully handling his knee. 'I have a problem with my knee. Here, I have taken a bullet.'

Having never met anyone who had been shot before, I found this fascinating and listened intently as Latif's story of a roadside ambush on his jeep had brought about his wound.

'My car pulled sharply and turned over and my driver was lost. Lying on the ground I found my Sten gun and as our attackers approached I stood up and let them have three long blasts...' Full sound effects accompanied this rather shocking disclosure. 'And they lay dead.'

My goodness, I thought, a killer as well!

'When my men came to me they said, "Oh Sir, you have blood," and yes I had taken a bullet, but in the commotion I had not felt it.'

The whole story was extraordinary and as tears welled in Latif's eyes it could only be true. Feroz and the others had paid little attention to the story; no doubt they had heard it before. It was obvious that the whisky was taking effect and proceedings at the other end of the table were becoming rather giggly.

'Mark, you must play for Latif's cricket team,' suggested Barbi and the rest of the assembled gathering excitedly voiced their approval.

'Yes, Mark, on Friday you must come to my house,' chipped in Latif, having regained his composure.

My cricketing ability had, I feared, been misperceived. A healthy interest does not a Test cricketer make, but Latif would have nothing of my excuses and protestations.

'The ladies will come, too, and Mark and Brenda, I will take you from my house to the field. We will see you on Friday at 9 o'clock!'

chapter eleven

Latif's residence, situated in the Cantonment, proved difficult to get to. *Bideshis* (foreigners) are not allowed in the Cantonment and at its entrance Masum was going through his whole repertoire of finger-pointing, shrugging and grimacing with the soldier on duty. Finally, he convinced the soldier that we were not a threat to national security and we were allowed to pass. We were given a withering look from close quarters as we drove through the checkpoint and I was  relieved the windows had remained tightly closed between those fiery eyes and me. One gets used to seeing guns in Dhaka—from the ageing *Lee Enfields* held by security guards to the highly polished automatic weapons handled by the Prime Minister's elite guards—but Latif's story had made me rather jumpy about guns altogether.

Squeezing between two parked cars, we approached the front door and rang the bell. After a protracted wait a servant opened the door. We were obviously not expected, but despite the unlikely event of two Westerners arriving at the door at such an ungodly hour we were ushered in and led through the house to a reception room. Heavy curtains were drawn back, allowing the bright sunshine a chance to fade the deep red velvet of the chairs' upholstery. The smell of invisible mildew in the soft furnishings suggested that the sun did not get much opportunity to do this. It was a sure thing that as soon as we were on our way the room would be closed up again.

'Saar, uppistairs,' announced the servant and disappeared.

Well, so much for the 5 o'clock start! The whole house was so quiet that the family could only be tucked up in bed and happily engaged in the time-honoured Bengali tradition of having a lie-in on the one rest day of the week.

Having encountered changing rooms of various standards on the village cricket circuit, I dared not consider what Dhaka would have to offer. I had therefore taken the precaution of changing into my cricket clothes already. Dhaka is the sort of place in which you could cheerfully walk down the street on fire and nobody would give you a second glance. Despite this fact I felt conspicuous and rather awkward, although when the servant reappeared with a tray, if he found my dress incongruous then he wasn't giving anything away.

Brenda and I warily surveyed the tray that had been placed between us. Four small oily, flying saucers and two cups of char. We would have to eat something and taking the plunge I nibbled the edge of what I now know to be a *paratha* and was pleasantly surprised. Brenda suspiciously followed my lead and within seconds we perversely found ourselves wishing that we had a couple more.

Finally Latif appeared neatly coifed and wearing a *punjabi*.

'My friends, so sorry you have been waiting for me,' he said, his arms outstretched in a munificent way, before lapsing in to a long explanation as to why he would not be accompanying us. Having established that Latif had consigned himself to the substitutes' bench, we were sent on our way with information that the Captain of the team was expecting me, and could be found at Gulshan Field.

Gulshan Field jaben which roughly translates as 'Gulshan Field going', got the desired response from Masum and soon we were picking our way down a

side road from the main Gulshan drag. A proliferation
of Corollas parked hard up against a shoulder-high
wall marked the spot beyond which lay the ground. As
we slowed, a jumble of small children eased themselves from their vantage points on the top of the wall
and hurried to our aid.

Many small dirty hands grasped at my kit bag after I had eventually got Masum to open the boot.
There was a bit of a gap in my vocabulary on car parts
and 'car backside' had eventually got the desired effect.

With so many willing helpers to choose from, I
picked a bedraggled child who, having been given the
go ahead, wrestled my bag from my hand and led the
way through a gap in the wall towards a collection of
men dressed similarly to myself.

Gulshan Field comprised two acres of thick coarse
grass bounded by a whitewashed wall that ran round
three sides of its square. At each end lay substantial
white-painted residential properties nestling in lush
gardens, separated from the ground by only a single
track road and the wall, while the remaining two sides
were flanked by a mixture of coconut palms and other
vegetation to ensure maximum difficulty in the event
of a lost ball search. Dead centre lay a smear of dark
clay which I presumed to be the cricket pitch, which
was being ministered to by two *lungi*-clad figures each
with a length of sacking.

A rotund figure fully kitted out to bat approached
and explained the function of the sacking.

'They are taking up the moisture from the pitch.'

I smiled and nodded knowledgeably, warily eyeing
the complete helmet and metal visor my companion
was wearing. Through the grille the chubby jowls of a
wealthy local were squashed into flabby rolls with a
sprinkling of unshaven stubble as garnish.

A tall, thin, bespectacled man who introduced
himself as 'Arshi the Captain' joined us. Evidently
Latif had managed to brief him about me and, having

established that I would be representing Renegades Cricket Club, he asked me in which discipline was my own particular forte.

'Do you bat or bowl Mark?'

Shifting uneasily on my feet I admitted to having no earthshaking talent for any part of the game, but could be guaranteed to run about in the field like a madman and that perhaps we should concentrate on this aspect of my game.

'Well you seem to have brought all your equipment,' he said, motioning towards my small porter friend. 'You can bat at no. 5.'

The cricket match was the place to be on a Friday morning if the facilities were anything to go by. As yet the sun was not at its hottest, although the noisy construction of a pink and white striped *shamiana* in a leafy spot on the boundary suggested that by midday we would require the shade. A *shamiana* is a marvellous makeshift marquee fashioned out of thick bamboo secured with coarse string and draped with brightly coloured material. *Shamianas* can be erected in double quick time and at a ludicrously low cost. Ranks of folding chairs arranged under the *shamiana* suggested that we were in for quite an audience, although by the looks of things we were yet to have a full compliment of players let alone spectators. Progress in that department looked slow, and Brenda, her interest on the wane, decided to pay a visit to our nearby Canadian friends, Peter and Sue, with the promise that she would return later to take in the action.

Finally each side appeared to have assembled at least ten of eleven men and with the toss won Renegades elected to bat. Our opening batsmen plodded out to the wicket and play commenced. I watched in horror as an athletic youth tore in from the far end of the ground and delivered the first ball of the match in a wayward but extremely speedy fashion. The balance of my side had taken up station under some trees adjacent to a small concrete building in one corner. This I would have loosely termed as a pavilion, although Brenda, with a North American view on just what constituted a pavilion, would have called it a concrete hut. My team mates howled support for our man, as he flashed an anxious look towards us through the grille of his hard hat. Our so-called friendly game had an edge to it and I was to find out later that the nucleus of our team were four ringers from local professional teams. Two to buoy up the bowling and a couple of batsmen to ensure a respectable score.

My porter was hard at work emptying my bag of equipment and I suppressed my protective urges as the other members of my team called for these precious items so that they could be inspected more closely. Throughout our ranks the amount of effort that was being applied to the donning of pads and the selection of bats suggested that faith in our openers was not running high. Sure enough, the clatter of stumps and the celebrations of our opposition heralded the fall of our first wicket. Followed swiftly by an other, which left me with the sobering realisation that I was next in. Doubtless having seen this pattern of events before, Arshi had contrived for both our senior players to be at the wicket after the surrender of the first two sacrificial batsmen. Taking advantage of the fast bowlers' initial exertions and with the shine having been taken off the new ball, our pair began to stamp their authority on the game. While I was riveted to the action, believing each ball to be a wicket-taker, my companions slowly lost interest in the proceedings. As our ringers accumulated runs, mobile phones were produced, newspapers read and raucous conversations entered into.

Feroz appeared in the gap in the wall and I did my best to attract his attention. My cricket garb for once had made me unidentifiable in a group and he and a group of friends walked over and took seats beneath the *shamiana*. Joining them, I was subjected to close scrutiny, the consensus being that I looked every inch a cricketer and that it would indeed be very exciting to see me take on the might of Dhaka. That moment was eventually heralded by a catch off a ball skied by one of our star performers. The outgoing batsman and his colleague had ensured that there was no pressure on me to contribute an enormous score to the total, but the pressure being exerted by the expectant, waving and smiling folk sheltering beneath the *shamiana* was considerable.

Once in the middle, I was surprised to find that the surface we were playing on resembled a large slab of leathery tarmac, which stood proud of the field some four inches. Small scarlet skid marks from where the ball had pitched testified to its durability and I hoped that this sort of impact would take the pace off the ball rather than allowing it to skid through. Whatever the merits of the pitch, I would have to wait to face a ball as the over had come to an end and my fellow batsman had the strike. Musing on how cool it was to actually be playing cricket in the sub-continent, I was brought to my senses by a sharp barking sound. My colleague had played the ball into a gap in the field and had called for a run. Once dispatched, the ball had shot off the leather pitch only to loose speed alarmingly as soon as it encountered the long grass. I had had to hurry to make my ground but I was still in and our partnership was worth one.

Now it was my turn to face the bowling and taking my guard I was relieved that the bowler hadn't appeared quite as fast at close quarters as he had from a distance. As the first ball bowled to me shot past my flailing bat to be greeted by an 'Oooooooofff'—an expletive in cricketing parlance meaning 'phew that was close'—I realised that I had just been kidding myself. Horribly fast is the official term to be applied and it was obvious that should the next ball be on target, then I would be done for. As luck would have it, the bowler erred in his line on the second ball. It looked to be distinctly legside as it left his hand. Yes, quite wayward in fact and as if in answer to a prayer the middle of my bat connected with the ball, sending it in a neat arc to the boundary pausing to bounce only once before registering four runs against my name. As the words 'Thank you, God' formed on my lips my colleague walked up to me and motioned for me to hold up my gloved hand. Dumbly complying he punched my glove smartly with his own made into a fist, which proclaimed me as one of them. Returning to face the next ball I settled over my bat only to notice that the handle had split from the main body of the bat. Play was delayed whilst a suitable replacement was found and rushed out to me. How many miles had I dragged that bat for that one shot? I thought as I took my stance, the bowler turning to start his run up, his final approach, the delivery. Again the ball was legside. I couldn't believe my luck and repeated my previous shot. Something about this stroke didn't feel so good. Not quite so much purchase and instead of helping the ball on its way: a rather uncultured club into the middle distance. For the moment, however, it looked just fine and for an instant I thought it would be making an unscheduled visit into the confines of the *shamiana* when a fielder, having made a well timed run, neatly caught the ball, much to the jubilation of the opposition.

It had been the perfect cameo. A minimum of humiliating scratching around, a crowd-pleasing slog and the *bideshi's* scalp for the bowler. However short my stay at the wicket, by the time I reached the shade I was perspiring profusely with adrenaline coursing through me. My porter, who had now taken to being my butler, produced a bottle of Pepsi. I drank as much as my urge to hiccup against the fizz would allow and my manservant relieved me of the bottle, draining the last inch and savouring every drop as he returned the bottle to the pavilion. Waiting for my heart rate to return to normal, I noticed a man sitting nearby with legs outstretched. He would soon be called upon to bat and was having his pads attached by one of the other boys who had been in my welcoming committee. Surely this was the height of luxury or laziness and I hoped the child would get his *baksheesh* for his trouble. To my amazement, on completion of the fitting the man drained a canned drink that had been under his seat and threw the empty can to the child. Having minutely examined the interior of the can for any morsel the child took the can over to a tiny bedraggled child with a shaggy mop of hair who had already started a collection. The ultimate in recycling. Tiny children sent out by their slum dwelling parents to scavenge enough plastic, cans, bottles, string or whatever to trade off against the next meal.

A meal was the last thing I needed after my exertion and in the sweltering heat of the midday sun. Wickets continued to fall regularly. Arshi, taking his captain's role very seriously, remained not out, making a stiff, defensive stand at one end, while a steady procession of batsmen whose optimism outweighed their ability spooned easy catches to waiting fielders or leapt down the pitch with eyes spinning and arms flailing, only to be unceremoniously dispatched by straight balls. My fellow players were displaying a healthy lack of concern about the situation of the game. By the time the last wicket fell lunch was the more immediate concern. Two dull black cauldrons arrived balanced precariously on the back of a flatbed rickshaw and my heart sank at the prospect of having to enthuse about, and worst still digest, their contents.

'Mark! Come! Take some food,' called Feroz, motioning for me to join the small crowd gathering by a table stacked with plates and thick smoked glass beakers. Great ceremony was made of ushering me through to the front to be presented with my plate of food - a substantial helping of discoloured rice and grey, bony meat.

'Ahhh *biriani*' were the words being voiced round me and I struggled to appear as outwardly enthusiastic about the fare on offer. Although to judge by the happy expressions of those peeling off from the group with laden plates, I was alone in the distrust of *biriani* camp. My other concern was the lack of cutlery. Although quite prepared to go local, up to a point, the prospect of plunging my hand into my oily lunch with non-existent ablutions was not a jolly one. A polite enquiry solicited a flat stainless steel serving spoon, which I was never going to get into my mouth but would save me from having to suffer spicy scented fingers all afternoon. Our wicket keeper certainly didn't share my delicate disposition and I winced as I watched him clear his plate and then plunge a *biriani*-speckled hand into his glove.

Lunch had been the big draw and with the resumption of hostilities on the field the spectators started to drift away. Even Feroz and his party were on their way, any novelty in the cricket having long since worn off. Oblivious to our lost support, Arshi was busy directing operations, which included placing me deep on the boundary fence under a canopy of shady foliage. I was pleased to be out of the sun and out of the direct line of fire as greasy mutton and chillies had just started to repeat on me.

Our opening bowler had paced out a magnificent run up and was starting his approach up for the first ball of our opponents' innings. Gulshan Field certainly had an agricultural feel and the outfield was mined with potholes, thick heavy clumps of grass and the odd cowpat. Having picked his way through these assorted hazards and run hundreds of yards, the poor boy was going to be exhausted. Our man, however, had not read the script and, bowling as though his life depended on it, dismissed the first opening batsman with the fourth ball of the innings. Joining the midwicket celebrations, Arshi walked over and informed me that the next man in had captained the Bangladesh national side and would need to be prised out if victory were to be ours. Eyeing this man with awe, I jogged out backwards to my station and watched as over the next few overs Faruque gave a master class on the chasm between the professional and recreational game.

Brenda and our Canadian friends appeared on the horizon and ambled round the boundary to come and talk to me. News of the *biriani* lunch was greeted with amusement and I was just trying to respond to the criticism that it was a very peculiar game that one could stop halfway through for a meal, when Arshi called over to me.

'Mark, take the next over at that end.'

His finger dictated that I bowl from the non carpark end of the ground, which meant that, in the event of Faruque getting to grips with my less than penetrating off spin, then at least the windscreens would be safe. Loping in off a short run, I was understandably tense and I watched in mild alarm as my first ball sat up invitingly in front of Faruque and was neatly sent on its way to the square leg boundary. Since even on the most helpful village pitch any spin I impart on the ball is normally attributed to it having hit a bump, I decided that on this rock hard shirt-front of a pitch damage limitation should be the order of the day. Spearing the ball in on the batsman's feet, I overpitched and a flick of the wrist helped my wayward full toss over the boundary for six. Needless to say, I wasn't asked to continue my spell and I returned to my fielding position to receive commiserations from Brenda and a ribbing from Peter.

The embattled Arshi took it upon himself to bowl the next over and I was greatly heartened as Faruque stepped down the wicket and heaved the ball into the air. My immediate impression was that ball had gone almost vertically but as it followed its course it became apparent that it was travelling in my direction. Starting in from the boundary, it spiralled above me and in my enthusiasm to retrieve it I over ran the ball and found that it had past me but was dropping fast. Halting my progress and backing out again I stuck up an optimistic left hand and as my fingers involuntary clamped on the ball on impact... I realised that I had caught it!

'I knew when first I saw you that you were a cricketer. Was that not the catch of a cricketer!' It was the most emotion I had seen Arshi display and on joining us in the outfield the whole team indulged in a spot of communal admiration while the next batsman walked out to bat.

With the dismissal of their star any hopes of victory for the opposition evaporated. Shortly before tea-time the last man was run-out in a shambolic mix-up and victory was conferred upon Renegades CC.

At the end of the game there was a charming impromptu round of speeches presided over by a small middle-aged man wearing a blazer and tie. Both teams were thanked for their participation and the winning Captain was presented with an envelope to the accompaniment of polite applause. Making my way wearily towards the car, accompanied by my small porter, a shout from over my shoulder stopped me in my tracks. It was Arshi.

'Hey Mark! Here is your share!'

'My share?'

'Yesss. Your share of our prize!'

With that he thrust a grimy hundred taka bank-note into my hand, a little over £1.50.

chapter twelve

Our meeting with Lisal Huque of 'Going Places Movers' in the lobby of the hotel was one of those where
good sense said that we should could keep this man,
the local agent for our removal company, on our side.
At the same time, it was one of those where the information he imparted was of such an annoying and
frustrating variety
that it was close to
impossible to keep
one's patience in
check. The *Bangla
Moni* had ap-
parently arrived at
Chittagong Port;
the container containing our worldly goods had been
located and was already aboard a train bound for
Dhaka. This was indeed good news and this initial
disclosure was met with jubilation. Then came the
frustrating part: we would have to compile a list of our
possessions complete with valuation for customs. The
purpose of this was to calculate the amount of duty
due on the contents of our container. In effect, we
were to pay duty on our own used belongings. Although we were assured that one day this money
would be returned to us when we took everything
away again, the prospect of that actually happening,
based on our limited knowledge of local procedures,
was infinitesimally small.

Feroz breezed into the lobby and spotting us at a
table came over to talk to us.

'I am on my way to my office,' he said, ignoring
our guest. 'Will I be seeing you there later?'

This was the sort of question that would send my
hand up in an involuntary action to scratch my head.

It would seem that the best-laid plans in Dhaka were never set in concrete. That despite the fact that today had been earmarked as our first day in Feroz's office. That elaborate plans had been orchestrated by myself to ensure the smooth transfer of the entire contents of makeshift hotel office to the new one. That Mala had called 'an important meeting' that afternoon to be held in the new office that all concerned should attend might somehow have been put on hold just for the hell of it.

Perhaps the nature of my previous discussion with Lisal hadn't left me too well disposed to local quirkiness and I proceeded to tell Feroz of the latest hurdle the authorities, in their infinite wisdom, had managed to place in our way.

'This will be a small problem,' was his considered response and he barked a series of commands to the startled Lisal, who rose and backed off in an obsequious manner.

'You must fax him a list of your things later today and he will arrange for you to meet with the customs people at the railway station. It will take just some small money.' With a careless wave and a 'See you later,' he was gone.

24 Dilkusha was the address we had been given and I minutely examined the buildings for numbers as we drove the length of the road. To one side of us ran a high wall, which Masum had already pointed out as the landmark.

'President here house have.'

To the other side there was a parade of commercial properties with the names of banks and insurance companies emblazoned upon them. A series of unpromisingly dark lobbies fronted by an arcade gave nothing away and I decided that I might have more luck on foot.

Having navigated a split concrete slab that served as a bridge from the road to the arcade over an open sewer, I spied a small '24' painted above one of the lobbies and gestured to the Masum that I had located the right address. Masum, who had been monitoring my progress, eased the car into a makeshift parking space in front of the building, scattering a disgruntled group of tea drinkers who had been squatting there. Brenda joined me and we entered the gloomy lobby, waking an extremely hairy individual who had been asleep on a weathered school chair in an alcove to the left of the entrance. Shakily getting to his feet, he saluted and gave us a quizzical look. Otherwise we entered the building unchallenged and having no other option climbed a concrete staircase in search of Feroz's office.

A pair of dark wooden double doors faced us on the first floor landing. On the door post a small brass nameplate with the name of Feroz's consulting company on it confirmed the office as our destination. Despite the fact that the whole building looked completely dilapidated and the offices abandoned, we knocked on the door and were relieved to find that there was someone in residence. A small rotund man with prominent teeth opened the door and ushered us into a large wood panelled room. With windows in just one wall it was fairly dark and depressing, but at a glance there appeared to be plenty of desks laid out like an old fashioned typing pool. Not ideal, but even as it stood it would at least be less cramped than our current arrangement.

'ASAD!' boomed Feroz's voice from behind a door in the corner of the room. With that the man who had opened the door shuffled off to do his master's bidding. Uninvited, Brenda and I walked over to Feroz's office and put our heads round the door.

'Come in, come in' said Feroz. 'You found the office without a problem?'

'Oh yes,' Brenda reassured him, ever the diplomat.

For such an immaculately turned out man it was strange to find Feroz secreted away in this shabby office. His own room had no windows and the electric lighting glowed yellow, dampened by the dark wood-panelled walls. Three telephones of various vintages and a fax machine on a small table were the only evidence that any business was ever entered into. A well-stocked ashtray and copy of the Indian TV magazine, *Starburst*, suggested that it hadn't exactly been a busy day.

'Come and see the rest of the office, you can choose where you will sit,' Feroz ventured and we followed him back out to the main office.

First impressions had been misleading and in all there were five smaller, again windowless, offices - satellites of the main office space—which, with the exception of the one occupied by Feroz, were all at our disposal. The largest of these, which housed both a desk and oval dining table was designated as Mala's. Brenda staked a claim on the next and another was set aside for Roger Barb, an Englishman who had recently arrived. Roger was something of an oddity inasmuch as he was an Englishman who spoke fluent Bengali. Married to a Bangladeshi girl he had met at university, he had strong local ties and was at present holed up with his mother-in-law. Brenda had met him London once before, but as yet I had only made his acquaintance on the telephone, but that would be remedied later at Mala's meeting.

The rest of us would be housed in the other two offices. Some of us in the typing pool area and those requiring a little more privacy in a cavern of a room sandwiched between Mala's and Feroz's. Saving me from the fairly dire prospect of being squeezed into a passable impression of Calcutta's black hole, Feroz suggested that I share his with him. Although I am by no means a lazy person, the idea of being tied to a desk all day, under the watchful gaze of others filled me horror, let alone the close proximity to Mala. I thought this an excellent idea.

Two more rooms remained on our tour: a small elongated cupboard of a room which housed a single gas ring supplied by a length of orange rubber tube and a gas canister, a large kettle and Asad. As we appeared in the doorway, he eased himself to his feet and stood eyes downcast while Feroz retrieved a worn key from a nail in the wall and held it at arms length for us to inspect. The key to the 'Executive' bathroom.

Plans were already well in hand to kit out the office. Brenda had pursued a rigorous examination of the local agents for various computer companies. This exercise had caused the two of us a certain amount of pain in as much as we had had to endure hospitality of a couple of the companies in the running. A painful evening at the American Club, which firmly decided us against that particular outfit and drinks with a giant of a man in a purple suit who, rumour had it, had been a freedom fighter and killed several men with his bare hands. He had doubtless tortured his American employers until he had been given the franchise for his computers. Although he was probably the most professional of all the people we saw, he too failed in his bid.

Brenda had finally opted for a company whose front man Shafiq was memorable inasmuch as he had steel grey hair and a bright orange beard. He rather boringly had met all the criteria for software and hardware and, more importantly, could actually deliver the goods. We had scheduled a delivery to coincide with our first day and I left Brenda at the office waiting for their man to arrive to plumb the machines in.

My own list of tasks was lengthening and I was keen to pay a quick visit to our local Mancunian bank manager, whose office was at the end of Dilkusha. Geoff Williams was as unlikely and unfriendly a figure as you were ever going to meet in Dhaka. Having already spent a year as Branch Manager, he was well versed in the techniques of handling the local bureaucracy and had plenty of experience in negotiating and side stepping, where possible, time-consuming annoyances. Perhaps it was this experience that had made him such a dour individual.

A firm believer in the Dunkirk spirit, I had done my best to exploit my own and Brenda's contacts, whenever and wherever they presented themselves. To a certain extent I laboured under the misconception that all my compatriots abroad would want to be my friend, to tough-it-out together in adversity. One such contact in Dhaka, a Scotsman whom we had telephoned out of the blue and who had good humouredly received us in his home, really couldn't have had a more bleak or jaundiced view of the place: taking advantage to the full of the good things Dhaka had to offer and cursing vehemently just about everything else.

As far as I could see, the one good thing for Graham was that if he hit his golf ball into a lake on the golf course then somebody would get it out for him. While the bad things ranged from his driver when given a direction driving into the middle distance for fifteen minutes, before admitting that he had no idea where he was going, to the simple fact that men pee in the street in Dhaka.

Despite his demeanour, Williams had the good news that, in principle, the Bangladesh Bank had approved our bank account, and that shortly he would be in a position to receive our funds. This was indeed good news, as we were still paying our hotel expenses with Brenda's credit card, while Mala looked after the bulk of other outgoings on what must have been a triple platinum Amex card. Dhaka, however, is a society dominated by cash and to a large extent credit cards are treated with distrust. Many of the things we needed could only be paid for with cash and the majority of local tradesmen were not as benevolent as Mr Haque at Haq's Bay. Mobile telephones, which were in their infancy in Dhaka, were—as far as we were concerned—a 'must have'. Even if we had had one, the local land lines being what they were any option was worth taking. However with the deals on mobile sets available at home in mind, the charges for the intermittent service in Dhaka were extortionate. We had planned to acquire three handsets for the princely sum of £1400 each, but no amount of charm or diplomacy would sway the proprietor from his stance that the money should be paid in advance and in full.

It was discovered that Schezade was a cousin of the man and he was wheeled out to see if he could work the oracle. In a meeting that seemed to take the format of which side of the negotiating parties could smoke the most cigarettes, we lost out dismally and once again I turned to Feroz.

'Hullow, I am Feroz,' came the voice from the telephone. 'I am in the hotel lobby, can I come up to your room?'

This was all very mysterious, but I complied and after a short time answered the knock on the door. Feroz stood in the corridor with a briefcase in one hand, which was totally out of character and perhaps the most energetic thing I had ever seen him do. Making sure the door was closed he walked over to the bed and put the case down. As if from a scene in a film he flicked open the locks and opened the case to reveal, laid out in rows the largest amount of money I had ever seen: forty neatly sewn up bundles of one hundred taka notes.

'I want this back you know Mark,' he said with a grin.

chapter thirteen

Mala's announcement really couldn't have come at a worse time. She had two snippets of information to impart and both of them affected me. The first and most pressing being that we were shortly to play host to an important businessman from Hong Kong. Mr Wong was currently humming-and-hawing over whether or not to make a substantial commitment, in terms of investment to the infrastructure of Bangladesh, or to look elsewhere. By all accounts this man had put the 'V' into VIP and we would be expected by our head office

to pull out all the stops in our handling of him. Mala was concerned that as well as putting on a first class show for the 'Great' man the new offices should be completed to coincide with his visit. This minor detail would require a small miracle if the current rate of progress were to be maintained. The second item on the agenda was more a cause for celebration than anything else as Mala declared her intention to disappear after the visit to the States for a month to pack up her apartment in New York and have her belongings shipped to Dhaka.

As if our life hadn't taken a complicated enough twist already. Brenda and I had arranged to be in Canada for a wedding in a week's time. The wedding was in fact our own and the date we had selected had been determined before the Bangladesh thing had entered the frame. It had been a precondition of the whole deal that we be allowed up to three weeks off and go ahead with our plans; and one that Mala had been quite amenable to. Now that the time was fast approaching a whole stack of things to prey on our minds was the last thing we wanted. However, perhaps, if one set the dominoes up in a neat enough line it would be a relatively simple task to delegate someone to knock the first one over. In theory it was a good idea.

The Mr Wong visit made us feel a lot better about our role in Dhaka. We had always felt slight social outcasts coming from the private sector whilst the majority of our friends and acquaintances were either working in development, on aid projects or teachers. We had a distinct feeling that somehow we weren't doing our bit. The multi-lateral view, regarding the development of Bangladesh, was that whilst aid is a marvellous thing, the encouragement of investment from overseas—particularly in infrastructure—was the way forward. If the latest story about a certain gentleman named 'Ivan' that was being bandied around the American Club was anything to go by; then the sooner the lead was taken away from the aid agencies the better.

The Thursday evening pizza night at the American Club was something of an institution and as the equivalent of a Friday night there was always a relaxed mood normally enhanced by the margaritas made by the fierce barman, Celestine. This particular Thursday the talk had strayed from the normal gripes about jobs, the country and errant servants to exited talk of Ivan's latest exploits. Ivan was a rather annoying and abrasive 'know all' type who managed at some time or other to put just about everybody out. Several heated arguments had already cost him his job however he had stayed in Dhaka and eventually found work with another program. His latest job had taken him out to one of the villages outside the city and a problem with a vehicle had meant that a return to

Dhaka and its relative civilisation would be delayed. Not wanting to spend another night away from his creature comforts he had taken his bosses jeep. Not surprisingly the discovery of which fact had led to the alerting of the local constabulary to the supposed theft of the vehicle.

The story starts to take a mythical turn as it appears that the local police force were successful in intercepting the vehicle and arresting the driver: the errant Ivan. It is however true and surely he can consider himself the unluckiest man alive to have been intercepted. Having been incarcerated it appears that whilst undergoing an interrogation he decided to take matters into his own hands. Managing to break free from his captors, he jumped out of a window and finding a police jeep idling in the yard below, booted the unsuspecting police driver from behind the wheel and was last seen disappearing down the road having smashed through the gates of the police compound. Bangladesh could appear at times to be a fairly lawless place, but not that out of control.

Members of the American Embassy were apparently carrying out polite negotiations on his behalf. With one well-known American national residing in a Dhaka jail for alleged drug offences, the considered opinion was that a slap-on-the-wrist would suffice and that the bounteous relationship between the Bangladesh and her largest donor would remain intact.

The considered opinion of the people in the bar was that everyone 'lost it' at some stage due to the abundance of day-to-day frustrations and that if it hadn't happened to such a disagreeable person, then it really would have been quite excusable. Brenda and I certainly felt better about our status as the 'bad guys.'

Polite negotiations with the local authorities would have to be entered into as well if Mala's master plan was to come to fruition. Roger and I, who had been designated as Mr Wong visit co-ordinators, were saddled with this unenviable task. As brand new in the organisation as he could be, Roger had yet to see the full force of Mala's capricious nature but it would not take long. I was sure I detected a slight twitch when in her description of Mr Wong's trip the words 'state visit' had been uttered.

Having neither of us staged what Mala termed a 'state visit' before, we put are heads together on how best to proceed. Roger, as the technical part of the double act, came up with a list of people Mr Wong should see, while I worked on the various logistical problems we would encounter. Before long the dreaded realisation dawned that the Board of Investment should be our first port of call and I steeled myself for a fresh encounter with the job-hunting director.

The Board of Investment was, if nothing, an approachable institution and a call to Mr Badruzzaman, a helpful but rather dopey secretary, would normally secure an appointment with the appropriate officer. On the day we called, my director was thankfully not at his desk, and after a brief consultation with Mr Badruzzaman, we were sent to the fifth floor of the building to see one of his colleagues. It seemed that the closer one came to the heavens in the accommodation the more rank it became. Even though the card we were offered stated that Mr Talukder was also a director of the August Organisation but given his inauspicious surroundings it was hard to image that his was a sort after role.

Mr Talukder, from outward appearance, was not a happy man. A permanent scowl underlined by a moustache-less beard, was broken only by an open mouthed expression of horror as the words 'state visit' were uttered in our explanation of the purpose of our visit.

'State visit is not possible. It is not permitted. This man can only have Government-sponsored visit. Government-sponsored-visit.' The measured repetition of these words served to underline the complete folly of our request and affirm his own authority on the subject.

'This is a very complicated question you are asking. You will have to meet with many people before this can take place.'

Time being of the essence, Roger politely requested if it might not be possible to arrange a meeting that encompassed all the relevant individuals, so that we might come to a concerted plan of action.

Lighting a cigarette Mr Talukder considered this request breaking his silence with a reverberating cry of 'L-O-T-I-K-A!'

This cry summoned a rather heavy lady, tightly bound in a sari, who on encountering two *bideshis* at such close quarters appeared to forget why she had come into the room.

'Ehhh Lotikahh.' Talukder broke in bringing her to her senses. He proceeded to reel off a list of instructions, which the hapless Lotika painstakingly noted down and content that she had got all the detail correct she left us.

'You will wait here, she is typing you a letter,' Mr Talukder explained and wait we did.

Some time later Lotika appeared with reams of tea coloured paper which, had been painstakingly typed with the aid of carbon paper in triplicate, three times over. A proofread from Mr Talukder produced all sorts of tut tutting and sharp intakes of breath and for a moment I feared a protracted session of alterations. Thankfully, however, we were spared this further agony and were eventually handed three envelopes each annotated in Bengali.

'These are letters requesting that the gentlemen from the Prime Ministers office, the Ministry of Industries and the Foreign Office meet with you.'

I stared at the hieroglyphics on the envelopes and could only take his word for it.

My mobile telephone had gone off while we were in the office: it was Feroz who had established that our container was ready to be cleared through customs and that I should meet Ismail there. Ever conscious of a

cultural faux pas I had apologised profusely to Mr Talukder at the intrusive call who responded by asking
me if he could make a call on my 'interesting little
telephone.' It was the least I could do and I helped him
with his number. It was the most animated I had seen
him as he explained to the person at the other end his
latest diversion in a flow of Bangla punctuated by the
words 'mobile phone'. Fearing the dreaded suggestion
that he could do with a mobile phone I said a silent
prayer to myself. But, content with just having a go
handed it back to me.

Leaving Roger, armed with his Bangla, to fathom
out to whom and where the letters should be sent I
headed for the railway station with the happy prospect
of being reunited the contents of our forty feet container.

Dhaka Central Railway Station despite being kitted out with rails and the odd train appeared strangely
inactive. Plenty of little people living in the confines
of the station area in various forms of accommodation.
The most daring being the nooks under the platforms,
housing a family complete with small children. It
seemed best not to dwell on the consequences of an
unsupervised child by a railway track. There were certainly plenty of people using the facilities—but not for
what they were intended—nobody seemed to be going
anywhere today. None of the hustle and bustle of an
Indian station which I am assured is due to the fact
that the middle class, the group of the populace most
active in train travel, has yet to establish itself in
Bangladeshi society.

Of course the only other area of Dhaka railway
station where the activity is frantic, is the heavily
populated corridor on the first floor of the Customs
and Excise building, that leads to the door behind
which resides the collector of 'duties payable'. Personal space is not a concept up for discussion in Bangladesh. I was never going to get used to the fact that
my every action was a spectator sport and that at

times scrutiny was going to be from very close quarters. We had not helped ourselves by arriving in force and Mala, Ismail and I joined a crowd of people eager to submit their own applications. Mala had come along in order to smooth the future passage of her own possessions. This in my view was a futile exercise, as any deal struck with a view to the future, would evaporate almost as soon as the sweat from the compliant handshake had dried. She was under the misapprehension that a tenuous link between Mr Doti and director of Customs and Excise was going to work the oracle, a claim that I would have given more credence to if we could have side-stepped the queue.

The door ahead of us opened for a fleeting moment and the crowd surged forward. An oily head came in contact with my nose which twitched with the smell of sweat and pan but staring at my feet to block out my discomfort, consoled myself with the fact that the ordeal could only be ten times worse for the precious Mala. Tight bellies thrust against me, bony elbows against my arms and teetering on my toes we finally made it to the door and struggled our way in as the last visitors struggled out when next it was opened.

The calm of the interior office was in stark contrast to the hubbub outside and I was dismayed by the lack of urgency in proceedings that the demand outside the door would seem to necessitate.

'*Moynul Islam khotai?*' Ismail asked of the only person in residence, a man seated at one of two desks in the room.

'*Se Chittagong Giyache,*' was the reply, the news that Mr Doti's contact was currently in Chittagong some two hundred miles from Dhaka, to my amusement, brought Mala's interest in the proceedings to an abrupt conclusion.

On a happier note, details of our container had reached the office, and to my concealed delight it was confirmed that an inspection of the contents could be performed immediately. This was excellent news and I inwardly cursed the old lags of the Canadian Club, who with their tales of woe regarding the handling of goods at the Port of Chittagong, had put my mind up to the direst imaginings.

Collecting his papers together and deserting his post, the customs official took us from his office and through the melee in the corridor. As we passed the crowd squeezed back against the wall just enough to enable to pass through sideways-on and then sprung back as attention was once again returned to willing the door of the now unoccupied office to be opened.

The containers were stored in a holding area, caged in with a wire fence and presided over by the obligatory armed guard. It was hard to believe that everything had arrived or that a tangible link with home was so close at hand. An expletive from the official roused the attention of a man who was hard at work examining the contents of another container. He emerged spotted with downy tufts of packing material and without pausing to dust himself down we all proceeded to the one identified as mine and set to work on undoing the seals.

My first view of the treasures lying within as the door opened must have been similar to that of Howard Carter on discovering the treasures of Tutankhamen's tomb. A slight exaggeration perhaps, but having not seen these items since leaving for work one morning early in May, it was a happy reunion tempered slightly by minute examination carried out by the officials.

'He wants to know what is this,' explained Ismail, as a ski boot was held up for my perusal. Having got bored with carting large amounts of stuff down to my long suffering parents' home we had eventually plumped for the take everything option. At least we would know where everything was but it did mean that a certain amount of our goods were surplus to requirements.

EXPATRIATE GAMES

The next morning, an excited John Cruze who had been leaning over the kitchen balcony as a lookout, announced the arrival of the brightly painted lorry bearing our precious container as it turned into Road 6. We had hired John long before we were ready to take up residence in our apartment. We had received an inquisitive call from him at the end of a crackling telephone line on a weekly basis, to see how things were progressing and if he was required to put in an appearance. Despite the fact that he was being paid for effectively doing nothing he had never really seemed to have completely understood the arrangement. Now 'Sir and Madam' were in residence and here were their things from England at last the promised job had materialised.

Standing in the road viewing the accompanying removal men and gauging their height against the drop of the back of the lorry; it was going to be a job not without its difficulties. A hundred and eight items, the list we received back from the customs official stated, and the total amount in duty: thirty thousand Taka (which amounted to about five hundred pounds), appeared to have been arrived at in an arbitrary way with little or no pattern to it. A computer printer we had paid a hundred and fifty pounds for attracted a hundred and twenty pounds in duty, while our other electrical goods were obviously not nearly as exciting and attracted little or no duty.

A hundred and eight items to transfer to our fourth floor apartment with the aid of a lift the size of a large fridge and ten undersized porters. What we did have in abundance were spectators from the smallest of young children clad only in a pair of grimy, baggy bloomers to the most wizened of old gentleman peering through glasses with lenses the thickness of tumbler bottoms. With Brenda stationed upstairs and myself at the lorry, there was a lot of scope in the space between us for things to go seriously awry.

Having spent such a long time in the hotel, we felt really quite vulnerable, spending our first night in our new home. It was obvious that we had been spoiled by the industrial strength air conditioning in the hotel. Our large units that had been fitted into the rectangular holes cast, for the purpose, in the concrete walls made a lot of noise and blared out only cool-ish air. Reunited with our sofa that evening we found its upholstery and our entire new environment quite clammy, but it was good to feel that we had at last established our base. John Cruze had excelled himself for dinner that night demonstrating a previously undisclosed talent for vegetable sculpture honed whilst working on a cruise ship. We had feasted on 'Shrimp P-ish' and salad garnished with a vegetable hedgehog fashioned from a melon complete with cocktail stick spines.

Having finished the washing up, John had gone out for the evening establishing what time we would like breakfast before taking his leave. He had left through the servant's door adjacent to the front door, but it felt like we had a roommate. Both Brenda and I felt uncomfortable about the fact that a complete stranger would later let himself into our home and take-up residence in the little room off our kitchen. We locked the door to our room and retired trusting to luck whether or not we would be murdered in our bed that night.

Lying in the darkness of our first night the background sounds of Dhaka were broken by the sudden silence as the air conditioning unit cut out. Cursing our luck, I got up and tried the light switch. Much to my dismay the light illuminated the room: which meant that it was a problem with the machine and not just a power cut. After a rummage around I found a screwdriver and removed the fuse from something I knew worked and put it in the plug of the AC. An empty click of the switch on the socket suggested something terminal and I cursed the man who had sold me the job lot of machines.

Climbing onto a chest of drawers to bring myself level with the machine I took off the front cover and had a poke a round. The room was already starting to warm up and I prayed that God make me an instant expert in AC engineering. There was no lightning bolt and after a frustrating hour I gave up and went back to bed, making myself as star shaped as possible and avoiding all bodily contact. It was an inauspicious start to our life in 'Apartment 401' but at least when we returned from Canada I would have a threshold to carry my bride over.

chapter fourteen

'D-V-A-I!' I called to a tall Indian queuing for the flight from London to Dhaka. I had never met him before; and he was obviously nonplussed to be greeted in such a friendly way by a complete stranger. I had recognised him from his photograph that I had touted round various Government offices in order to secure a work permit for him.
By the same token I  recognised his girl-friend, Catherine, and was able to make introductions to Brenda as though they were long lost friends.

'You look much smaller in your photograph,' I said to Dvai, which was not as ridiculous as it sounds as he was solidly built and well over six feet. We all examined his passport photo so that my argument could be borne out and everyone agreed that the tiny figure peering out from the page did look about five feet tall.

Catherine was following Dvai out much as I had done Brenda: engaged and unemployed. Boredom was going to be a major factor for her and she would need as much help as possible in finding her feet in Dhaka. Being of Canadian extraction, Brenda shared some common ground and explained the intricacies of how to beat the system and wangle a membership of the Canadian Club while we waited to be boarded.

We were seated in the bubble of the jumbo a couple of rows back on the opposite side of the aircraft.

'Are they drinking anything?' Brenda asked me in a stage whisper.

'Hang on' I said craning over. 'Yes I think so.'

Roger's CV had proclaimed his teetotal status which had got us worried and since Dvai and Catherine were potential social life for us it would be a disaster if they too were abstemious. Any worries we had on that score soon evaporated as the steward attending to their area seemed to be doing fairly brisk trade. Leaving us wondering whether we would be able to keep up.

The monsoon had left the landscape more water logged than ever. Inaccessible humps of land poked up through the muddy water giving way to the weather scared white concrete blocks of Baridhara as we reached the edge of metropolitan Dhaka and eased down into Zia Airport. Arriving back in Dhaka for a second time was not a cause for celebration. The inevitable scrum to leave the building did nothing to ease the transition back into the sub-continent. We were relieved to see that Masum had got his times and days right and was there to whisk us home to the apartment. We had been away for fifteen days and it was hard to believe that we had been back to the UK, over to Canada, seen friends in both countries; acquired all the items on a lengthy shopping list and got married in such a short space of time.

We had kept our promise to call in to the office on a regular basis and we were already aware that all the other expatriate staff had arrived during our absence. The Board of Investment had stipulated in their allocation of work permits that there be a ratio of one expatriate to every three local staff. We had made a start to reel that statistic in with two new signings. Brenda before our departure had managed to entice one of Shafiq's computer staff, Mutton, to join us to look after that side of the operations and I had acquired Rana as an assistant (another product of the Feroz stable). With the Wong visit fast approaching and the prospect of more local hires, the sooner the office proper was complete the better. With that in mind the telephone lines issue would become one of some urgency and I had heard nothing from Feroz since I had given him our completed forms.

Jute House was a ten storey, curtain wall edifice situated in the remains of its own building site near to the Lalbagh Hotel. A mid-point between the commercial heart of the city and the less urban residential areas. It was the perfect situation in terms of commute and for visiting overseas business people to access from the hotel. We had tempted fate somewhat by having our Jute House address printed on our business cards. The impression this had on recipients amongst the local business community of the proffered card was one of awe. The first building in Bangladesh to be constructed with its face entirely clad in glass set it apart from the dreary local architecture, but would I was sure make it unbearably hot in high summer.

I was looking forward to seeing what progress had been made at the site in our absence as I took the lift up to the seventh floor or rather the renamed eighth. Mala's insistence that to ensure good Feng Shui we use the Chinese lucky number eight to label our floor had added confusion to plans and negotiations that were already complicated enough. That all documentation appertaining to our lease and renovation work be so annotated had been a hard one to explain and since the lift buttons would always proclaim our location as being on the seventh floor it all seemed faintly ridiculous.

Stepping out of the lift I disturbed a security guard who catching forty winks was sat with his head on his knees on some piled bags of cement. A procession of three labourers in the standard issue *lungi* and vest passed in front of me each carrying a pile of bricks on his head. The only protection being a paper skullcap fashioned from an empty paper sack and held in place with coloured nylon string. Sixteen flights of stairs they had brought those bricks and easing their loads to the ground they set off to start the process again. Bricks were a bad sign as it meant that actual building work had yet to be completed and on entering our proposed office I was dismayed by what I saw.

When I had posed with Mr Hashem, the owner of the building, for a photo on taking possession of the floor we had four thousand square feet of empty space. Into that we would need to introduce walls, partitioned offices, a false ceiling to house a multitude of cabling, air conditioning and something approaching western plumbing. Desks and chairs were being assembled off-site. The crowning glory would be the grey carpet tiles imported especially from Singapore. The architects had promised great things in my absence. And the sum total of these good works? The same empty space, bar two hurdles supporting a plank of wood, which in turn supported a sleeping child and a hastily constructed brick wall which had been erected in the wrong place. There were, however, building materials, which suggested that action was planned but that the Wong deadline had evaporated. It was a disaster and I stormed off in a rage to the offices of our contractors.

'What the bloody hell have you been up to Habib?' I fumed.

He looked downcast and said nothing.

The precaution we had taken of adding a penalty clause to our contract should the work not be completed on time looked to be an odds on certainty of being imposed. However, even with the threat of a substantial cut in their fees hanging over them there was no sign of any urgency.

Remembering my cultural sensibilities and realising that humiliating Habib was going to get me nowhere, I decided change my tack.

'Alright then, let's go and have a look at how you are getting on with the desks.'

The smell in the adjoining workshop took me back to carpentry school a pleasant whiff of sawdust and glue. At least there were signs here that progress as being made. Non-descript desks stuck with the two tones of laminate Mala had chosen stood stacked to the ceiling in one corner of the building and work was in progress on another.

'Where on earth did this wood come from?' I enquired suspiciously eyeing the dark brown weathered plywood that the desk was made from.

'It is from Chittagong,' replied Habib. 'It comes from the ships they are breaking there. It is very good to make furniture with because it is very well weathered. It will not warp in the heat and wet.'

It seemed an excellent idea but I made a mental note to check just how much we were being charged for these second hand materials.

Friends again I explained my plight to Habib. The imminent arrival of Mr Wong, and the pressure I was under to deliver the completed office from Mala. He seemed to take all of this on board and I left him having been promised a concerted effort.

Rocking on the back legs of my chair I asked Feroz what I could do to chivvy along the architects.

'You can do nothing,' he chuckled with a smokers rasp.

'But what about the penalty clause, if they are not careful they will loose a substantial amount of cash.' I reasoned.

'They don't care about this; they have so many jobs that they do just a little bit, a little bit, a little bit everywhere.'

'Well, any luck with the telephone lines?'

'Actually, I can't really say. Mr Doti he is taking care of this, you must ask him.'

Wearily I reached for the most modern looking of Feroz's phones.

Mr Doti's advice had taken me to the office of the divisional engineer, in the Nilkhet Exchange. I was slightly wary of the location of the building as it was just off the rather charmingly named Elephant Road on the not so charming frontline of Dhaka University campus.

The University, by tradition, was the focal point for political agitation and most Dhaka inhabitants of sound mind preferred to keep clear of that area. Ismail had taken me through the area once before by accident and I had marvelled at the war torn buildings which looked as though they had been the site of a jolly good punch-up and that no-one had turned up later to clear up. Small encampments of police testified to the fact that these punch-ups were still happening from time to time and, I hoped, that when the time came these men had the strength to run away encumbered, as they were, by solid looking knee protectors and heavy hard hats. However, the comings and goings of young people carrying books suggested that as a centre of academic excellence the University was still in use. Although as both Ismail and Rana reliably informed me it might take several years to complete your course or sit undisrupted finals before being conferred with your degree.

It was a symptom of our policy not to pay baksheesh: that I would find myself in these ridiculous situations. The Nilkhet Exchange was a building that had never seen an Englishman before, let alone one wearing a tie and I was an object of some fascination as I navigated my way through the building. A helpful man took pity on me on the stairs and walked me up to the second floor leaving me seated in a waiting room. But, what were these people waiting for? There was no system, no secretary to announce 'Thank you Mr Islam the divisional engineer will see you now.' So playing the trump card of dumb foreigner I marched into the adjoining office.

Somewhere in the archives of Dhaka Museum there must be a blue print for 'Conducting business in an office environment'. Detailing the following advice:

Under no circumstances must the officer be left alone at any time. That two chairs be placed either side of the desk to accommodate at least two friends who will disrupt with animated conversation whatever task it is he has been elected to perform.

Thus the four of us sat and listened to my tale of woe.

Roger and I were entering our third meeting with the various parties involved in the Mr Wong visit. We were at last making some headway after an abortive first and then acrimonious second attempt. A certain battle of wills as to which department was the most important had emerged but it would not be terminal. Held in a conference room in the Board of Investment, Roger and I had waited in the long sunny room sat at a boardroom table for the best part of an hour. The doleful Mr Talukder had been the first to arrive sporting a white crash helmet with a blue band down the middle of it. I hadn't seen one like it since the early seventies and doubted its life saving properties. However, from my observations of the wearing of protective headgear in the sub-continent whilst riding motorised transport a hard hat was designed to protect from the unlikely occurrence of objects falling on to ones head, rather than the wearer head butting the ground at speed.

The tall and extremely self-important representative of the Ministry of Industry who had joined us next, took up station at the head of the table and sat staring impassively from shiny silver, mirrored sunglasses. He was neither impressed with proffered hands nor with being summarily booted from his seat as the chairman of the BOI's representative entered with attendant acolytes and a mass of files. A small, round man full of smiles who, if depicted in a cartoon, would be followed by a cloud of dust. He leant a levity to our the proceedings which was most welcome since there was obviously no love lost between the Ministry of Industries and the deputation from the Foreign Office who made there own customary tardy entrance.

Thankfully the Government had agreed to sponsor the whole event, which made the logistics of the visit considerably easier for me. I had so far not found my colleagues particularly helpful when it came to parting with their transport and justifiably so since to do so would strand partners and children. Masum could normally be pressed into action in such cases, but he would be pushed to handle the entire Wong entourage single-handed. With the Government involvement transport and accommodation of central figures would be dealt with for us and to ensure that the billets were up to scratch I was invited to inspect the state guesthouse.

The Foreign Office was the most stately building I had yet to enter in Dhaka and showed a distinct British influence. Set back slightly from the road amongst palm trees it was a welcome change from the crowded pavements of the commercial area and considerably more fragrant. Equally unusual was the fact that I was carefully quizzed about my business at the entrance and given precise instructions on which way to turn having reached the top of the grand staircase without which finding my man behind the numerous panelled doors, would have been something of a lottery.

Mr Harun was hard at work applying a bluish purple ink to papers with a rubber stamp when I found him. His office for some reason had no door at all and I had fought my way through a heavy brown, blanket-like curtain to get into the room. With shutters closed to keep out the bright sunlight the darkness of the room was in sharp contrast to the light and airy corridors I had negotiated on my way there. He shared this space with two other men I was rather pleased that I could take him out for a break from this dreary setting.

In the car on the way to the guesthouse he smoothed out a sheaf of papers between us on the back seat.

'This is the VIP request to the airport. You must take a copy to Mr Talukder, one to the chairman of BOI and one to the director of the airport,' he explained

It seemed simple enough; although the trip to the airport had I not have to take Brenda there for a flight to Hong Kong the following day would have demanded a huge dogleg. Could this be all there was to it? I was amazed to see that this hallowed document was no more formal than one I might have produced on my computer back in the office.

Masum slowed at the gate to the fortress like state guesthouse. Having established that we were not a threat to national security, we were allowed to pass into the compound to follow the drive through the walled estate. Winding through well-kept gardens of lawns and tropically planted borders we came to a standstill in a neat roundabout in front of a featureless but substantial residential property. The sound of our car bought out a dapper man in a fawn jacket who appeared delighted to have guests to attend to.

'Come please, you are most welcome,' He greeted us directing us up a couple of shallow steps and through a porch-covered doorway.

Had the guesthouse been as full of style as this man was of good intentions then, it would be a truly splendid place. However embarking on a guided tour up a sweep of staircase I somehow doubted that this was going to be the case as the rather unlikely figure of the 'Laughing Cavalier' beamed down from one of the walls at me.

Any building that is in a permanent state of suspended animation is going to suffer from a feeling of neglect, without undergoing Dhaka's extremes of temperature and humidity. The approach we had taken with our apartment was the hot country look, of as little clutter as possible and floor that could be easily swept or better still mopped. The fewer soft, damp, potential breeding grounds for cryptogamous plants the better. It was a game plan that might have quite advantageously been applied to the guesthouse although there was obviously quite a chasm between what was deemed practical and essential to the comfort of that strange breed, the foreigner. Heavy carpets and chintz in the drawing room was obviously a must whilst the most outrageous moulded plastic headboard in the master bedroom, would definitely contribute to a memorable stay. However, on concluding my inspection with a brief glimpse into a bathroom with hideous maroon fittings, I pronounced it a most comfortable residence vastly superior to any of the accommodation available in either of the two local five star hotels.

The man in the fawn jacket beamed in satisfaction. I wondered if the mysterious Mr Wong were he to find out that I had made this stupendous claim and committed him to this sanctuary, free of mod cons and a mini bar would have thanked me. With the substantial kudos he would acquire in local terms from being a guest of the Government he would have to lump it.

chapter fifteen

My first appearance for the Canadian squash team had left me walking like John Wayne and it was a painful business lowering myself into my seat at the head of the table set carefully set for two. This painstaking attention to not doing *quite* what we had asked of John was a common occurrence, but more a symptom of us not driving home the point that 'Madam' had gone away, than a conscious effort on his part. Brenda had missed the heroic Canadian team of four men and one  lady crashed to defeat at the hands of a well-drilled representation of the Dhaka Club. We had scored a resounding victory in the ladies leg but it should be noted that the lady from the Dhaka Club had taken to the court in *sharwal kemeez* and *plimsolls*. Otherwise short on volunteers we had all played a couple of places out of position and I had left the court not quite sure where I was, having been run into the ground by a seemingly near professional number two.

A buzz on the intercom announced Masum's arrival and I walked out to the balcony and dropped the car keys the four floors down into the forecourt and his cupped hands. More often than not he would make a well judged, if painful catch of the missile and having acknowledged his wave I ducked back into the apartment. John had made a neat parcel of sandwiches which he handed to me and I wondered what other than the onion, that had tainted my chopped pineapple breakfast, lay between the two coarse slices of bread.

The drive to work was rather a pleasurable experience. Once the overpowering smell of fly spray that Masum had blasted the interior with to deter stray mosquitoes had dispersed and one acclimatised to the dampness. Due in part to the exposed nature of our parking space and Masum's liberal splashing of water around the interior to clean out the previous day's dust. Yes, reading a four day old copy of *The Times* bought second hand from a street vendor, AC on full, windows tight shut while Dhaka swarmed around us. One had to admit that it knocked the spots off the Northern line or queuing for the 137 bus, at the crack of dawn in London. This morning's peace was broken by a call on the mobile.

'Maurrk can you join me in the hotel for breakfast?' It was Mala wanting to go through the Wong schedule. It was going to be a long day.

Having had a break from the hotel breakfast it was quite nice to have a bowl of cornflakes. We had found an aged box on the market but resisted the temptation to part with the best part of a fiver for a small taste of home. Mala, for a small person, had an enormous capacity for food and had doubtless considering her high-maintenance status an opportunity to hone the most exquisite table manners in some of the world's finest eateries. This opportunity she had apparently flouted as I sat opposite a tiny individual freckled that morning's breakfast.

'We must have complete office facilities at the guesthouse, do you think you can organise that?' she asked.

It was possible and would just require taking one of everything from Feroz's office and sufficient time to set it all up at the guesthouse.

'Good. One other thing. I met a lady at dinner last night who has organised conferences here and I have asked her to join us and handle the events this evening.'

The fiasco with the architects had shaken Mala's confidence in me and this latest turn of events would appear to be a slap-on-the-wrist. I had plenty to do as it was and frankly, I was happier doing the running around behind the scenes anyway, so I would survive the ignominy.

Mutton and Rana both looked worried. Neither of them was enjoying the frenetic activity around the office with presentations being prepared and information packs photocopied and assembled. The news that the photocopier was to be transported to the guesthouse was met with universal distress and a great deal of head shaking from Mutton. With the flight not due until 4.30pm there was plenty of time and as long as the machine was in place by 5pm then we would be covered.

Dinner that night was planned at the roof top restaurant of the Sheraton Hotel and my visit to check on them was deemed unnecessary by the food and beverage manager who assured me that he had everything under control. However, I had been in Dhaka just long enough to know that it was worth taking the time to visit the twelfth floor to make sure and that one of the few decent places to get a loaf of bread was the Sheraton coffee shop. Now that I was no longer a prisoner of the hotels I found a visit to either of the two upmarket hotels a welcome diversion. To witness the comings and goings of other Western faces, browse through the peculiar selection of English titles in the paper shop and perhaps pick up a Curly Wurly chocolate bar, if fortune had smiled on me, and they had them in stock. If I was completely desperate, I would occasionally crack and buy some Indian Cadbury's chocolate and brave its odd texture and after taste. Zinc added to the mixture to prolong the product's life in the heat of the sub-continent was something that one would have needed to have been weaned to, from a tender age and occluded from all other brands to believe that metallic Kit-Kat was as good as it gets.

125

Rana called to tell me that the Biman Bangladesh Airlines flight from Hong Kong had been delayed and that the Wong-ites would not be arriving until 8.30pm. This would squeeze our schedule to a point where all activities would have to be entered into at breakneck speed. Clearing the airport, even with the VIP passage, and the drive into central Dhaka would take us to 9.30pm; a brief stop to change and then the short drive to the Sheraton. Dinner at this rate would be finishing in the small hours. As a result of this development Rana had been given the thankless task of trying to track down the chairman of the airlines telephone number so that Mala could insist he keep his aircraft to its timetable.

Mala's attempted intervention had, not surprisingly, failed to expedite our visitors' passage and it was obvious that the airline were not letting-on that 8.30pm had been a conservative estimate. Mr Badruzzaman and I walked out to the arrivals area at the airport to scan the screen for more news. We had arrived in a convoy of vehicles, with which we would transport our guests, who comprised a party of six. Mr Badruzzaman, who had thankfully advised me that I could abbreviate his name to Zaman had opted to travel alone in the splendour of a large, four wheel drive vehicle intended for the Mr Wong while Masum and I had brought up the rear.

We had followed the signs marked 'VIP' round to one side of the airport complex, down a slip road to find our way barred by a metal, white painted gate which was opened speedily for Zaman and closed again to bar entry of my less splendid mode of transport.

I wound down my window, allowing a blast of warm Dhaka night and a number of mosquitoes into the car, and handed a copy of the Foreign Office note to the man on duty. He, having studied it for a moment, handed it back to me with a shake of his head.

'No, no, look here,' I ran my finger under the words enunciating them slowly. 'Mr Mark Trenowden will meet Mr Wong arriving on flight...' Taking the note again he went over to a small sentry box and compared my name against those in his logbook. Returning only to post my note back to me through the half open window, resolutely unmoved. Getting out of the car in frustration I walked to the gate and eyed the horizon for Zaman who to my relief was in sight just getting out his vehicle.

'Zaman,' I bellowed 'Come and sort this man out, will you!'

'Expected 9.15', read a furry announcement, glowing from an archaic screen. I did a spot of mental arithmetic. Dinner would start at 11pm. I called to tell Mala the bad news. The pressure was beginning to tell on her and my hesitation in coming up with suitable answers to barked bizarre questions about the incoming flights' whereabouts, that no one could have possibly answered did nothing to put her at her ease.

'What do the people in the control tower say? Where is the plane at the moment? When exactly is it going to land?'

Finally the magic word 'Landed' was screened and we walked through to the VIP area from which we could access the gate and intercept our visitors before they disappeared into immigration. Zaman proudly produced a hastily prepared 'Mr Wong' sign with letters of varying height and case, which he held out expectantly. I knew Mr Wong from various photographs and pointed out the middle aged man to Zaman as he appeared on the ramp. He could not contain his excitement and rushed up to deliver a rather charming but ill-timed speech of welcome. The progress of other travellers forced our slightly alarmed party forward cutting Zaman short and having briefly introduced myself I directed them towards the VIP lounge.

I was amazed at just how unsophisticated the VIP process was, as we forced our way to the head of the immigration queue. For the guest, however, it was a seamless exercise. We had left them seated in the VIP lounge having relieved them of their passports with the assurance that we would return with the necessary entry stamps and their luggage. Behind the scenes Zaman and I were going through the normal procedure for arrival at an international airport with the added excitement of doing it for six people at once. Leaving Zaman to tough-it-out with the immigration people, I searched the baggage carousel for their luggage. We had taken the precaution of asking them to identify their bags with a coloured label prior to departure, and by the time Zaman had completed his task I had located six bags with neat red ribbons tied to the handles and plucked them from the conveyor.

Johnny Ho, Mr Wong's assistant, introduced himself and the two younger members of the group to me as the luggage was ferried through the lounge and out to the waiting cars.

'I'll take you three to the Lalbagh Hotel where you are staying while Mr Wong and the other gentleman are driven to the Government guesthouse. Between you and me I think you've got the better deal,' I added as an aside.

Johnny was very friendly and, with Brenda away, I was pleased to have this link with civilisation. His sartorial appearance revealed that trait of young Hong Kong Chinese to frequent the most exclusive of designer establishments and my eye settled on the small polo player emblem on the base of his tie, which I thought a bit twee given our third world setting. I envied this evidence of access to real shops and hoped that Brenda was hard at work ticking off the items on my wish list.

With the visitors safely dispatched Zaman called me over to him and looking about him furtively before speaking. 'Saar...It is most difficult for me... I have spent money on tips.' From his shifty appearance and hushed tone this was a blatant lie but he had been extremely useful and I slipped him a fifty taka note.

'Now going?' Masum enquired.

My tentative use of the Bangla 'taratari' effectively 'step on the gas Masum' had the desired effect and bowling along the airport road we soon caught up with and passed the Government vehicles which were proceeding at a more stately pace. At this rate I would be able to initiate proceedings at the check in desk in the hotel.

'Yes M-A-R-K, I confirmed them yesterday,' I said irritably. 'Three rooms booked by Mr Mark for Ho, Stewart and Ryan.' It was the first time I had used this sobriquet myself but increasingly in my daily activities I was being referred to as 'Mr Mark' and I had subconsciously picked it up.

'Ahhh, yes Mr Mark.' said the duty manager who I had called upon in my frustration. 'Your company is paying for these rooms.'

'Err...no! I think...' I was interrupted by the arrival of Johnny and the others.

With a promise to meet them all at the Sheraton and directions on how to get their driver to take them there, I headed for the guesthouse to make sure that things were going as planned.

Walking into the room, which had been designated centre of operations I found Rana seated on a sofa looking worried. He brightened up when he saw it was me and I asked him if there had been any problems.

'None of the plugs on the machines match the sockets in the guesthouse, they are too old and Mala is very angry.'

Rana needn't have worried: the blame would squarely be laid at my door.

'Well, Mark we will just have to use the office in Dilkusha,' said Mala who had by now joined us. This was impossible as the offices would by now be locked and the key safely in the possession of one of Feroz's employees.

'But, Mala it is now 10.30pm it is unlikely that after their trip and at this hour that any of the party are likely to need an office and besides if we are really desperate there is always the hotel business centre.'

The lip trembling fury that met this suggestion was extraordinary and I made a mental note not to incur this ferocious wrath again. The pressure of time saved me from further punishment and I ducked out of the room after a severe reprimand for suggesting the obvious, to return to the car.

Rana stopped me in the hallway.

'Mark, I need to get my wife. It is very late and she gets worried about being alone in our house.'

'Well Rana you can't go now. If she calls get her to take a baby taxi and come here. The office can pay.' It was not what he wanted to hear but it was the best I could do.

'Oh and Mark, there is one other thing. Mrs Wadood has just taken your car to the Sheraton.' This was the frightful woman that had been drafted in to preside over the evening's proceedings. Now car-less and with no other option I trotted out of the guesthouse and down the drive to the gates.

Hailing a rickshaw that was meandering down the street I leapt into the back.

'Sheraton Jabo,' I said to a rickshaw *Walla*. Not a glimmer of recognition from the figure in the darkness.

I had never travelled in a rickshaw alone before. Rana and I had been in one together in the commercial area, which had been very exciting for me from a tourist's viewpoint, but I hadn't had to do any of the driving. Now we sat stationary. Like a horse that senses a novice rider we were going nowhere until from the recesses of my mind I drew the word for 'straight' and we eased off down the street. By the time the Sheraton came into view I was feeling fairly pleased with my-

self having made the whole trip purely on the commands left, right and straight when a large rain drop
brushed my cheek.

'We welcome Mr V-wwong to Dhaka.'

It was a gratifying moment as Mrs Wadood's lisp
put in a late and unplanned appearance. The upside of
her having taken over, was that I had been asked to
attend the dinner and I sat in silent triumph as the
wretched woman struggled to enunciate the intricacies
of the Chinese and western names. I had been sat at
one end of the table next to a gruff, older man who
was an Australian and an engineer. The combination
of these genes had produced a gnarled wildman intent
on consuming as much beer as was possible in the
time available and I wondered how he would have
survived had he been confined in the Government
guesthouse all evening.

At the end of he evening, having dispatched all
parties to their respective lodgings, I located Masum
and having settled his *baksheesh* for the extended overtime sent him on his way. I had decided to take advantage of the now deserted streets to make my first excursion behind the wheel. I had driven round the expatriate area as a number of people did but the causeway
beyond DIT 1 in Gulshan was definitely the end of
the earth, as far as the majority of foreign drivers were
concerned. Having set off from the hotel, I was just
musing on how wide the roads were without the usual
chaos when the mobile rang. It was Rana, who having
been reunited with his wife was now stranded at the
guesthouse.

Having now driven beyond my last recognisable
point of reference I was entering no mans land. I
looked over at Rana in the passenger seat hoping for
some pointer that we were nearing the end of our
journey but there was none. A left turn, off the main
road onto a side road, was good news and we slowed to
negotiate the undulating surface. I made a note of a
small cinema complete with miniature painted hoard-

ings advertising the latest show and on we went. Side road gave way to sandy track and bumps to potholes. We were now relying solely on the headlights and I swerved to negotiate two individuals having a late night confab squatting on the verge.

'Here turn left Mark,' Rana directed and we turned off the track into what appeared to be an area under construction dotted with rectangular concrete pill boxes three floors high. Despite their regular shape they appeared to have been put up rather shakily and untrimmed iron supports protruded from the topmost roofs suggesting that there was some fine tuning to be made to the design or addition to be made.

'There is my house, Rana said, proudly pointing to a single lit window, glowing in the darkness.

With the car teetering on a steep slope from which I would have to reverse to extricate myself I suggested that if it were possible it might be advisable to walk from there and having exchanged thanks Rana and his silent wife left me to find my way home.

Feeling quite vulnerable I did my best to retrace my route along the dark and dusty track. Potential threats to my well being came to mind. What exactly was a *dacoit*? And would I meet one, I wondered, as I progressed through the deserted suburb, when to my relief I came across the cinema. Up to the top and turn right and then I would be back on the road to Dhaka. The eight lane road in front of the National Assembly, Sher-e Bangla Nagar was a landmark that I knew well, and relaxing I set a course down the middle of this extraordinary slab of tarmac, and picked up speed. Traffic lights suspended on a gantry brought my progress to a halt just by the entrance to the Cantonment.

The traffic light had always been a mystery to me in Dhaka. There seemed to be no obvious rule to follow since heavy traffic would often be seen to be challenging the authority of a red light. When I had first started driving near our apartment I had been soundly tooted for stopping at a red light. I queried this with

Feroz who put it down to the incident taking place on a Friday, the weekend, when everyone's obedience to such things was relaxed. Now following slightly more orthodox rules I obeyed a green filter arrow shining brightly in the darkness. No sooner had I driven through the light when the shriek of whistle had me looking in my mirrors. I slowed to the side of the road and got out of the car to confront the approaching policeman. Safe in the knowledge that whatever either of us said we would neither of us understand, we set-to, each of us putting our case eloquently, supported by elaborate sign language. Short of clapping me in irons and leading me to the local station, there was no course of action other than to let me go. However, strong the local culture of slipping the officer a couple of taka in such incidents; with my patience fast deserting me I resolved that he wasn't getting a penny out of me. Having detained me long enough for this fact to become obvious even to him he dismissed me from his sight with a flourish of his swagger stick.

However, innocuous the incident it had given me a bit of a shock and as the trauma abated I returned to turning the day's events over in my mind. Suddenly a dreadful thought occurred to me. Does the hotel think we're settling Johnny's bill?

chapter sixteen

After a restless night, I woke convinced that as I had left it the hotel was under the misapprehension that my company would be settling their account. After the previous day's showdown with Mal, a bill for five hundred dollars was all I needed. I would have to intercept Johnny and I was up early to do it.

First thing in the morning was a pleasnt time to be up and about. With the sun bright but not yet hot and traffic fumes at a minimum I enjoyed the sights of a Dhaka morning. A long

stream of colourfully clad ladies streaming over the Gulshan Lake Bridge disappeared into garment factories. Rickshaws ferrying implausibly large loads of fruit and vegetables, complete with their purveyor perched on top or piled with enormous, evil smelling fish from the market barely down wind of the Lalbagh Hotel.

I had had an event free drive in, save a near miss with an extremely long bamboo pole that had suddenly appeared from an alleyway followed by a man at the pivotal point, who failed to think just what he was doing through properly. Once at the hotel, I asked the doorman to call for Masum on the *tannoy* and he emerged sleepily from the car park. It had seemed pointless in dragging him all the way across town for such an early start, although my leniency would have been frowned upon by the likes of Feroz.

I had plenty of time in hand and I took the opportunity to sit and have a coffee and read one of the local papers 'AWAMI LEAGUE CALLS HARTAL.'

The headline took me aback as it announced an unscheduled day of national strikes the following day. For the whole time we had been in Bangladesh there had political rumblings between the Government, led by the then Prime Minister Khaleda Zia, and the main opposition party: the Awami League led by Sheikh Hasina, daughter of Sheik Mujib Rahman, the founding father of the country. One got the impression that for these two formidable ladies the quarrel was not only political, but also personal but for the time being the point at issue was one of the constitution. The trouble had started in 1994 when the opposition resigned en masse from the parliament to press for immediate parliamentary elections under a neutral caretaker Government. Over a year later nothing had been resolved and the calling of a *hartal*, which would effectively bring the country to a standstill for a day, had become common practice.

We had so far experienced three or four of these days of political agitation but the rumours were that they would be becoming more frequent and violent. Whatever the rumours, the reality of the *hartal* would mean rethinking the Wong visit. Previous calls to strike had been answered by small gangs of political activists, whose anger had turned to violence directed in the main towards property rather than other's flesh and blood. Vehicles were a favourite target and reports that senior Government officials had resorted to riding in ambulances on strike days to avoid attack had been recounted in the press. However desperate we were it was an unlikely scenario helping the entire entourage into a fleet of ambulances in order to get them to the airport the following day.

Johnny and his colleagues appeared, and waiting for the cars outside the hotel, I managed to split him from the pack.

'Why don't you come with me?' I offered holding open the back door of my car.

To my relief without the slightest suspicion that I had an ulterior motive he accepted my offer and I joined him in the back of the car.

'Mark,' he said with a laugh rather unnervingly stroking my knee. 'You've worried all night about that.'

The relief that swept over me at his response to my nervous enquiry about the hotel expenses, was tempered a little by the concern that the friendly pat I found relieving, was still being given to me. I had found the male of the species generally a lot more tactile in Asia, and had on more than one occasion, found myself holding hands with hairy individuals in unlikely settings. Mr Badruzzaman had accompanied me down four flights of stairs at the Board of Investment, fondly holding my hand, and even the super tough, Colonel Latif, given half a chance would grab parts of me for protracted fondling.

The approaching maroon Bentley of the British High Commissioner caused Masum to pull over to one side of the drive as we approached the guesthouse. It is a measure of how quickly one adapts to a new environment that I found myself gawking in wonder at this magnificent mode of transport. Few vehicles would turn one's head in Dhaka, other than the ones in such a magnificent state of disrepair that it was hard to believe they still went, or those that were extravagantly overloaded. I had seen a silver BMW on one occasion and found myself thinking, *Wow a BMW!*, before coming to my senses. The one vehicle I had yet to see, however, was the mythical red Ferrari that belonged to the proprietor of the mobile telephone company. Like a tale of a ghostly, headless horseman it was said that in the small hours of the morning he could be seen driving it on the airport road, the one surface sufficiently lump free to accommodate it.

Arriving at the roundabout in front of the building we joined a semi circular line of assorted vehicles which had backed up in a clockwise direction. This bottleneck was due to the fact that the representative of the Ministry of Industry still wearing his mirrored sunglasses had chosen to make his entrance from the opposite direction. Lest this vehicular snarl up attract further condemnation of my organising abilities, I nipped out of the car and barely suppressing outward signs of my frustration asked him to: 'Be a nice gentleman' and move his car.'

I'm not sure where the expression came from but I think that in trying to word my request without using the words silly ass it was the best I could come up with.

Mala was in a state of excitement within. The *hartal* was playing havoc with her moment of glory. My sympathies lay with Roger whose efforts to organise all the business aspects of the visit were being undermined. I was sure he was being given the Mala treatment as well.

'The British Ambassador...'

I didn't have the heart to point out that he was a High Commissioner.

'..tells me that as no one is sure how the political situation will develop it is best not to travel tomorrow. So Mr Wong and his colleagues have decided to take this evening's flight to Hong Kong and you have to get them on it.'

Reza, the travel agent was dumbfounded by my request.

'Six tickets, Mr Mark, is very difficult.'

By the look of his heavily populated office our party was not the only one taking this course of action. With the pile of six passports stacked like roulette chips I gambled on the promise of putting all the office business through his agency in future. He played with a stumpy sixth digit below the thumb on his left hand while he considered this offer and then made a call. Still transfixed by his extra terminal member the news that the flight was full took an instant to register.

'Nothing at all, not even economy?' I pleaded.

He consulted his timetable and made another call.

'They can travel by Indian Airlines this afternoon to Delhi but you will have to visit the office to confirm the seats. And give them the passport information.'

The Indian Airline office was situated in a small parade of shops in the car park of the Sheraton Hotel and on finding the office open but unoccupied I walked the length of these to pass the time. By the time my circuit brought me back to the office there was still no sign of an official and my agitation grew as my wait became more prolonged. Eventually a lady in a crimson sari emerged from the hotel building and swept across the car park to the office. Hard on her heels as she entered the office, I quite startled her and I apologised profusely for my eagerness, explaining my predicament. This did little to allay the distrust that leaping out on her from nowhere had instilled and our dealings were conducted with me grinning inanely so hoping to dissipate any threat while she maintained a scowl.

Indian Airlines could get my group out of the country but how I would pay them was something I had yet to address. In an act of unintentional self-destruction I had allowed, Brenda, one of the joint signatories to depart Bangladesh without signing a couple of standby cheques. With our cheque book rendered impotent and neither the ability nor inclination to squeeze six business class fares onto my credit card I would have to think again. Doubtlessly bringing local Anglo-Indian relations to an all time low I left the office with the assurance that the bookings should be kept and that I would be back to settle the invoice. Resolving to chase round all the locations of the day's meetings in the hope of catching up with Johnny and his flexible friend, Masum and I shot off. The guest-house was nearby and we would have to drop in there to collect a copy of the itinerary. Entering the building at a trot I bumped into the Australian engineer having a crafty cigarette in the hall.

'Is Johnny around?' I asked him.

'No mate they've all gone on some helicopter ride.' This unlikely and unscheduled event had skippered my chances. In desperation I explained my plight.

'All you had to do is ask!!' He said reaching into his breast pocket and produced an impressive wad of dollars, his craggy features betraying no humour. Meanwhile my emotions were a mix of relief, delight and disbelief. It was a stroke of luck indeed and I returned in triumph to collect and pay for the tickets.

That afternoon at a farewell tea party at the guest-house Mr Wong's second in command sidled over to me and thanked me for getting them onto the flight. I sensed that there was relief in his gratitude. It had been a trying twenty-four hours for everyone involved. Rather than shatter the illusion of the miracle I had just performed, I decided that I would leave him in ignorance of the song-and-dance it had been to acquire the tickets. As we spoke, Mrs Wadood continued to pontificate from a small raised platform, detailing the conclusion of the visit and disclosing the hitherto secret information that they would all be presented with going-away gifts of varying magnitude and usefulness. The chairman of the Board of Investment struggled with a large framed, hand-embroidered picture for Mr Wong; which would take an expert in the negotiation of hand luggage allowances to transport. Meanwhile the rest of the group were presented with small, framed photographs of Mala shaking hands with Mr Wong. The desirability of which was clearly registered on the faces of the recipients as they opened their packages.

Determined to go out in a blaze of glory, we had mustered just about every vehicle that had so far been employed in the extravaganza. Masum and I had at last been reunited and he brought up the rear of a splendid cavalcade complete with military motorcycle outriders. The loading of all the protagonists would take a while and, I took this opportunity to duck back inside the guesthouse to the room in which we had all been entertained to tea. The waiting staff had lost no time in tucking in to the remaining vitals, and I went unnoticed as I relieved the establishment of a souvenir ashtray complete with Governmental insignia.

Our daily routine had been disrupted, with Brenda away and my time-consuming schedule, and John Cruze seemed pleased to see me when I got home. He greeted me with exciting news.

'Table coming, Sir!'

This slightly misleading information actually translated into 'the new table is here' and I was curious to inspect our latest purchase, which to the untrained eye appeared to be standing fully intact in the dining room. Local craftsmanship was of a reasonable standard and having investigated the three main options for the expatriate home-maker we had approached the glamorous Tahera Alam—she of the failed office tender—to design and build a table for us. My past dealings with her company had been left on a decidedly frosty note and I was relived when her assistant, Qamrul, fielded my preliminary call.

With his boss out of the country, he had delighted in visiting me to discuss my requirements and with the aid of a heavily thumbed book of western interiors we came up with a traditional oval design supported by two pedestals. Qamrul, who despite finding the time to report on local sporting events as his business card declared, assured me that he would take care to preside over the construction of the table from start to finish. That had been in the early days when my benevolent trust was misplaced and I believed what I was told. In this case it was not a far fetched claim as the company had furnished the hotel in which I had been incarcerated in its entirety I had no reason to think that my table would provide and insurmountable hurdle from them. Lack of interest, however, a glut of local football matches requiring coverage or a conscious effort to go slow out of spite had dragged the projected completion time from eight to twelve weeks. Completion had then been followed by the promise of a bicycle-powered delivery, which had had to be abandoned on account of a torrential downpour. Then when we thought we could take no more without warning the finished product had arrived unannounced.

But could this be the table that we created together. The promised light oak effect of Chittagong teak, which in reality gave the effect of brownish cherry coloured and creamy white stripes. The solid top of so-called seasoned wood, which had so much movement in it, was almost rippling. The attachment of the pedestal legs, that on close inspection betrayed a job so incompetent in its execution, that it was hard to believe that the egotistical Mrs Alam had let it leave her premises. Noticing my examination of the underside table John joined me on all fours.

'Table here broken,' he pointed out running his hand over the pitted surface of the solid block, which provided contact between table and pedestal.

'Here sir, I have mended table.'

Mended table he had indeed. Mended table with 'Sir's' hammer' and the pock marks of the metal hammer head were clearly visible where, in my absence, he had taken upon himself to make running repairs and given the joint a good whacking to secure it. Despite his attentions the joint was, as we examined it prizing apart and, bearing the weight of the table top it would only be a matter of time before the joint gave way completely and the structure collapsed upon itself.

I emerged from the bedroom having changed to find that John had secured one end of the table with an assortment of books, which with the aid of this minor design modification, was now completely operational. Dining on emaciated chicken and the string bean and carrot melange that whatever season we were in was regular fare, I concocted an elaborate story with which to shame my furniture provider. Visions of the table laid for an elaborate dinner party, the legs parting company with the top, smashing crockery, scalding soup cascading over influential guests, I was in no doubt that I would get my own back.

There was also the issue of Mr Cruze, who had not only taken matters inadvisably into his own hands, but had also had a pretty good rummage through our belongings to find his hammer. The *American Woman's Handbook* suggested that personal effects where possible be kept under lock and key at all times to deter household staff from spiriting them away. We had decided that with the exception of obvious valuables life was too short to lock *everything* away, however, the American women of Dhaka would not have approved of this course of events and I would have to give him a talking to.

'John, you are very good at helping in the apartment and we appreciate your help but you must understand that this is our home. Our things are private and if you need something then you must ask,' I said in the most authoritative tone I could muster.

I couldn't decide whether the tears that welled in his eyes were instantaneous and an involuntary reaction to being told-off or whether they were the product of more considered hurt. Whatever, their cause they had the desired effect and back tracking to extricate myself from the painful situation I helped him take the dishes into the kitchen.

The following day's *hartal* was well-timed as far as I was concerned. The thankless task of putting in enormously long days, the frustration of all things local and the absence of Brenda left me feeling not too kindly disposed towards my situation. Thankfully, however, Peter and Sue had allowed us a chunk of their alcohol allowance on their passbook and I got myself a beer from the fridge before gloomily installing myself in front of the television to watch a fuzzy broadcast of *Inspector Morse*.

chapter seventeen

Steeling myself, I made a call to Mala in the States. However well-primed I thought I was, she could be guaranteed to floor me with an impossible question. One such question earlier that week:

'Well, what colour are the framed partitions in the other offices of the group around the world?'

Had seen me dispatched on the first available plane to Bombay to see our offices there and consult with my opposite number.

The suddenness of my dispatch had given me little time to worry about the prospect of a flight but I put it to good use and being consigned to the national carrier I was entitled to have cause. A delay of seven hours in the airport, while some part had to be bolted back on to the aircraft, had added to my concern. By the time we had taken off I was a wreck. I had taken a Tamazapan before the flight to calm my nerves but it was no match for the adrenalin coursing through my veins. It was the first time I had travelled at five hundred miles an hour and, been aware of it as the internal fittings did their best to detach themselves from the interior, with assorted unwanted noises. The toilet was however still intact and I had been a regular visitor. On one occasion whilst standing in a line waiting to use the facilities a small man had sauntered past the line and up to the head of the queue. It would be ridiculous to expect the sub-continental art of queuing to be to be as finely developed as that of the Englishman but I was a man without reason. Meting out my own justice I grabbed the man by the lapels of his jacket and placed him in his rightful place in the line. This act was accompanied by the sound of stitches becoming detached and as I resumed my wait I caught a glimpse of him out of the corner of my eye dumbly inspecting the damage to his jacket.

Leaving out this particular detail, I ran through the highlights of my trip on the telephone to Mala and the developments that had been made on our site. I was just about to inform her that we could be in the new office within a week when she returned to her previous topic.

'So what colour is the frame?'

'Well white actually but...'

'And ours?'

'Brown, but that's all there is available in Bangla..'

'Change it!'

'Mala, we can't possibly change it at this point.'

'Change it!' She spat and the phone went dead.

Aside from the fact that Mala had actually chosen the frame, its installation had been at an early stage in the building work. To change it would necessitate the removal of glass and the false ceiling which, even had the materials been available, would have put us back weeks.

Habib had relocated his office and acquired a mobile telephone. Were we over-paying Mr Shifti and Co. that much? The new office in residential Banani was considerably easier to access than the seething area of Malibagh where the workshop was situated. Malibagh had long years ago been part of the old European zone an area especially established by Moghul rulers so that they could isolate the foreigners from the rest of the population. Any traces of my predecessors were sucked into the local scenery long ago and today, with its proximity to the railway station and commercial area, it is choked with humanity and a white face is something of an oddity. In relocating the foreigners to the distant corner of Gulshan and Baridhara someone had done me a great service.

Habib's reaction to the news was predictable, but I did my best to allay his fears. Common sense would hopefully prevail and if not then we should come up with a contingency plan. But wait a moment what was this? Here at one end of Habib's office was a small cubicle constructed from the required white framework.

'This is experiment. You see here the paint,' he said ruefully examining a worn patch on the sliding door of the cubicle, lifting a small flake with his fingernail.

'We have already tried to turn the brown frame to white.'

From the way the paint had come off the surface the wear and tear of a heavily populated office would render our frame shabby within weeks of installation. But this was perfect. The means to complete the transformation and a valid reason for not seeing it through.

'Habib, can we get more paint like this?'

'It is very difficult, maybe in the market,' he replied screwing up one side of his face in a pained expression.

'Good, then we must go to the market.'

I loved an excuse to go to the market for anything and spending someone else's money, even if was just for paint, made the experience all the sweeter.

The covered market at DIT 2 roundabout was the nearest to the office and just a short drive down the wide main drag of Banani. So unlike the main roads in central Dhaka with there high raised pavements which provided sanctuary in times of flood or else shop fronts for hawkers. Here the tarmac stood proud of sandy soil, with sparse grass grazed by angular cattle and goats or supporting small colonies of flat-bed rickshaws and their accompanying *wallahs*, whiling away the day in the hope that trade would come to them. The pace of life here was less frenetic and one could see why some of the expatriate inhabitants restricted their movements to this area and for whom Bangladesh was a country two miles big. Certainly for members of the begging fraternity pickings, were richer in this part of town and the sight of a *bideshi* driving into DIT 2 market bought a gaggle of grubby children, to the car as we came to a halt, all crying.

'Me *chowkidar*, me *chowkidar*!'

'Me driver have!' I would reply, but I was no match for them and I relented selecting a particularly spindly looking child to mind the car, who in the event of a hoard of marauding hooligans attacking the vehicle would surely be squashed flat. My choice made, the crowd grudgingly dispersed.

The United Hardware Company looked promising from the assorted collection of brooms, cast-iron tools and galvanised buckets, slung from the shop front. Our entrance was greeted by the illumination of the interior as the proprietor rose from his seat behind the counter and flicked the light switch behind him. The shop was a depository for all things oily and rusty. Laden shelves of oxidised paint cans, sweaty brown cardboard boxes, coils of wire and neatly piled local cooking utensils seemed to be his stock in trade.

Habib did the talking.

'He says he must go outside.' Came the news after some discussion. We would wait.

I took the opportunity to wander up to the first floor and have a look round the galleries and antique shops. Business had been slow and Queen Victoria still stared out of Saju Arts. The leather shops provided a new diversion and I was in no time standing on a sheet of brown paper while a chubby man with a busby of black hair knelt on all fours and drew round my socked feet. He had assured me that he could make me a serviceable pair of shoes and having between us fashioned a design for a pair of chukka boots it would only be a matter of time. Habib would be wondering where I had got to and as I made to leave the shop I noticed a dusty suitcase on the floor by the door. A chestnut brown leather bag that in days-gone-by expatriate predecessors might have acquired from the Army and Navy catalogue and nowadays one might only purchase in Jermyn Street having first arranged a mortgage. The smell of petrol used to cure the leather would fade and I resolved to return with the dimensions of my cricket bat for a bespoke kit bag.

Mr United Hardware had managed to purloin an aerosol spray of white paint and having eventually got Masum to open the 'car backside' we secreted it there. As Habib stepped into a rickshaw we reaffirmed our unwritten pact to demonstrate it only as a last resort.

Bound for the office we were halted in our progress by a man waving a tree branch in front of the lowered barrier of the level crossing by the Lalbagh Hotel. The wait as the blue and white Intercity train past us with its assortment of passengers both official and unofficial and housed both in and on its compartments gave me sufficient time to divert Masum.

Though lacking in originality 'hotel backside' was the accepted command to circumnavigate the main hotel building and whisk me straight to the rear entrance of the hotel, and in particular the cake shop. On this occasion we were brought up sharply behind a troop carrier, parked outside the main entrance to the hotel lobby. This was not an unusual sight in the hotel confines as functions attended by the Prime Minister would often require the deployment of several vehicle loads of smartly turned-out ceremonial guards in camouflaged combat fatigues topped with a bright scarlet cravat and matching beret. As we skirted round the vehicle and drove by the hotel entrance it was apparent that these were soldiers of a much more serviceable and everyday appearance and that they were stationed to bar entrance to hotel.

The lobby area was essentially an enormous, glass encased corridor with the main entrance at one end and bordered on one side by the check in desks and the other by a cafe and meeting area of tables and chairs. At the far end of the lobby the corridor tapered to a narrow arcade of shops and the rear entrance and its double doors through which I made my entrance.

The first person I encountered was a security guard propped against a wall. He was without his regulation headgear and his hair dishevelled. The epaulets on his shirt stood proud of his shoulders and the points at which their restraining buttons had been attached were two small ragged holes. He was visibly upset and by the looks of things he had been grasped by the shirtfront and given a good shake. My next encounter was with a chef who came around the corner with the look of a man on the warpath. He cut a dashing figure complete with blue and white checked trousers and white double-breasted tunic albeit unbuttoned to reveal his chest and a large shiny tanned belly. With his appearance the guard took to his heels and the doors to the outside world banged closed behind him.

This bizarre sequence of events proved to be nothing in comparison to the sights and sounds that met my eyes as I entered the main lobby. The place was in uproar bordering on complete and total anarchy. Reports would later pick out the personalities involved and details behind the uprising but from my viewpoint it was a free for all straight from a wild west saloon contained in a giant goldfish tank. Crockery spiralling through the air, chairs broken over heads, a figure prostrate and star shaped in the centre of the fracas being ministered to by an anxious group of kneeling figures. Faces I recognised from the restaurants, business centre and front desk contorted in anger. All orchestrated by the reservations manager who spurred his forces on to victory by leaping up and down on the counter of his desk and shouting maniacally.

The following day's papers would picture this individual being led away in handcuffs, but his actions and the subsequent mutiny were soundly applauded by those who had had the misfortune to work or even reside, under the despotic rule of the hotel manager and his cronies. They had jumped to safety through windows and disappeared into the middle distance at the first sign of trouble. I had arrived as the army was attempting to contain the combatants while the Minister of Tourism was summoned to hear their demands. Neither wishing to spectate on what had the makings of a bloodbath or to become embroiled in the melee I slunk out to the car park reasoning to myself that John Cruze could always toast stale bread for breakfast.

At the sorry prospect and its associated joys namely the steamy primeval turquoise bathroom home of countless nasty creepy crawlies of having to spend the rest of the afternoon in the Dilkusha office I directed Masum to the Foreign Office. I had a favour to ask of Mr Harun who had helped me with the VIP passage of guests at the airport.

A friend in London had managed to get a letter to us with details of his new address in the Bangladeshi dominated area east of the city. On his way to work he would pass the various establishments of expatriate Bangladeshi's and one in particular a travel agent advertising an offer on flights to Dhaka had caught his eye. Would we be able to do deal on return tickets to the UK he wondered. In principle it was a good idea but I wasn't sure I had the strength to pursue it. It did however sow a seed in my mind and within hours of my fax home my father had responded in the affirmative. The various plans that were now afoot regarding his visit included my own determined one to make his arrival at the airport as painless as possible.

Expecting to be greeted like a long lost friend I was taken aback at being forced to jog the memory of my contact at the Foreign Office. The thick blanket in the doorway was a familiar point of reference I was definitely in the right place, perhaps all *bideshi's* looked the same to him.

Undaunted I put the case for our illustrious visitor.

'This man is a famous historian.' It was a pardonable exaggeration and despite my impassioned plea Harun would have nothing of it. This was not the same man with whom I had masterminded the Wong visit. Then unseen forces from above had been at work in softening his demeanour.

'He is a very old man and it will be very difficult for him at the airport.' This was stretching things too but the humanitarian angle I was sure would make him crack.

He remained unmoved and I decided that rather than aggravate him and so threaten any future work related visits I would think again.

Doing my best to banish uncharitable thoughts about Harun from my mind I rummaged in my briefcase in the back of the car. Examining the request to the airport authorities to afford me the privilege of accompanying VIP visitors a hitherto unrecognised devious side to my character started to emerge. There was no mention of the Foreign Office at all in the document and I reasoned that their previous involvement had only been necessary because of the magnitude of our VIP. I had approached the wrong man, Mr Talukder of the Board of Investment, had signed my document and here was an example of the innocuous looking letter. I would make my own VIP document and having returned to the office I set to work.

It being Thursday evening if we left at a reasonable hour we would be able to catch happy hour at the Canadian Club. Brenda had delighted in my story of the fisticuffs at the Lalbagh and I was looking forward to being able to recount my story of having witnessed the goings on at first hand.

The clang of the metal door to the Canadian Club closing behind us was a delight at the end of any week. Picking our way round the lawn in front of the clubhouse as the light faded we were pleased to return the friendly greeting of the ball boys sitting beneath a single light bulb outside the squash court. The sound of laughter and chat spilled through the open windows of the bar and opening the screened doors there was no perceptible change in volume. We spotted Peter standing a head above a group engaged in lively conversation causing his fellow Canadians to throw their heads back in laughter.

'Hey you guys!' he called across to us spotting us in the doorway. Making crab like progress across the crowded room we joined him and his party.

'Have I got a story for you two,' he boomed, his grin a credit to his orthodontist.

'Well you won't get a better account of it than we have,' boasted Brenda. 'Mark was actually there!'

'At Sally Jones' house?' he responded incredulously.

'No silly the Lalbagh.'

The High Commission had already been informed of the events earlier in the day and had lost no time in circulating the news. Their most vociferous spokesman an annoying character called 'Larry,' who had bored us loud and long on the various shortcomings of our newly adopted homeland shortly after our arrival. Tales of gloom and doom and insights into the local ways of the world. It was ironic really that it should be him who revealed that for a relatively small fee one could arrange to have someone 'taken care of' since by the end of our conversation—he was a prime target. Now having done the rounds, he had unwittingly spoiled my scoop.

Peter's story, however, came from a different world. One to which we, being neither teachers or parents, had no entry. An inner sanctum of that stratum of expatriate society just a step below that of those conferred with diplomatic status—the American School and its associated community. Sue taught English at the school and had been the source of the story, but Peter had claimed it for his own.

'So, Sally goes away and asks Kelly Dean if she can look-in, occasionally on her two dogs. After a couple of days Kelly goes round to the house to make sure the dogs are okay. When she can only find one of them she asks the cook where the other dog is.'

"Dog in kitchen Madam,' says the cook," recounted Peter, embellishing his story with his best local accent. 'But when she looks in the kitchen...no dog.'

"No Madam dog inside!' and with that he opens the lid of the freezer and there he is...paws in the air!' Peter lifted his hands to the ceiling to demonstrate.

There was a simple explanation in as much as the dog had died and not knowing what to do with it in the absence of his employer the cook had sought to preserve the remains of her companion. Which however resourceful was not the first conclusion the 'dog-sitter' had arrived at.

As the green chits of happy hour were exchanged for the normal blue the beer continued to flow and every dog story emerged. From the litter of puppies that had been purchased one-by-one by a Korean man. To the incredible tale of an unfortunate male dog who whilst in the safety of his own home had taken the fancy of the *chowkidar*. In his struggle to molest what was not a small dog he had made such a noise that the dog's owner had been woken, and on investigating the noise, had found the couple in *flagrante delicto*. I was told that, if it were of any consolation, the mental image of the happy couple would leave me after approximately twenty-four hours.

chapter eighteen

The ease with which my colleagues took to their desks situated in our new offices in Jute House came as something of an anticlimax. With Mala still away, and the nod given to go ahead by the architects, the resident heads of departments and I took the executive decision to negate the Mala factor by providing her with a *fait accompli*.

Surely the sight of heads bowed over assignments, and in their respective offices, and workspaces would soften her resolve.

I was delighted with my own office set at the exact opposite end of the building to that of my illustrious boss, affording a panoramic view of the city area. The reaction of my colleagues was favourable, too. A mixture of relief to be out of the gloomy Dilkusha surroundings and amazement that quite such a close approximation of a western environment could be achieved against a third world backdrop. Indeed, Jute House rose out of a water logged slum community whose daily activities were played out in a fascinating tableau some seven floors below us. Bamboo panelled homes raised on stilts with access gained by delicately picking a way along a single sturdy bamboo pole supported above the water with finer poles tied to posts sunk into the water as makeshift handrails. These precarious structures were negotiated by the even the most senior of the local inhabitants and served to link small satellite dwellings to more permanent looking corrugated iron shelters and communal areas. The concrete washing area served by a single tap did almost non-stop trade and occasionally a lone figure would pick its way out along a bamboo tightrope to one of the small rectangular cabins for a period of solitary cogitation.

The pressure I had endeavoured to exert on the Nilkhet Exchange had still resulted in a conspicuous lack of telephone lines. Now with no land line to call upon, my mobile telephone was on constant walkabout amongst my colleagues in the vicinity of my office. Although it was an accepted practice to borrow it, answering it was a different matter. Despite my protestations, its trill would attract no response until I could bear it no longer, dashing out of my office to locate it before we lost the call.

'Hello, it's Dad here,' were the words I was least expecting to hear on answering the telephone, having located it amongst a pile of cables and computer disks on Mutton's desk.

It was resourceful of him, since we had no home telephone nor had I ever seen anything approaching a public telephone box in Dhaka. Since there was pretty much an open season on the interception of telephone lines, which might result in the unsuspecting account holder running up thousands of taka worth of bogus calls, presumably making one a landmark would make easy pickings.

'Where are you calling from?' I asked wondering how my father had succeeded in an area that so far I had dismally failed.

'Noel, the servant in the apartment upstairs let me call.' He replied his tone rather matter of fact.

'So what's up?' I enquired.

'Well. While I was out this morning a man from...wait a moment,' he paused while I imagined him searching for a card. '...Banani Decorators. Filled your flat with coloured lights. Was he meant to do that?'

Christmas had come to Dhaka at much the same time as my father. His arrival had brought with it the realisation that really there was very little to do in the city and we were relieved that there were a number of locally planned events to brighten what might otherwise have been a dreary stay. To a certain extent there was entertainment to be found in the day-to-day peculiarities that we had become accustomed to and for which he had come unprepared. At the airport I had spotted him at a distance, he having taken the precaution of camouflaging himself with a blazer and bow tie. I was greatly relieved that my bogus documentation had got me through the VIP gates, and I could spare him a rude initiation in the ways of the subcontinent. Now by the sounds of things he was starting to find his way.

'Is he still there?' I asked.

'Oh yes he's out on the balcony with another sack full at the moment.'

'Get John to tell him to wait and I'll get Brenda to come over and help you out,' I advised him.

Entering into the spirit of the season we had decided to throw a party, and on the advice of a friend, had visited Banani Decorators, one of a number of establishments dotted around the Gulshan area styled as party outfitters. For a fee they would provide a venue for a function, as in the case of the *shamiana* for the cricket and/or, as in our case, bedeck whatever you wanted with coloured lights. We had seen a number of buildings completely covered in oscillating lights and as someone said to us, 'It's just one of those things you have to do before you leave Dhaka.'

With this axiom in mind we had discussed our requirements with the proprietor and had made an appointment for him to plan the layout of our lights and deliver plates and glasses on the eve of our party. However, in best local tradition, the plates were delivered, but the lighting consultant was not with them.

We could console ourselves with our Christmas tree acquired locally, complete with its own ants' nest housed in the pot. This, with our own decorations and

countless others acquired from just about every charitable organisation known to man at the American
School Christmas fete, would provide more than
enough festive decor without the lights.

Having secured an allowance from a friend's passbook we could offer our guests an assortment of alcoholic beverages and with Siddique, the barman from
the Canadian Club, we would have someone to hand
them out. John, whose performance had been greatly
enhanced by the arrival of the awe inspiring Fardda,
had been hard at work in the kitchen. Brenda had left
work early to police our now numerous servants and
ensure that everything was in order.

'Hi, it's me.' It was Brenda.

'Everything OK?' I ventured.

'Yup.'

'Sure?'

'Yup! When were you planning to get home?'

'You've sent Masum back to the office?'

'Yes, ages ago.'

'Well in that case I thought I'd leave at about 5.30.'

'OK, no need to rush.' She was gone.

It was a cryptic call, the full meaning of which
was not apparent until I got home later that evening.

Driving up Road 6 in Baridhara, having dropped
Masum at a good place to pick up a baby taxi, I ducked
between the car sun visor and steering wheel and
looked up to the fourth floor of our apartment block.
There, identified by the small Union Jack and Canadian flag flying from the balcony was the pleasing
sight of neat lines of cascading coloured lights on our
balcony. So that was what all the secrecy had been
about.

The sound of my key in the door brought John out
of the kitchen. His oven gloved hand raised in welcome gave the impression that he had been strangely
mutated since the glove was a product of our last visit
to Canada and in the form of a lobster claw. Putting it
to further good use he ushered me in and directed my

gaze to the extraordinary spectacle that was now our sitting room. All available wall space had been adorned with strings of multicoloured walnut sized light bulbs strung from what on close inspection proved to be two inch nails driven into the wall just below the ceiling at six inch intervals. Would this assault on our decor have been confined to the sitting room? Instead the lights having done numerous circuits of the Christmas tree spilled out of the sitting room into the adjoining dining room snaking round the walls and out into the hallway.

Brenda joined me.

'You should have seen it an hour ago!' she sighed and proceeded to recount the events of that afternoon.

With the discovery of our illuminations, Brenda had put a damage limitation plan into action. Knowing that my reaction towards those responsible was likely to be colourful, she had wanted to keep me out of the way while some of the lights were removed. Having left her mobile with her colleagues she had called upon the offices of the unlikely named 'Noel' and telephoned me from the apartment upstairs in the hope of stalling my return. The first part of her plan complete she had returned to our apartment which was emitting the distinct smell of something burning. Having checked the oven and found nothing, a wider search led to the discovery of a small electrical fire running up a string of lights in the dining room, which, after some impromptu fire fighting with a tea towel by John, was extinguished.

The man from Banani Decorators, despite orders to the contrary, was obviously well aware of the idiosyncrasies of his equipment and had wisely stayed on the premises. John had found him holed up with the guards in the car park and while he set about running repairs, an inspection was made of the damage. A scorch mark ran up the wall, pausing at the join between wall and ceiling before fanning out in all directions, leaving a sizeable sooty smear. John had tried to scrub the blackened wall and ceiling which had little effect. My father had helpfully offered a macramé angel wall hanging, purchased at the American School fête, to disguise the damage but Brenda had diplomatically declined his offer pointing out that it would only serve to draw attention to the spot. With paint the only sensible option, John was dispatched to the market.

I had left my 'favourite' and most precious cricket sweater on the back of a chair and the fire had caused molten plastic to drip onto it. This was now Brenda's chief concern and she had taken it into the kitchen to perform major surgery. A bang, accompanied by a squeal and a crash, brought her swiftly out again to find the man from the decorators akimbo prostrate on the floor unconscious and festooned in a funerary way with his own lights.

With the odds stacking up against her—a potentially homicidal husband on the way home, forty people due shortly, a home decorated like a fun fair, a charred dining room and now a dead man on the floor—she called my father. A short inspection resulted in the painful prognosis, that the man would unfortunately survive and that he was coming to his senses.

Having been briefed on the afternoon's dramatic events, it seemed we had got off relatively unscathed and after all it did provide us with an excellent conversation piece later that evening. Particularly when much to the delight of some of our guests, and consternation of others, the lights flickered on-and-off in such an alarming manner that it was decided that in order to preserve our dwelling we should pull the plug.

The cold season that old hands had promised us established itself: and we enjoyed sunny days with blue skies and cool evenings. Dhakaites took the operative word 'cold' very seriously, enjoying the opportunity to take woolly hats and jumpers out of mothballs, and at this time, street vendors of brightly coloured paisley scarves did steady business. For people that evidently felt the cold, wrapping up well to keep warm was an activity, which eschewed the virtues of sartorial elegance. Respecting this we would acknowledge the deferential salute of our guard, keeping a straight face as we went to and from our building despite the fact that he appeared to have taken to wearing a tea cosy on his head.

The expatriate community embraced Christmas wholeheartedly, taking advantage of the comfortable evenings to stage various festive activities. It was a joy to participate in traditional pastimes with their own local and international embellishments. The candlelit carol concert held in the splendid tropical garden of the Australian High Commissioner was one such event. Massed under the stars two hundred or so participants rushed through an enormous number of carols accompanied by a tuneless upright piano. The highlight being an Australian version of 'The twelve days of Christmas' with its 'five kangaroos, four platypuses, three koala bears, two pink gallahs and an emu up a gum tree'.

The Americans, not wishing to be outdone, organised a splendid carol singing tour with a difference, taking in the network of residential streets of Gulshan. Swelling the coffers of the local rickshaw *wallah* fraternity, a convoy of fifty or so three wheelers wound their way round a carefully mapped out route. Pit stops were made at designated houses, and refreshments provided while carols were sung, delighting a posse of local children that had formed in our wake. It was my first experience of the American corruption of the well-known British arrangement of 'O Little Town of Bethlehem' and an introduction to others that will always remind me of that evening. The flat bass of the broadest man I have ever seen, a black US

Marine, mangling 'Joy to the World' has left such an indelible impression on me that surely it is the only way for it to be performed.

The reserve of the British High Commission showed signs of cracking with the club hosting the inter-club tennis party. This was such a boozy affair that we encountered Joanne from the Canadian High Commission doing a passable impression of Ethel Merman being helped out of the gate as we arrived. The ball boys from various clubs suffered, too. Good Muslims all, their annual association with alcohol behind the walls of expatriate society was a messy business. When finally I was coerced onto the boards of the open air dance floor, several of them were whirling about in a trance-like state.

The Canadians outdid the Brits and their no nonsense catering with their Christmas dinner. Due in part to the club manager's clandestine links with the American Commissary, we dined outside on all the traditional fare. This included some well travelled turkeys, whose ambition to survive Christmas, must surely have been superseded by the momentous contribution they were making Anglo-American relations.

Before his departure my father had unloaded all sorts of goodies dispatched by my mother with which to bolster our own arrangements. But however well-prepared we were, and however much we tried to replicate what we would do at home, Christmas morning came and both Brenda and I were homesick. The *BBC World Service* at 7am ensured that we, at least via the airways, were live with Christmas in London it being half past midnight there.

There was, however, a positive side. In working hard to create the Christmas spirit there had certainly been a concentration on the more wholesome aspects of the celebration rather than the commercial ones that have all but taken over in the west. A service was held at the American Club and, despite a clergyman in

Roman legionnaire's sandals and shorts and the accompaniment of two folksy guitars, we were glad to have made the effort of going.

Peter and Sue hosted an evening meal for which Brenda had cooked another one of those unfortunate American turkeys. He made his last journey across town on Brenda's knee, while we sweltered in the evening sunshine, the car's AC doing its best to keep us cool. We had dressed as any self respecting Bangladeshi would for an evening in the cold season in hats, scarves, and coats, barely able to contain our mirth at the thought of being met at our friends' front door. The joke had rather fallen flat when a complete stranger answered our knock. Shortly afterwards, Pete had appeared scantly clad in a *lungi* and T-shirt and made introductions to Mike, an American, and his wife, Sheryl. Excuses were made for our behaviour by dint of my being British, and by the end of the evening and several games of Pictionary, we were all firm friends. Another new friend, Kim, had turned up towards the end of the evening having attempted to leave Dhaka only to find that a transport workers strike had blocked all exits out of the city. This was an interesting turn of events since those members of the expatriate population who were not already on leave were planning getaways on Boxing Day. Although a piece of local intelligence that no one had seen fit to share with us consigning us to a gloomy run into and beyond the New Year. The 6th of January was the day to set our sights on and the return of Mala.

chapter nineteen

Our progress had been halted at the roundabout just a hundred yards shy of our office. Brenda and I played out our daily ritual of feigning deafness to the urgent tapping on the car window. Fortunately for me the small child in stained and ragged clothing was on Brenda's side and while her heart strings were undergoing a major tugging, I made a minute inspection of my fellow road users. We were side-by-side with a rickshaw and I examined the toes of the driver as he held the weight of his vehicle by standing on the pedals. I wondered how long, if I were cast out on  the street shoeless, it would take for my own feet to take on this appearance—skin that a small elephant might have been proud of and toe nails trimmed and rearranged by various encounters with solid inanimate objects.

From the footplate behind him rose two eight feet, high well stuffed opaque plastic bags. A third wedged between them and the seat for good measure. Another rickshaw *wallah* had done me the service of up-ending a similar load on a previous morning, spilling his cargo of puffed rice and so satisfying my curiosity as to their contents. This delicacy was destined for the market, to be decanted to smaller bags and sold at sunset by street traders to those good Muslims observing Ramadan.

As we started to move and the sound of finger nails dragging down Brenda's side of the car subsided, we edged past the cause of the obstruction. A portly policeman his stomach straining against the blancoed-

163

webbing of his belt had restrained the early morning traffic with nothing more than a hard hat and umbrella. Disappearing up a spur of the roundabout were those he had protected. A string of magnificent looking mounted policeman and as the last one trotted away from us topped with a khaki *sola topee*, I made a note to look in the yellow pages for police outfitters.

In Mala's absence, a pleasant calm had descended upon the office and the advent of the holiday season had compounded this. The Holy month of Ramadan with its shorter working days was the ideal way of easing back into her more demanding regime. 'Cultivating piety' was however playing havoc with the punctuality of our staff. The accepted method of getting through a day of fasting being to rise before dawn, eat a gargantuan feast, jump back into bed and then rise at the usual time. This was fine in theory but in practice the getting up factor was the most difficult to implement. An almighty fuss had been kicked up one morning, when by 9am, only Brenda and I had made it into the office before Mala had arrived, resulting in a hastily convened office meeting.

Assembled in the boardroom, it was evident that we had come quite a way since Brenda, Schezade, and I had fought over a single laptop in the hotel. We had added to our numbers and in so doing a considerable weight had been lifted from my shoulders with the recruitment of a fearsome, local lady accountant. Having confounded every mathematician that had ever had the misfortune to teach me, I had derived a certain amount of pleasure in tracking the office finances. It was however a ridiculous state of affairs that a mathematical incompetent be faced with this responsibility and my repeated protestations had eventually borne fruit. We were now fourteen in total, but with the amount of *peons*, drivers, guards and cleaning staff that we had behind the scenes we were easily double that.

Recruitment for the support staff had been a hit and miss affair. Without the benefit of a designated agency an advertisement in one of the local papers was the only course of action. I had assumed that, being a foreigner, I was being overcharged for space in the classified section, and had fought long and hard in the office of the *Bangladesh Observer* trying to negotiate the rate down. Determined to strike some sort of deal, I had finally accepted a free inch in which I inserted a small note announcing the fact that Brenda and I were now married and residing in Dhaka.

The bundle of mail that we received in response to our recruitment submission was substantial, and of dubious quality, although there was a certain scholarship in the ingenuity that had gone into some of the applications. One gentleman so elderly that, however well qualified, we couldn't possibly consider; sent a photograph of him taken at a time when he was considerably more youthful. However, the extraordinary nature of his then hairdo growing in one direction and beard in the opposite, was lost on him but not on me. The halo of hair standing proud of the top of his head and chin was so magnificent that, in disbelief, I faxed it to a friend of mine in London. On the strength of his luxuriant locks and qualifications, he was called for interview only for me to discover that, by the look of his thinning grey hair, the intervening years had not be kind to him. Perhaps he should have considered the approach taken by another applicant, who unable to send a photograph, had drawn a small, and not too flattering, picture of himself.

Whatever the quality of our applicants, for them, the prospect of an association with a foreign company was an attractive one. Although not necessarily straightforward. The facilities would prove hazardous, and within a week of our first influx, I had several complaints from colleagues of footprints on top of the sanitary ware. Rana fielded a complaint from a deputation of slum dwellers who had endured a competition

for the longest spit, which may or may not have emanated from our floor. And following Mala's assembly,
I was left to council those fasting who were left reeling by the news that their day would not be ending at
sunset for *iftar*, the meal to break their abstinence.

No doubt recognising that she was doing her countrymen a terrible injustice I had been beeped on my
intercom and determined not to miss-out on the fun,
set off with Rana to purchase *iftar* for thirty people.
My experiences with local food ranged from the uncomfortable to the debilitating. The best restaurants in
town had laid me out. If some dormant nasty didn't
get me, then the sheer quantity that generous hosts
would lavish upon me, would. At the opposite end of
the food chain, my fascination lay more in the ritual
than the sampling.

From my office a bright neon sign picked out
'Pushpa Plaza,' a monumental concrete shopping complex that housed Dhaka's one and only escalator. I had
investigated it one lunchtime only to find that what
promised so much from its signage merely housed the
obligatory fancy goods stores with their strange mixture of kitsch, toys and western toiletries. The draw of
its escalator, however, provided sufficient passing
trade for a number of restaurants including Big Bite
Burgers. I noted that the proprietor had taken care not
to mention what sort of burgers he served and I shuddered to think what unsuspecting animal might have
found its way into his fare. Hopefully he did not frequent the same butcher as his neighbour Penguin
Pizza. Whatever the ingredients, we would surely be
able to find something suitable.

Iftar was a much more sophisticated institution
enticing local restaurateurs out onto the roadside to
cater for the brisk trade. Hastily erected stalls and
trestle tables supported piles of neat brightly coloured
square boxes. Large woks of boiling oil bubbled behind
them cooking up orange oil-soaked local 'fast food.'
Spilling onto the road the crush of ravenous people

took little interest in the traffic grinding by inches away in a fug of dust and exhaust. The urgency of knobbly elbows was all around me, the press of hot flesh through cotton shirting pressed against mine.

'So Rana, ten taka or fifteen taka *Iftar* boxes?' Could there really be a difference in quality for a difference of pennies.

'Fifteen!' His indignant response suggested that there was and shouting our order at a stall holder we watched as thirty fifteen taka boxes were hastily assembled. Each containing five different pieces of fried dough and *bhajis* and a twist of cellophane containing a yellow brown sauce.

An aged *Hoozur* in white robe and hat stood at one end of the table, watching the process through thick black rimmed spectacles of a prehistoric vintage.

'Tiris ek box!' I asked of the man making up the boxes, distorting the Bangla but not the gist. I had read regarding Ramadan that anyone who can afford it should feed someone less fortunate and I was happy to comply.

On our return, we found that Mala had left for the day. I had been looking forward to dispatching one of the *peons* to her office with one of the small greasy boxes. Instead she had gone home to unpack her shipment of which, acting as her factotum, I had overseen the arrival. Although marshalling hordes of removal men was a job that I would rather have not repeated, her request for me to do so did display an element of trust in me on her part. Although as my role in this particular quarter developed, some of her requests were perplexing. The failure of her washing machine to function was solved by adding that crucial element of water to the equation. A guard was hired to keep a watch over the guards already posted at her building. That the air conditioning had been installed incorrectly allowing the ingress of little 'salamanders' had tested me. Surely a person with local roots would know that geckos were a fixture in the most five star of dwellings.

The frustrations of living in Dhaka, whether associated with our work or domestic surroundings, had a debilitating effect. So much of my work in keeping the office up and running was reliant on the services of local contractors, and it was an almost daily occurrence to be let down in some way—from the late production of proofs for printed matter to the no show of the air conditioning engineers after an entire system shut down on a sweltering day. An intensification of the opposition party's 'non co-operation movement' in the run up to the election had increased power cuts and resulted in water shortages. A severe bout of what Winston Churchill would have termed 'black dog' was brought upon me when whilst enjoying images of home, a power failure in the middle of a broadcast from Hong Kong of the Five Nations rugby match between England and France.

That other cause of annoyance had still yet to resolve itself. I was a regular visitor to the Nilkhet Exchange in my quest to obtain a telephone line. Interspersing my calls with visits to the Board of Investment in the hope that they would live up to the line in their bumph that described that August Institution as being:

> *Vested with necessary powers to take decisions for the speedy implementations of the new industrial projects and provide operational support services to the existing ones.*

Ah, it sounded so good but sadly it seemed the other parties involved in the process were unaware of this fact.

I had established quite a routine during the course of my visits, and had discovered that there was in actual fact, a system, which relied upon registering one's arrival with a clerk on the ground floor before trekking up to the second floor. Having done this, after a short wait, I was dealt with in a reasonably efficient way, being called into the divisional engineer's office for an update by one of his flunkies. My patience had been stretched on my last visit. Having waited for half an hour and read the *Bangladesh Observer* two or three times, I let myself into the office to find it empty.

'Engineer *Shibe khotai?*' I asked of the clerk downstairs, which roughly translates as 'Engineer Mr where is?'

'*Sylet.*' Came the reply.

I had neither the Bangla nor the strength to continue our conversation.

My association with the Exchange was however about to come to an end. On this occasion my entrance to the office of the divisional engineer and subsequent greeting received no response.

I took a seat and waited patiently until the great man collected his thoughts. Taking a pen he slid it between sheaves of paper bound in a cardboard file and flicked it open. Scanning the page through the lower lenses of bifocals he sucked his teeth noisily.

'Mr Mark, Jute House,' I said hopefully hoping to solicit a response.

'Old eschkool estreeeet.'

'That's the one.'

'There eis no line here.'

'Precisely.'

'You have made application.'

'Yes sir, you have seen me many times before!'

'No, never.' It was the most extraordinary untruth.

'I don't think....' I thought better of it there was no point in antagonising him.

'There eis no lines Old esckool estreeeet.'

'But, the Lalbagh Hotel is in the same area it has lots of lines.'

'Eis not same place.'

'The other offices in my building have lines.' He could not deny it, the fact of the matter was that so far no *baksheesh* had been forthcoming. He changed his tack.

'No demand note have.'

'Now look here, I made my application last year. We have paid thousands of takas for our connections. I have my demand note. Mr Shamsul Alam from the Board of Investment has telephoned this office on many occasions regarding these lines. I have been in this office many times. Before you have said that the lines are coming. One week, maybe two,' I lapsed into local speak, emphasising my point with my forefinger on his desk.

'Never!' he responded firmly.

I resisted the temptation to enter into a round of 'Oh yes you dids.'

'So when can I expect my lines?'

'There eis no lines.' He closed his folder and swatted me away with a dismissive wave.

'Call Mr Alam at the Board of Investment,' I said as I started to lose it.

'There eis no lines.'

At a tender age my father had shown me, as a means of warding off bullies, a karate chop under the nose made in an upwards direction. As a diminutive child, it was an implausibly difficult blow to land. Thirty years later the strength of ten men coursing through my veins I picked my spot. The voice of reason however sounded out through the red mist.

Fuming, I made my way towards the stairs, the slam of the divisional engineer's office door resounding behind me. It had helped a little but I owed this man, the bane of my existence, more than that. The perfect riposte to his intransigence presented itself as I reached the top of the stairs. Slung from a bracket was a faded red fire bucket containing a pleasing amount of sand and tens of cigarette butts. There was only one place for it and without hesitation I unhooked my weapon and returned to the office of the divisional engineer.

I had hoped for more of a sandcastle effect but the sand was very dry and liberally spilled around the desk. The 'Ivan factor' had accounted for me too. The product of a childish tantrum, but what a fillip.

'Now going?' Masum enquired.

'The Board of Investment I think, Masum.'

chapter twenty

Whatever the merits of the people or the cause, Bangladesh was a hard sell. I could see Mala's point in playing down talk of civil unrest, but the parliamentary elections having been boycotted and the ruling party returned unopposed, the once sporadic outbreaks of violence around the city were becoming more common. Despite being largely uncontested at the polls, allegations of vote-rigging to exaggerate voter turnout had been made. Peter and Kim had been drafted into a  team of independent election watchers and had encountered some pretty unsophisticated methods of increasing the vote. Namely the stuffing of large quantities of ballot papers into the boxes when they were unattended.

The American Embassy had caused a ripple of panic amongst the expat community. It had advised that everyone have their prized possessions at hand so that a hasty exit from the country could be made at six hours notice. To some extent the diplomatic quarter played up the threat, erring on the side of caution. But one sensed that to a degree, their sense of satisfaction in being able to justify their existence. In the confines of the Canadian Club, Larry from the High Commission swaggered about with a large and very visible walkie-talkie. This was no crisis, he was loving every moment.

Mala's views were changed somewhat having witnessed one lunchtime, her nose pressed against the windows at the front of Jute House with the rest of us, a swarm of ant like folk engulf a car leaving the car park. Trapped on the street once the car park gates were closed, the miscreants had made short work of all the breakable pieces of the car before frantic tooting had alerted the gatekeeper to let it back in. The report in the local paper the next day under the heading of 'Police and musclemen fight in Kawran Bazar', which reported: 'The mastans fled the scene when a large contingent of police rushed to the outpost' was not quite as we had witnessed it.

Such naked aggression was disturbing and later that day, Feroz called Mala with news of a huge demonstration scheduled to start by our office at noon, the following day. Looking north from the opposite side of the building to my office the massive concrete mass of the Sher-e-Bangla Nagar, the National Assembly was clearly visible. This was the target for the demonstrators and the scale of the turnout being predicted would choke the area around the office. The decision was taken to close the office for the day of the demonstration. The news was greeted with a flurry of activity. Plans were made to relocate computers in people's homes under cover of darkness, and I was given the task of getting Mala on the next morning's Thai flight to Hong Kong. These eleventh hour requests were tiresome particularly as it could be guaranteed that Mala would not be alone in wanting to escape a city on the verge of a standstill. A constant engaged tone at our travel agent bore out this theory. The calm her absence would bring to the office atmosphere was, however, sufficient incentive to make me brave the streets and cross the roundabout to the Lalbagh Hotel, wherein lay the office of Reza.

'Where are you?' Brenda's voice came out of my mobile.

'At the Lalbagh.'

'Are you a complete idiot?'

It was fair comment.

'Bad news,' she continued 'I have to go with Mala to Hong Kong.'

Brenda hadn't been too keen on leaving me on my own in the country, offering to revoke my employee status temporarily and demand that I be evacuated as her defenceless spouse. It was a kind thought, although on balance, a couple of days on my own were preferable to the flight. That is to say completely on my own. Our honourable bearer, Mr Cruze, whose behaviour had over recent weeks become more erratic, had 'Gone my village'. A small, apologetic, beautifully written and horribly spelt note left under an upturned bowl on the breakfast table had told us this. That he was gone was fine, it was the lack of warning that irked me. That evening, in a return to the ways of a bachelor, I called Spaghetti Jazz restaurant and ordered a take-away pizza. Home-delivered pizza in the third world one might argue is extremely civilised, and within an hour, a buzz on the intercom from the guard down below signalled its arrival.

'Surrr, man!' Was remarkably fluent for our guard but rather than enter into a prolonged bout of 'Hullows' as the conversation took a more complicated twist, I walked down the stairs to collect my dinner. The doorman from the restaurant had bought it on his bicycle and he greeted me sweating and beaming from beneath his pillbox hat. Dressed as a bellhop, clad in maroon with gold stripes running down the seams of trousers, he was the most spectacular pizza delivery-man you could wish for. Relieving him of the limp square box, I settled the account and tipped him far too much. He was worth every taka.

I had taken the view that hot and dry, rather than cold and soggy, was the best way to enjoy my culinary delight and I closed the oven on it with a metallic clatter repairing to the sitting room to see what was on the telly. Sitting on the sofa I heard an indistinct clatter similar to the one I had just created, but dismissed it as something on the television or simply someone elsewhere in the apartment block slamming a door.

We were used to background noise, the rattle of the AC and buzz of the transformer for our television and hi-fi but there was something different about this latest addition to the cacophony. There definitely had been a new noise and there it was again. I knelt next to the television and listened intently. It certainly wasn't coming from there. Perhaps it was coming from the back of the apartment. Another block was going up ten feet away from ours and the view from our bedroom was now directly onto a building site. Complete darkness suggested that it was not the source. Back in the kitchen the sound was more distinct and I stood absolutely still to listen.

Shouting, I could definitely hear shouting. Banging, metal on metal. Yes banging, too. Louder shouting and more banging. I went onto the balcony between the kitchen and John's room and stood amongst the drying mops to listen. The heat of the night exaggerated having left the cool of air conditioning I leant on the rail. The sound drifted in on the warm air. Whatever, it was there was a hell of a lot of people on the move and by the sounds of things they were coming my way.

My mind started to work overtime. The demonstration. The whole city has gone crazy. The musclemen are out for blood. Of course they'll start with the expatriates. Oh my God!

'BANG, CRASH, BANG!' It was getting closer.

My cricket bat. I can fend them off with that for a bit. 'Oh yeah Larry where are you now with your walkie-talkie.' I thought to myself.

'BLOOD! BLOOD! BLOOD!!' The angry mob bayed, its progress relentless.

Light spilled onto the street below from Elizabeth House, the British High Commission Medical Centre, situated adjacent to our block. Through the foliage of a tree the legs of a figure leading the pack came into view. As the main body of the group appeared the noise rose to a crescendo. They were dragging something down the road. Two ropes manned by lines of figures attached to a solid object...a cement mixer.

As quickly as the panic in the city had been drummed up it subsided. Much to my relief the scheduled Marylebone cricket club tour went ahead as planned. It was an unlikely event, an English professional touring side's visit coinciding with our stay, and not wanting to forgo an opportunity to see my fellow countrymen do battle on the cricket field, Masum and I attended an important 'meeting' in Motijheel.

The National Stadium was not only the centre for sporting excellence but also the hub of the electrical trade. Masum and I had been there often, paying our five taka to enter the stadium confines to seek out a bargain or simply to exit at the opposite side, a tried and tested short cut into the heart of the business area. A battered white coach parked on threadbare patch of grass beside the stadium indicated the presence of the players. I would have loved to see the faces of them as they boarded what, by local standards, was an excellent conveyance. Although there were dents on every visible panel and a length of brown tape plastered over a large crack in the windscreen, the alignment of the chassis did look pretty square. In local terms this classed it as tiptop.

Beside the bus, a crowd queued for tickets. An excited mass converging on a low, concrete building in a disorderly scrum. Hovering at the back of Dhaka's cricket going public, the situation looked hopeless until a policeman came to our aid. Flashing a smile, he took my arm and led me up one side of the crowd. I could now see their goal. A pair of geometric openings cut into the wall of the building. One rectangular through which to make one's request and one circular to plunge an arm into to accept the tickets.

Raising his swagger stick the policeman made to beat a path for me to the head of the queue. I hadn't realised this was how he had meant to effect my queue-jumping and restraining him with a blurted 'Na! Na!' he shrugged his shoulders and left me to my own devices.

'Never mind Masum! I'll forget it I think.' I reasoned as we walked back to the car.

'I'll just have a look down here to see if I can see the pitch.' I mimed looking through binoculars and walked over to an entrance and tunnel into the stadium labelled 'Players and VIP' Making unchallenged progress past two security guards I walked down the tunnel at the end of which a set of stone steps manned by another guard led up to a backdrop of sky surmounted by a grill. Gesturing skywards he ushered me up the steps and Dhaka Stadium stood before me. Caged I might be, but it gave me a sense of the atmosphere. A reasonable crowd, dotted around the stadium, the dark track in the middle of the ground with wickets pitched and an imposing scoreboard towering over the proceedings bearing names I recognised. I felt a strange kinship with these people, their names picked out in whitewash, who knew me not.

'Please, please!' One side of my cage opened. 'You are England team.'

'Err, no actually but I am from England.' Quickly establishing a reason for my interest in the proceedings.

'Ah, you must sit with the British High Commissioner.' He motioned to a bank of seats above us.

'No really I'm fine here.' Fine was an under statement, I was delighted to be in and, having shrugged off my host, took a wobbly seat on a folding chair built to accommodate a child.

People were generally inquisitive of a white face in a public place. Sitting alone in an empty area of the grandstand I stood out rather and, for a group of children seated in front of me, I was spellbinding. If I caught one of their glances they would turn away giggling, their heads bowed in consultation. Eventually one of them plucked up the courage to approach me proffering a small notebook and a pen. If he wanted my autograph, who was I to deny him?

More people filtered in as the game began and a character that remembered me from one of my local games joined me. I greeted him like a long lost friend although, if the truth be known, I hadn't the faintest idea who he was. He was pleasant and chatty and politely made excuses of climate and conditions as my countrymen started shakily losing two quick wickets.

'Ah this man is good batsman.' His judgement obviously based on the incoming man's propensity for swinging his arms around like windmills.

'Oh yes very fine,' He cooed, as expansive squatting warm up and other stretching exercises were performed before the player took his block in front of the stumps.

'Unlucky, very unlucky.' This comment accompanied by tut tutting after the batsmen's middle stump had been sent cartwheeling from the ground first ball.

It was obvious that there had been no dramatic development made in English cricket during my absence. Deciding to leave the ignominies of the game to be etched in the memories of the players and some faded page of *Wisden Cricketers Almanack*, I retraced my steps in search of Masum. I found him sheltering from the sun in the shadow cast by one of the stadium floodlights. It was very resourceful of him to remain so visible without cooking himself when he could have so easily disappeared into the scenery around the stadium and its associated market.

For almost its entire circumference, small shops had been established in the area below the tiered seating of the stadium. Amongst those dealing in electrical goods was the odd sports shop. I could never resist a visit to examine the splendid cricket bats stocked in old dark wooden cabinets. A scene from a bygone age with nineties prices. At over a hundred pounds each I wondered if they ever made a sale. An illicit purchase of two cheaper specimens on another occasion had earned me a severe reprimand from Brenda. Although the ancient boxing gloves and an old laced medicine ball were tempting curios, I could hardly justify them. Instead I contented myself with a small shiny alloy trophy which would remind me of this place one day when I added it to the collection of assorted paraphernalia displayed in the pavilion of my village team.

The opportunity for similar sneak outs was removed by the return of Mala. Although I was delighted to have Brenda back. Her return coincided with a renewal of the tension before and the bellicose posturing of the two central political parties. With a literacy rate of around thirty-five percent, the visual had played a strong part in the election. Symbols representing each of the political parties were in evidence on fly posters throughout the city. Although the outcome had been a foregone conclusion: the sheaf of wheat being returned unopposed by the boat. I had a theory that if I were to start the cricket bat party owing to the popularity of the game in the sub-continent I would score a runaway success. The prospect of explaining to family that our return home would be delayed for a number of years because I was now Prime Minister had however proved sufficient deterrent.

The absence of John Cruze was starting to become rather tiresome. Brenda and I decided that we would give him one more chance and having drawn the short straw I was designated the mean, old disciplinarian who had to deliver this ultimatum. However, when he did eventually put in an appearance it was so late one evening that we were on our way to bed and in no mood to embark on lengthy discussions about the future path of his career with us. The morning was the time to settle the matter and his explanation would keep until then.

The poor devil had obviously been on tenterhooks all night and I was pounced upon in the corridor as soon as I had emerged from the bedroom. The sound of the hair drier from the bedroom suggested that Brenda was still some way behind me, which as far as he was concerned would give us a chance to speak man to man.

'Saar, my need speak with you.'

'Well John, I think that you need to tell us why you keep disappearing.'

'Oh Saar!' The tears started. Not theatrical beads down the cheek, copious tears expelled from his eyeballs like windscreen washer jets. At the best of times he was difficult to understand. I listened intently to his assorted sobs and sniffs in an attempt to decipher what was the problem. With such a shameless display of grief it was the least I could do. Finally he caught his breath and gulped.

My old Saar, Saar, he my new job giving.'

'Ah!' I said nonplussed.

'My old Saar he going Kuwait and want me going to him.'

So John had a new job overseas. Three times his monthly wage he had been promised which having done his sums was an opportunity too good to miss. I did not envy him his choice, which would take him away from his family for two years.

'So when are you going?'

The tears continued unchecked.

'Today Saa, eleven morning time.'

'Oh dear, oh dear. Poor John.' I commiserated putting a comforting hand on his shoulder. It was too sad. Uprooted from home and taken to a strange country. Having had his farewells with his loved ones he had spent his last evening in Bangladesh with us and I had been curt with him. It was just too much and I felt my bottom lip tremble.

'Now my Saa and Madam no cook have.'

'Well don't worry about that we're just sad to see you go.' Now my eyes were damp as well.

Brenda joined us and restored some order fetching a tea towel from the kitchen with which to staunch the flow of John's tears.

Never have I seen an individual cry so much and he left us a forlorn figure still blotting his face with the towel Brenda had given him. I hoped that when he eventually hung it out to dry the picture on it of a big, yellow tiger and the legend 'Bangladesh' wouldn't start him off again.

In the kitchen we found a note propped up against the toaster with the heading:

'God's Almighty

Dear Sir and Madam,

At first you take the best wishes. I am happy for your kindness. I'll forever miss you. Really your memory will remain forever in my heart. Then may you be happy and live long.

No more today.

John Cruze'

There was not a dry eye in the house.

chapter twenty-one

The expatriate community lived their lives to a carefully timetabled schedule and we fell into their ways following the pattern without question. The Muslim festival, *Eid-ul-Fitr*, celebrating the end of Ramadan had prompted a mass exodus out of the city and we had joined it. Calcutta was the nearest destination for a little rest and recuperation and on a subsequent visit I would set the world beating time of two hours from leaving my front door to  standing on Chowringee Road. This journey was more memorable for the lengths the party of Brenda, Peter, Sue and Kim had gone to get me there. Having developed a severe case of 'not wanting to fly if it isn't necessary syndrome', Brenda had conceded that if it was going to make me a nervous wreck then it was better to stay in Dhaka.

However, a day spent wracked with guilt for having spoilt everyone's plans convinced me that I should endure the flight for the common good. All manner of frightening drugs were available freely at local pharmacists and Sue, having consulted with a friendly doctor, had purchased a sedative and delivered it to the apartment. My bag packed, and Peter and Kim on standby to carry me onto the plane if required, I was filled with local valium and sat on the sofa to await its effect.

A suitably dopey figure was led out onto the tarmac at the airport, which to the dismay of the attendants was instantly revived by an adrenaline rush from the sight of an aircraft of the local airline with twin propellers. There is a certain mystery in the jet engine. The lack of visible moving parts is faintly reassuring in its mystery. The propeller however is a much more functional device liable to stuttering to a standstill or falling off. But things were out of my hands by then, and Kim and Peter each taking a firm grip on an arm, led me to the foot of steps into the plane.

No sooner had I recovered from the Calcutta ordeal then the spectre of another flight hove into view. The election result rejected, the opposition party intensified its campaign to depose the Government by launching an indefinite 'non co-operation movement'. Instead of juggling small pockets of the staff and assorted hardware around the city, it was decided to close the office in Dhaka temporarily and dispatch the staff to other offices in the region. India was the most cost effective destination and for the office new blood, it was an opportunity to gain some experience in a more established office and business environment. Fortunately for me, Brenda was more useful located in Hong Kong and in my combined role as employee and bedfellow we would save on accommodation. The Hong Kong Sevens rugby tournament would be in full swing at the time of our proposed stay, and to our immense good fortune, it was only possible to get a room in one of the more upmarket hotels. Although by the time the logistics of the whole operation was complete I was in need of some pampering.

Many of the local staff had never travelled before and the rapid acquisition of passports for them with its attendant local obstructions was a struggle. One girl had a passport that was being held by her estranged father who had to be persuaded to part with it. Indian visas took time we didn't have. Flights to India were heavily booked and the route to Bombay that was finally arranged required an overnight stay in Delhi, which in turn, meant more accommodation. It was either impossible to get a line to India to make the arrangements or having finally got through a sickening ping would sever the connection. Designated roommates refused to share with each other. Disputes arose over rank and accommodation, the distribution of cash for everyday expenses and the prospect of daily travel on Indian trains. Where was the Dunkirk spirit when I needed it most?

A *hartal* called the day before our departure gave me a day off to celebrate my birthday, and with the England cricket team playing a crucial game in the World Cup being staged in India, I was keen to monitor their progress. Our television connection had always been something of a hit or miss affair. The route up to the roof was one well trodden by me on maintenance missions to the large satellite dish fixed to the flat roof of the building. It said something of the precarious nature of its fastening that despite being five feet in diameter its ability to transmit could be interfered with by a strong wind.

Ten minutes before play was due to start I switched on the set to be confronted with a snowstorm on the screen. Taking the stairs up to the roof two at a time I arrived breathless to be confronted by an aberration. Strung from the satellite dish to a fixed point elsewhere a clothesline complete with wet and dripping washing. Reattaching one end of the line to a less vital piece of equipment I gave the dish a wiggle in the vain hope of returning it to its previous position.

Back in the apartment there was no improvement. Calling Brenda I asked her to monitor any change while I returned to the roof to make fine adjustments. It was useless we needed to be able to communicate while I was on the roof. Having surrendered my mobile telephone to Dvai and Catherine telephoning each other, which would have been a flagrant misuse of company property, was not an option. The situation called for some lateral thought.

'I told you this would be useful.' I said playing out the ball of string that had caught my eye at the local market because of its twisted strands of red and white.

'You hold one end and when the picture comes back give me two yanks for 'yes" and if I yank it I'm asking you for an update. If there is no change then it's one for a "no", ok?' Brenda raised her eyebrows and I shot off back up the stairs taking my end of the string with me.

Too many twists and turns on it tortuous route made a pull on the string impossible to recognise so I tried an alternative course off the roof, over the side of the building and in through the balcony door. Repeated single pulls greeted my pulls and having twisted the dish in every conceivable direction I had to admit defeat. There was only one thing for it and it was a last ditch desperation measure. I would have to go and watch the television at the British High Commission Club.

Since the deserted club bar and its particularly tasteful collection of saucy seaside postcards is possibly the most depressing place on earth: it was a wonder I escaped to Hong Kong with my sanity intact. Mala had done us the good service of opting to head off in the opposite direction around the globe to complete a convoluted itinerary. I had been given the unenviable task of trying to arrange a hire car for her from Delhi Airport to Dharamsala for an audience with the Dalai Lama. The arrangement I had come to down a crackling line from Dhaka with a local Indian car hire company would rely upon an intervention from His Holiness to proceed without incident. Save a special request that I book her a room in the hotel we were staying in for Passover, which seemed a strange request from a Bangladeshi American, we were free.

Hong Kong provided a setting for a return to a more structured day. Although the environment was rather sterile in comparison to the one we had left there was novelty to be found in mundane things. Our fascination for the telephone that connected on the first attempt and allowed a conversation to take place without the background noise of several other distant calls invited queries about our adopted home from colleagues. 'Bangla. . .where?' and 'Do we have an office there?' were comments that didn't entirely fill us with confidence about our struggle to put the Dhaka office on the map.

Of the treats available to us the ability to walk about unchallenged was perhaps the one we had least considered. However, Masum and his services had made us soft and we both suffered blisters after a prolonged shopping trip to Kowloon. Our shopping list for other people was long and varied with requests ranging from pine nuts to squash rackets. One item on our own list that one might think was peculiar to seek out in Hong Kong was an extension on our Bangladeshi visa. An operation uncomplicated by thinly veiled requests for *baksheesh* and a desire to see you return as soon as possible to go through the process again. A seamless three hour process at the Spartan, but functional Bangladesh High Commission reuniting us with our passports by lunchtime, the ink having just dried on a twelve month stamp with unlimited visits. In Dhaka circles this was an item to die for.

Our bubble burst after a week with a long call from Mala, whose attention to the bottom line of her projected budget, was giving her cause for concern. Enquiries were made of the ever helpful Larry at the Canadian High Commission in Dhaka regarding the political situation. He suggested that we read the local newspapers, which left us none the wiser. Peter was more helpful in response to our call, and without prompting, volunteered to provide us safe passage from the airport in one of the more rugged vehicles in his agency's stable.

Mala's call had resolved one thing and that was the Passover question, which had already required a telephone call to a Jewish friend in London to find out the exact date.

'Would that be this year's Passover?' I had politely enquired.

'NO! Next year,' she responded indignantly. 'You know the one from Britain to China!'

We had thought Pete's precaution of collecting us in a large white four wheel drive vehicle a mite cautious. Rattling down the airport road we appeared to be the only vehicle on the road.

'Look at this guys!' He shouted above the din pointing at a bus careering down the opposite carriageway. It was a regulation Dhaka single-decker bus listing precariously as it thundered along the road but with one slight design modification. The windscreen had been removed and the driver issued with a crash helmet.

It was clear that in our absence the local situation had changed. One sensed an air of muted concern and we were alarmed to find troop carriers stationed at various points around the normally sleepy area of Gulshan. The cab of each lorry topped with a youthful soldier manning a heavy machine gun. It was clear that the authorities were prepared for the worst.

In response the expatriate community encamped in their homes or behind the walls of the various clubs endeavoured to put a brave face on things. The British contingent sported t-shirts bearing the legend 'With a stiff upper lip I survived the 1996 Bangladesh Elections', but was this tempting fate?

For those attempting to do business it was a frustrating time. One encountered the bravado of those that claimed they had masses to do and how they got so much done at home only to find them sheepishly acknowledging a wave from beside the club swimming pool.

Shortages of various commodities became commonplace: fresh milk was a thing of the past and supplies of fresh meat and vegetables scant. One Bangladeshi Canadian, with perhaps more money than sense, had taken the precaution should things get worse of acquiring thirty live chickens with which he was sharing his garden.

Days of being house bound provided us with the opportunity to sort out the filling of the position vacated by John Cruze, and having no other suitable applicants, we agreed to a trial period for a friend of John's who had made himself known to us. By his own admission, Anil was not a qualified cook/bearer if such a thing exists, describing himself as a farmer. This was useful up to a point as due to scorching weather and warm winds we would wake to find a fine layer of pale brown dust over our balconies which it would take him a good hour to clear. Whilst the nurturing of our retained Christmas tree, with the next season in mind, was obviously a task of major importance.

Living off what fat there was in the land had not been kind to Anil's physique and his girth was more a trait of white blobby expats than Bangladeshi's. Perhaps it was this factor that accounted for his being possibly the slowest moving person in the country, which in an uncharitable moment we might have claimed, was quite an achievement in Bangladesh. This coupled with several bouts of severe incompetence, we found within days was driving us crazy. A spate of dipping into the house keeping sealed his fate, and having not really had to sack John Cruze, it was decided that I should be the one to mete out our judgement.

'Saar, this big problem for me.' Started pangs of guilt that were quickly dissipated by his clumsy and sluggish collection of his belongings. So much of what went into the rubbish was sorted and stored by servants for resale that an unprepared sacking involved the loading of this booty into the lift. Wine bottles, plastic water bottles, coat hangers, tin cans, plastic packaging, newspapers it was all good stuff, and that was just at the first stage of the refining process. Small slum children would sift through whatever did not pass muster upstairs in attempts to find edible morsels. The sobering sight of a child sniffing an old wrapper to determine its age and suitability for digestion had prompted us to bag all left over food and hand it out. A process that normally required a walk of only a few hundred yards before a suitable recipient came forward.

So with the words 'Big, big, problem' ringing in my ears we were once again servantless. Not for long however as an American friend knew of a lady who had been looking for work for some time. If poor Anil was the slowest, than the next likely candidate, put in a healthy bid for smallest servant in Bangladesh. It was a measure of her diminutive stature that a glimpse through the spy hole of our front door on hearing her knocks revealed only empty corridor. She was a pitiful figure with a tired look and a faded and worn sari. She had obviously been looking for work for weeks, and although this did not bode well, we could not turn her away. We had got rather bored of sharing the intimate layout of our apartment with a third party, so with the promise of two new saris to smarten her up and a supplement to her wages to ensure that she lived out, our vacancy was once again filled.

The *BBC World Service* kept us abreast of world events but failed to mention us. Local economists were more vocal in the thin editions of local newspapers about the country's plight. The gloomy prediction was made that it would take three years for the country to recover from the harm done to the economy by the last year of strikes and disruption. Whether or not these comments were the catalyst, some relaxing of the non co-operation movement was then announced.

The not too earth-shattering concession was made for the *hartal* to be relaxed from 3pm. This gave only the most die-hard of local institutions sufficient time to get people into their offices. As a fair proportion of our staff were still in India, the dubious honour of checking the office and monitoring our new fax line fell to me. In desperation, we had coerced our landlord into pairing off one of his lines just in time for office activities to come to a shuddering halt.

Since the time keeping of the local ruffians in the pay of the opposition party might be none too exact, I decided not to tempt fate in the car. These people certainly existed, and the experience I had had whilst on a rickshaw of coming face-to-face with a wild eyed individual brandishing a length of chain at a road-block, was an experience I was in no mind to repeat. Preferring not to put my getaway—should one be required—in the hands or rather feet of a rickshaw *wallah*, I dusted down my bicycle. Having dragged it four thousand miles it seemed a pity to leave it propped up against the wall of out spare bedroom for the entire duration of our stay.

The bicycle provided a sense of freedom I had up until then not encountered in Dhaka. I meandered down the leafy back streets of Gulshan, enjoying the heat of the sun in the gentle breeze created by my momentum. Once beyond the causeway and the Gulshan limits, what had been a trickle of cars breaking the curfew, became more serious traffic and the journey became much more of a struggle. Through the more aggressive environment of main thoroughfares with their dust, baby taxi exhaust fumes and uneven surfaces. For some the sight of a *bideshi* haring along the road was just too bizarre, for others, it was a delight, and for the more competitive cyclists, an opportunity to prove that when Bangladeshis put their mind to it they could cycle like the wind.

My approach to cycling in the main city area was tireless and workmanlike. An encampment of troops, on a traffic island opposite the office, had convinced me that there was no incentive for idling from A to B; particularly when my route involved passing the barrel of a heavy machine gun set amongst sand bags and played on the open road. The headline 'Expatriate Cyclist Riddled With Holes Mishap' was one I preferred to keep in my mind's eye.

My first appearance at Jute House caught the security guard posted outside the door to the office on our floor completely by surprise. A clattering of hobnailed boots rang out on the tiled floor as he struggled to his feet from a reclining, boots on table pose. For these poor boys stationed at a small desk relieved at seven hour intervals the day was interminably long and my appearance at least provided some diversion.

One particular guard called 'Selim', who had always seemed rather goofy I discovered reading an extremely elementary English book. The length of time it might take for me to send a fax from the machine in our reception area provided him an opportunity to try out his language skills. He had a sad tale to tell, it transpired being forced out of school to work and contribute to the family coffers. A tragedy that one so keen to improve himself should be consigned to the fifteen hundred taka, about twenty-five pounds, a month existence of a security guard and I resolved to squeeze him into our organisation when a suitable opportunity presented itself.

So the days past until rumblings in the newspapers heralded the announcement that the Prime Minister had announced her resignation. The 'indefinite period of non co-operation' was called off and everyone prepared to go back to work. I say prepared as the announcement coincided with a national holiday. The guards could put their feet up for another couple of days.

chapter twenty-two

Arrangements for the night of festivities to celebrate the first *Eid* at the end of Ramadan was an exciting time for people in all walks of life. The traditional bonuses the local staff considered a God-given right, and which Mala was eventually coerced into parting with, had been readily accepted and spent on all manner of exciting vitals.

The second *Eid* was awaited with equal eager anticipation. 'Cow *Eid*,' the expatriates called it and the 'know all' contingent gleefully told the less well informed to 'pray for rain'. More correctly the Feast of the Sacrifice a re-enactment  of a scene from the Torah. Instead of God testing Abraham's faith by asking him to sacrifice his son Isaac, Muslims sacrifice a cow or goat and it is a messy business. We were assured that the streets were awash with blood, and although it was hard to imagine sloshing through ankle deep gore in the gutterless streets of Gulshan, there had to be some basis to the claim.

Fortunately the warning had come early from a better informed and more reliable source. Peter and Sue had suggested that we all get out of Dhaka for the duration of the festival. We had heard great things of our proposed destination, the tea gardens situated in the hilly countryside near the eastern border with India. Owing to Sue's foresight, we had secured a bungalow at the snappily named 'Overseas Development Administration British High Commission Compound

Srimangal' and we eagerly awaited the opportunity to get out of Dhaka.

I tentatively approached Masum on the subject. Would he want to miss out on the fun in Dhaka to take us on holiday? He always gave little away and his undemonstrative acceptance had left me feeling as though I had bullied him into it. Had we shared a common tongue he would have allayed my fears. At our rendezvous at Peter's office, it was obvious by the excited chatter between him and Tasleen, Peter's driver, that the two of them were about as well travelled as us in Bangladesh and were looking forward to the trip.

Our journey out of Dhaka after work bore an uncanny resemblance to struggling out of London on a Friday evening to some distant destination off the M4. A hundred yards from the top of Dilkusha, two stone gate posts marked the entrance to Shishu Park, and a narrow artery to the old city, funnelling two lanes of traffic in two directions into one and a half. Needless to say the obdurate nature of Dhaka drivers combined to make the negotiation of this hazard a painful process, and we were glad to follow in the wake of Tasleen's four wheel drive vehicle which had considerably more presence than ours.

We had seen enough of the open roads around Dhaka to know that after dark they were no place for the faint hearted. The prospect of six hours spent playing chicken with heavy goods vehicles travelling without headlights was one we felt we could happily forgo. We had assumed unlit vehicles were another local myth, but they were much in evidence as drivers attempted to make their journeys whilst supposedly conserving the life of their battery. It was no wonder that the morning papers reported motoring 'mishaps' on a daily basis and sadly they were normally of an apocalyptic nature rather than light prangs.

Instead we had opted to spend the night at a field station belonging to Peter's aid agency. Situated on the outskirts of the small town of Comilla, we had driven through dark deserted streets until metalled road gave way to dusty track. As we bounced about in the back of the car, it was obvious that our little Toyota was ill-equipped for this sort of excursion. The bluish night sky disappeared as foliage encased us and as we eased further down the track until we arrived at what appeared through the gloom to be a courtyard bounded on two sides by stable blocks. The only light source our headlights and the yellow glow of dimly lit rooms above us, gave our arrival in darkness at the lush compound an unreal feel. We emerged from the vehicles sleepy, disorientated and blinded by the beam of a torch.

'Welcome Peter!' Came a voice from behind the torch and introductions were made with the warden to the rest of us and a great fuss made of Sue and Peter's little girl, Aysha.

In this short time, our car decided that it had done enough for the evening, and refused to start for Masum to move it once we had unloaded our bags. It was a bore, but not an insurmountable problem, and while we discussed possible contingency plans, Masum and Tasleen set off back to the town to wake up the local mechanic. Masum had taken this sequence of events as personal slight, accompanied by a great deal of sighing and self-castigation. Already Tasleen had a superior vehicle, and now that his inferior one had conked out, his loss of face was complete.

Shamelessly leaving them to it, we were lead up a narrow concrete staircase and found ourselves in the dining room of a spartan dwelling on the first floor. Home to several expatriate workers engaged in 'the field' there was scant evidence to suggest their presence. A cassette recorder and tapes appeared to be their only concession to the outside world and a disparate collection of books. The regulation local colour scheme of grey concrete floors, cream painted walls and dark brown wooden furniture was much in evidence and I was glad that our stay in these depressing surroundings was going to be a short one. The resident cook had prepared a meal for us which, added to my depression and having struggled through it, a power cut sent us feeling our way to our beds.

In the darkness of our room, I went to the window and looked out into the Bangladesh night. Shadowy trees and vegetation gave way to a flat landscape and despite the close proximity of the town I felt uneasy about how remote this place seemed. There was no sense of joy and excitement that here was the subcontinent in the raw more that surely this was the middle of nowhere.

Aysha made sure that we got an early start the next morning, and Masum and Tasleen, having done a sterling job, presented themselves to us having not only got the car going but had managed to do so for a ludicrously small amount of money. We left the field station, which, in the daylight had the appearance of a small walled stronghold and headed north east towards Srimangal. The traffic was much lighter in the early morning and we made good progress along straight roads against a monotonous landscape. Lush, green fields punctuated by small distant villages of bamboo mat houses built on raised ground. Occasionally we would pass through a squalid market point where crowds waited for we knew not what and char stalls did steady business.

We had expected more of the countryside and it is remarkable that the most memorable sights were those of upturned buses in fields or crushed vehicles protruding from the under growth. One dared not to think what had happened to the occupants in these roadside 'mishaps'. One could see how it happened as the sight of another vehicle was a rare occurrence and this prompted a total recklessness that Masum was hard at work cultivating.

As we neared our destination, the landscape changed and we wound our way through the small hills of the tea estates. Little ladies could be seen plucking the leaf tips from the neat regimented lines of bushes, an undulating rich green carpet under a canopy of widely placed shady trees. Having topped one such hill, we could see the white washed gateposts of the ODA Guesthouse compound. The sight of a Union Jack inwardly made me feel rather smug that my countrymen had the foresight to provide such a facility.

The compound comprised a two acre site perched along the long gradual incline of a picturesque tree covered hillside. A sandy drive threaded its way between compact white bungalows and we followed it up to an L-shaped annexe that housed various facilities and the office of the compound manager. Glad of an opportunity to stretch our legs, we all walked round the side of the building and were pleasantly surprised to find a swimming pool enclosed by rhododendrons with a view across the tea plantations beyond them.

A local man appeared in response to our 'Hellos' and introduced himself as 'Reginald Andrews'. He greeted us and with the air of one long associated with the establishment and confidently ran through a list of dos and don'ts and times for meals provided in the adjacent dining room.

'Now I will take you to your bungalow.' He apologetically ducked between us and led the way back the way we had come.

'My father was soldier British Army.' He offered in explanation to our unvoiced inquisitiveness as we walked.

'See!' He proffered a small leather wallet containing a small vinyl window out of which peered a small black and white private soldier in a forage cap.

'My father, he also Reginald.'

We thought it impolite to enquire whether there was any other legacy of the original 'Reg' and instead concentrated on the guided tour of 'Bungalow No.8' on which we were about to embark.

The journalist James Cameron's expression 'Equatorial Ealing' neatly describes our leafy suburban setting and our abode was fully fitted out with home comforts. A sitting room complete with fireplace, chintz furnishings, a leafy view and throughout and an air of holiday home mustiness. With two bedrooms and en suite rustic bathrooms we were well catered for. But what of the drivers?

It was apparent that they were itching to be given their liberty, and we packed them off with the equivalent of twenty-five pounds each and our car. Masum had always struck me as a shy and reserved character. It is an interesting exercise to try and get a feel for someone's personality without actually being able to engage him in conversation, and in the year or so I had known him, I had seldom seen him more animated. Perhaps it was a national trait but I was always impressed by his ability to strike up a conversation with passers-by, and I would often return to the car to find him chewing the fat with a stranger. He and Tasleen appeared to have struck up an instant rapport and we sent them on their way with orders to return in two days time.

Enjoying the opportunity to be in Bangladesh, without the sense that you were actually there, we embarked on a regime of extreme slothfulness, managing the occasional visit to the swimming pool or a lethargic game of tennis on an ageing court. I had managed to inject some excitement into the proceedings whilst searching for an errant tennis ball. Thrusting my head into a bush I instantly became aware of a prick on my forehead. Almost instantaneously several others around my face and scalp followed the initial strike. Reeling out of the bushes my cries from what had developed into searing stings quickly brought my fellow players to my aid who brushed my attackers from my hair and shoulders. I had inadvertently stumbled upon a colony of large red ants and their unwanted intruder had received short, sharp, shrift.

Sue, armed to the teeth for events of a calamitous nature, had been able to soothe my wounds, which had manifested themselves as small burns.

Still feeling rather sorry for myself, the discovery of a table tennis table proved to be a distraction and an annoying one for the girls. Peter and I became obsessed with this new sporting discipline, grabbing every available opportunity for an international challenge match barely allowing ourselves to be prised off it at meal times.

Around 7pm each evening a meal was served in the annexe. Other residents of the compound appeared for a beer, served from a tiny bamboo bar in one corner of the dining room, before settling down to food of the very English and school dinner variety, the proceedings watched over by a framed photograph of Her Majesty the Queen. Our fellow guests were a mixture of nationalities, all of whom were involved in aid or development projects. One other gentleman joined us by open invitation, swelling the numbers of Englishmen present. He was a clergyman who had lived in the area for thirty years and was obviously a regular, a dinner.

They were indeed pleasant surroundings in which to live if one could cope with the isolation. We had ventured out of the compound and followed the hilly road through the tea gardens and the occasional pineapple plantation nestling in the hollow between two small hills. We had all been delighted to come across a working elephant and his mahout retrieving a twenty feet tree trunk from the cover of trees by the roadside. The mahout had been rather protective of his charge as we tentatively approached, taking a stance under the elephant's eye, one arm hugging his trunk. His manner relaxed significantly after his request for *baksheesh* had been met and I was happy to play the tourist and inspect our wrinkly friend at close quarters.

Our visit was characterised by our involvement with the fauna of the region and we were to have one more encounter. Playing cards before bed on the eve of our return to Dhaka a loud chirrup startled us all into silence.

'What the ...?' I exclaimed only to be hastily 'Sshhhed' by the others in order that we might listen for the noise again.

Sure enough there it was again 'CHIRRUP!'

'Is it coming from the roof?' Sue enquired.

We all assembled under the middle of the ceiling and looked skyward.

'CHIRRUP!'

'It sounds like a big gecko.' Peter gave his considered opinion.

'Do you think it's on the roof?' Brenda asked.

'Maybe.'

'Well would you two like to go outside and scare it off!'

Peter and I went outside and having selected a reasonably sized stone lobbed it onto the corrugated iron roof. A spectacular clattering ensued and we went back inside our job done.

'CHIRRUP!'

'This is really creepy,' said Sue.

After four years in Bangladesh I was of the opinion that Sue and Peter had probably encountered most things, and for them to be concerned, it was bad news.

Our unwanted visitor issued another mighty call and we pinpointed it as having come from behind a dresser against the wall.

'It definitely came from behind there.' Sue confirmed what everyone else was thinking.

'OK Pete you look.' I said bravely.

Carefully he looked behind the dresser.

'As anyone got a torch I can't see anything?' He asked adding to the tension and the hunt was delayed while Brenda fetched her torch.

Peter looked again.

'Whoa! My God you should see the size of this thing!'

Whatever it was we never found out. We had all abandoned Peter who joined us outside our respective bedrooms having secured all the doors of the sitting room. In the morning he and I tentatively looked behind the dresser but the lizard was nowhere to be found. Whether or not this was a good thing we failed to reach a consensus on but there is little doubt that it hastened the tidying and packing up process.

Tasleen and Masum appeared at the appointed time and made a big show of displaying the watermelons that they had bought on their travels. We had decided to travel back into Dhaka on the actual day of *Eid*, which would enable the drivers to have some time with their families, and would also make the journey back into Dhaka easier. So having taken photographs of Tasleen and Masum as souvenirs of their holiday, we set off back towards Dhaka.

Comilla, as had already been demonstrated, was a good mid-way point and we decided to visit the World War II Memorial Cemetery there. By all accounts, including that of my father, the cemetery was beautifully maintained and well worth a visit, and it was to provide the most bizarre coincidence.

On the drive I was reading the autobiography of Hilary Hook an old Indian Army Officer who became something of a celebrity having appeared in a BBC television documentary. In his account he detailed his experiences whilst convalescing in east Bengal:

> 'We were put aboard a DC3 and flown to a tented hospital in east Bengal. One morning I was sitting when two orderlies passed by with a body on a stretcher.
>
> 'Who is it this time?'
>
> The reply came, 'a Major Nixon.' 'What is his regiment?'
>
> The orderly bent to read a card 'Major Guy Nixon, Royal Deccan Horse.'

It was a sad blow; for several days my friend had lain wounded and dying amongst strangers a few yards from my tent.'

As I read it, east Bengal had not translated itself to me as Bangladesh and I thought nothing more of it. The cemetery as we had read was immaculately maintained and having located the caretaker we gained access to the tranquil hillside grounds. We walked through the neat rows of nameplates of British, Indian, Irish, Australian and Japanese troops up to a stone cross overlooking the site at the brow of the hill. It was a sobering site and by far the most ordered environment we had encountered in Bangladesh with its neatly trimmed lawns and manicured shrubs. I was pleased we had made the stop and as we came to leave I walked along one of the lines of memorials and what I saw stopped me in my tracks.

The nameplate of one 'Major G.B.Nixon M.C. The Royal Deccan Horse'.

Outside the confines of British maintained property the rest of Bangladesh was up to its elbows literally in *Eid ul Azha*. The first reminder we got was when we came across two bearded gentlemen robed in white, sharp knives in hand a liberal splattering of what appeared to be tomato ketchup on their clothing. They had just delivered the coup de grace to some unfortunate beast and were on their way to their next appointment. As we carried on past them a gap in the bushes at the roadside revealed a small group of huts in the centre of which lay their last kill. In the aftermath figures bent over the carcass paring off the meat for distribution amongst friends, family and the poor.

As we pressed on we encountered a line of cows with painted horns and paper adornments slung about their necks being driven along the roadside on their last journey. In poorer districts, goats stood patiently, pegged out awaiting their doom. While nearer the city, the evidence of the next process was already in

201

evidence. Passing through a small town, a pile of twenty or so flat cows lay by the side of the road. Horns and tails at each end but just a flat brown slab of hide between them destined for the local leather industry. It was all rather fascinating in a macabre way.

The other aspect of *Eid ul Azha* was that many people unaccustomed to large quantities of meat made themselves horribly ill. Doubtless they were all hard at work inside doing this as we deposited Masum and I drove us back through the near deserted streets of Gulshan. We were pleasantly surprised to find the rivers of blood had run dry in Baridhara although we did come across the odd splash of blood soaked grass but otherwise we had got off lightly.

Back in the flat our intercom buzzer sounded.

'Man coming!' Announced the guard and I wearily walked down the stairs to see who it was.

'Please Sir, don't mind.' Pleaded the man as he leant forward with a blood smeared plastic bag held in two out stretched hands. It was Colonel Latif's bearer with our very own piece of raw cow.

chapter twenty-three

Over the ensuing weeks the substantial pile of bones deposited on a piece of waste ground by the side of the road at the Gulshan Causeway shrunk and blackened. The disintegration of the heap represented a passing of time that brought significant change.

A second attempt at an election had provided us with a new Government, indeed a new party as the Awami League over turned the BNP majority. There was a palpable sense throughout the com-  munity of a 'new age' having dawned and a general air of optimism with a return to a more predictable working week and normal everyday life.

I had timed a visit to the Board of Investment to collect a letter of invitation to meet the chairman of Telecommunications Board to plead our case, with the morning after the election results. Only to find the building full of exhausted people who had spent the night watching the drama unfold on the local television station. In his office, Mr Talukder and colleagues lounged around on all available seating and as I appeared in the doorway I was waved into their midst with the exaggerated movements of a bar full of drunks.

So welcomed, I was subjected to a cosy morning of gossip, char and cross questioning on a variety of topics mainly concerned with my relationship with Brenda and why it was we had no children. Unseen, Lotika, the long suffering secretary had laboriously typed my letter and the upshot of my patient vigil an introduction to the one man in Dhaka who had the power to magic telephone lines where others thought it impossible.

In addition to establishing the traditional twentieth century method of communication before the anniversary of our application, the office gained three significant new personalities:

Momin joined us from a local bank in the guise of an assistant to our accountant. His appointment was presented to me as a *fait accompli* and in my first meeting with him he demonstrated an admirable but potentially truthful streak when I queried his suitability for the position on the account of the fact that his resume was devoid of any accounting qualification. In response to my asking whether or not this had posed any problems in obtaining employment in the past he had replied.

'Oh yes, most definitely. Plenty of problems!'

Having slipped through the net and received an offer, extracting him from his present employer proved a difficult process. The comfort of routine, his long-standing association with his employer of some ten years and the uncharted waters of employment with a foreign organisation, left him in turmoil. Eventually a compromise was reached that he should take a bogus holiday from his present job to try us out for a trial period. Further uncertainty existed when it came to approximating his true age. This was by no means a trait unique to him as almost the entire population seemed to be rather vague about the time and place of their birth. Eventually it was accepted that he was approximately forty-five, which made him the most senior member of staff in years. Although only a tendency to wear half moon spectacles on the end of his nose and the need for regular colouring sessions at his barber were his only concessions to age.

This innocuous, congenial man represented an affirmation that whatever the imported ways of the office, the more despotic local conventions for running an office would establish themselves when we eventually packed up and left. Momin represented no threat. A compliant and subservient foil to our accountant and first of a number who would be hired to dilute my influence.

Despite this as yet undeveloped trend, the soul searching regarding his decision took place in my office on a daily basis. When one day he arrived at the momentous decision to accept a full time post, I made a point of buying him a special pen to commemorate the occasion. This small action it seemed guaranteed a special place for me in his affections, and although not under my remit, he would always approach me with his problems. As his confidence grew, his visits were more likely to tell me his latest joke or to recount some bizarre anecdote. His patent remedy of rubbing the appendage of a young boy on the affected area as a cure for an inflamed eyelid was one I recommended he keep to himself. That he had been a radio announcer, in the days before Bangladesh Independence, was a much more palatable topic and he needed little prompting to give a demonstration in thick, hushed accented tones of his past profession 'I am your newsreader Anisole Momin, Radio Pakistan.'

Asia was the son of a wealthy businessman and a very visible member of the young 'Dhaka set' who frequented the American Club. More often than not on a Thursday night, he would be amongst the full of beer, die-hards who at the end of the evening would play pool against the barman. He had come in to the office for an interview just after the move to the new building but had been considered unsuitable. We had first encountered him in an ill tempered and tensely fought battle of the titans in the inter club squash league at the Dhaka Club. He had taken our star player, he of the thirty chickens, to the wire in an acrimonious game of posturing and gamesmanship. This had not endeared us to him and we were surprised one evening when he lurched up to Brenda in the bar and offered her a drink. Several tequilas later, such was his ability to sell himself, he had secured himself another interview.

Having learnt from his previous experience, it was a very different Asia that turned up in a dapper suit with his all his wits about him. Educated in the States, he had returned to Dhaka a potent combination of skills. He was the ultimate salesman and although something of a wheeler dealer, it was decided that his knowledge of local sharp practices and connections within the business fraternity would make him a valuable asset. A live wire like Asia, however, needed to be kept in line and it was our next overseas visitor to whom this dubious delight fell.

We had seen rather than met Douglas in the Bombay office. A pallid, black curly hair topped, beanpole of a man, immaculately turned out, as ex-guards officers tend to be. There he had appeared aloof, and despite my readiness to discuss the merits of dear old Blighty with any likely candidate, had studiously ignored our presence. Consequently without prejudice I had derived a certain amount of pleasure in steering a hassle free course for him on his arrival at the airport when he came to Dhaka.

His whirlwind fact finding visit to get a feel for the local market had provided him with more than he had bargained for. I had sent him off to Bombay with one of my unofficial VIP departures and an offer from Mala in his pocket and the unenviable task of breaking the news of relocation to his girlfriend.

Although fully justified in her own mind of bringing Douglas on board, Mala had unwittingly added to the imbalance of expatriate to local staff. My application for his work permit had set off alarm bells somewhere in the system which brought about a visit by two officers from the Dhaka Special Branch who arrived at the office unannounced one morning.

'Mark, these gentlemen are from the Special Branch.' Rona's nervously introduced the two moustachioed, shady individuals standing in the doorway to

my office. Dressed in shirts with regulation char stain-
ing, left undocked and billowing over corpulent bellies
each of them could have done with a good wash. It
was apparent that these were not the most distin-
guished investigative officers of the force. The lack of
warning however had taken me aback and the words
'Special Branch' had registered quite positively.

'Could you get one of the *peons* to bring us some
tea please Rana.' I suggested fixing a smile on my
guests.

'Now Gentleman, what can I do for you?' I offered
them both my business card.

'Mark Tree...Tree...Tree...' His halitosis hit me in
a wave as the larger of the two on my left laboriously
read my card out loud.

'...now den,' I finished for him.

The two consulted and the one on the right removed a folded sheaf of fawn paper from his breast
pocket which once smoothed out on the desk revealed
a list of names. Each running a finger down the list of
names they reached the bottom before starting again at
the top.

'Here!' I pointed out my inverted name.

'Mark Tree...'

'Yes, that's it!'

'Work permit?'

'One second.' I swung round on my chair to the
draw of files behind me and ran through the hanging
folders containing the documents relating to each
member of staff.

'Yes, here we are.' I handed them a copy of my
application for a work permit and the actual document.

Laying the papers between them they examined
them minutely.

'Photocopy?'

'Yes of course, I'll be right back.'

I watched them through the glass partition of my
office while the machine churned out its copies. One

leant back in his chair and rolled his eyes round the room while the other picked up a small wooden figure holding a football that was sitting on my desk.

'Your child?' He enquired on my return. I thought it simpler to say yes than explain that Dvai had awarded me it to me for beating him 5-0 at computer soccer one evening.

Having examined the photocopies the officer on the right folded them into four and forced the bundle into his pocket.

'So gentleman is there anything else I can do for you?'

They returned to their list.

'Mala Arune work permit.'

Spotting that a trend was starting to develop here I went through the list with them.

Before too long they had copies of every conceivable document relating to the legal residence of all our expatriate staff. Mala had been so pedantic about adhering to the very letter of the law in all our dealings. It had definitely slowed down the process of the telephone lines but I was delighted to be water tight in this department.

'Is that it?'

'Yes.' The one on the left said.

'Err... No!' The other interjected.

'We need...' from the left.

'....gift!' from the right.

'Na, Na, Na.!' The left spoke to the right in an admonishing way and turned back to me.

'Calendar.'

The handing out of calendars was indeed a popular pastime at the start of the New Year but Mala had taken the view that rather than forget someone and put them out it was better not to produce one at all.

'I have no calendar.' I held out my hands in supplication.

They consulted again.

'Diary?'

'No, I'm sorry.'

'Pen?'

'Well yes I have a pen, hang on a second.'

So they left me, each clutching his Japanese 'Rolling Writer' and my interview was at an end.

A little while later Rana tapped lightly on the glass partition of my office.

'Yes Rana, what can I do for you.'

'The officers they are still here. They are using the telephone.'

When Douglas had rejoined us from Bombay I jokingly said, 'I hope you realise your bloody work permit application brought the Special Branch in here!'

'You don't want to worry about them, just tell them to bugger off!' He replied disdainfully.

'Well, actually I don't think that would have helped us very much in this situation.'

'Look, doing business in these countries is like close quarter, hand-to-hand fighting!'

I begged to differ but in the interests of the entente cordiale I bit my lip. It was to become apparent that there was little I could tell Douglas about subcontinental living. The neatly manicured toenails protruding from silver Chanel flip-flops of the glamorous lady who accompanied him on his return suggested that there was, however, a gap in their local knowledge. It is a statement of fact that within the confines of the office there was no better informed source of information regarding setting up home in Dhaka and I freely availed Douglas of my services.

'You'll find that despite the fact that all the accommodation is pretty hideous in Gulshan and Baridhara at least everything works and it's a comfortable environment. I'll go with you one afternoon and point you in the right direction if you like.' I ventured.

'Look that's awfully kind of you to offer but we thought we'd have a look around the old city for something with a bit of character. You know, something along colonial lines.'

'Ah, have you been to the old city yet?'

'No, but reading in my guide book it sounds as if that is the place to find somewhere interesting to live.'

'Umm, yes...certainly interesting. You'll struggle with your car there you know!'

'Look old son, we've thought of that already. We're going to get one of those rickshaw things. Tabitha wants to paint it up with Dalmatian dog spots.'

Who was I to argue with someone with such a firm grip on reality. I pictured them marooned in their colonial residence. Powerless, waterless, lavatory less and joyless. Attempting to escape the old city through the narrow route through Shishu Park in their three wheeled Dalmatian mobile.

They had poured scorn on the aspects of expatriate life that I detailed for them. Wrinkling their noses at the mention of High Commission Clubs, their various assorted activities and generally the whole Gulshan area of the city. Admittedly it was the sub-continent, sanitised, but with good reason. I thought it best to leave them to their own devices until Tabitha went back to Bombay for a few days. I had, in conversation with her, realised that we had a common acquaintance in a friend of mine in the wine trade. In a call to him I had mentioned this fact to which he had responded 'I give her two weeks at the outside.' Bombay was certainly a different world to Dhaka in what it had to offer. Our own visits there had been like a breath of fresh air, and in expatriate circles it was a far more *puck* posting, to borrow a hackneyed expression.

From my own experience I knew Dhaka to be a fairly miserable place to be stuck alone, and it being the end of the week, we offered to take Douglas to the American Club.

'It will give you an opportunity to meet some people and maybe make some contacts for Tabitha.' I assured him.

'Love to, but Asia is taking me to some nomadic disco run by a friend of his. Says they just pick a new venue each week and off they go. Some other time perhaps.'

Douglas's approach to life in the city left me querying our own life style. We had arrived lost and with the help of Feroz found our feet. Were we now too staid and boring caught up in the petty goings on in the expatriate community? Perhaps Douglas had the right idea. To go out there and stamp his personality on the country and grasp all the opportunities and experiences there were to be had.

Saturday saw the return to work after the all too short weekend. Looking up from my desk I noticed Douglas had arrived and was making slow and painful progress towards his office.

'Are you alright Douglas?' I called out.

Stopping in his tracks he turned awkwardly and deliberately towards me to reveal a heavily blackened eye and split lip.

'You, fine!' He said with a sheepish smile.

The shirt Douglas had been wearing at the time that his views differed from the proprietor of the disco was extraordinary, in as much as the collar was intact, but the rest of the shirt fell from it in tatters. He took the jokes winging their way around the office regarding the potency of the British Army's presence in good part. Protesting that:

'It's jolly difficult to fight back when there is an enormous man sat on one's back!'

This caused further hilarity at the idea of the British Army being rendered impotent by a force of large Bangladeshi's sitting on them.

Some days later Douglas came to my office.

'I've found an apartment in Banani.'

'Oh good whereabouts?' I enquired.

'Just overlooking Banani Lake.'

'So you didn't find anything in the old city then?'

'Well one quite nice place, an old school.'

'What was the problem with that?'

'The school wouldn't move out.'

'Ah. Anyway at least you didn't crack in taking somewhere in Gulshan in Baridhara.'

'Well it's spitting distance. No, it seems we've taken your advice. Brand new, two floors of featureless concrete walls, three bathrooms, holes already in place for the air conditioning. OK, I admit it, it has to be the most spectacular one hundred and eighty degree turns in history.'

chapter
twenty-four

'Can you hear that?' Brenda sat up in bed and asked.

It was one of those mornings when one awoke to nothing but the background chatter of workman on the adjacent building site and the 'tack, tack, tack' of little ladies breaking bricks with a hammer down below us at street level.

'The air conditioning has gone off that's all we must have a power cut.' I reasoned.

'No lie still and listen.'

I strained my ears.

'There it is again, can you hear it now?'

'Yes, that crunch, crunch, crunch noise.'

'That's it!'

'Where do you think it's coming from?' I asked.

'It sounds like it is coming from behind the chest of drawers, go and have a look.'

Not relishing my mission, I fought my way from beneath our mosquito netting and approached the bamboo chest of drawers we had bought locally some weeks previously. Putting my ear to the side of the object I listened intently.

'Crunch, crunch, crunch,' was clearly audible, like a colony of ants simultaneously stamping up and down in tiny hob nailed boots. Tentatively I moved the chest of drawers away from the wall and sprang back lest the offending beastie take a dislike to me. Plenty of fluff but no intruder. We listened again.

'There definitely is something,' said Brenda. I could not deny it.

'You'll have to take the whole thing out onto the balcony and empty everything out of it.'

I grudgingly agreed.

Having fashioned a probe by straightening a metal hanger I removed the top drawer of three and laid it on the floor. Carefully taking the probe I fished out the first item of clothing. Whatever it was that was making the noise it was staying pretty still and I repeated the process until the drawer was empty. I had mixed feelings about not having found anything in the first drawer as it stacked the odds rather about finding something in the other two.

The final item successfully removed from the second drawer I steeled myself to pick through the contents of the third. As I cleared the final drawer I reasoned that whatever it was it couldn't be very big and confronted by a final pair of knickers I returned to the bedroom to arm myself with a suitable weapon to dispatch my foe. Rolled magazine in hand I approached the drawer with my probe I hooked the last item and making sure I had a good grip on it I flicked it swiftly out of the drawer and pounced.

'There's nothing in here!' I called to Brenda.

'What about the frame?'

I cleared a space and toppled the main structure over on to its back expecting my quarry to scuttle out and across the floor. Still nothing.

'That is just too weird!' said Brenda inspecting my handiwork putting her ear to the piece of prostrate furniture in disbelief.

Later in the office I told Rana about my exploits.

'Cane mites,' he said chuckling.

'No!' I said in disbelief.

'Yes every house has them. You must pour boiling water or petrol on your furniture to kill them.'

The good news was that the power having turned off our electric alarm clock we would have overslept had it not been for our small guests. I had one of my big days in prospect with the arrival of a private aircraft load of American gas company executives hoping to tap the country's natural resources and exploit the massive potential for growth in the energy sector. I had been asked to do many strange things during the course of my working life in Dhaka, but to arrange air space for a private aircraft I felt was stretching my powers somewhat. Undaunted I had visited group captain, Namely Haque, at Zia International Airport and detailed my hopes and fears. Much to my delight: it couldn't be easier as far as I was concerned as the pilot, who doubtless encountered the same problem on a regular basis, would contact them well in advance of his arrival to get the go ahead.

My ability to tick things of Mala's list of 'improbable jobs for Mr Mark to do' was sometimes more of a hindrance than a boon. Next on the list for our gas company was the hire of three 'luxury' four wheel drive vehicles. A commentator on the country described 'a style called Pager' the ultimate four wheel drive vehicle that in Dhaka society says more about you than money ever can. Whether this is an accurate view these days is open to debate, but for Mala this Rolls Royce of all terrain vehicle was a must have to ensure the smooth passage of our guests.

Car hire however is not a sophisticated business in Dhaka. Those vehicles for hire, although presumably deemed sparkling examples by the proprietor's of the limited number of establishments providing such a service, would not pass muster with Mala. After a morning spent on the telephone I ventured out to a back street garage where I was assured I would find what I was looking for.

'Three very good ka-lean Pager. You come. You find out!'

Masum and I had found 'Khan Trading and Rent-a-Cars' secreted down a dead end side street littered with vehicles in various degrees of distress. The road tapered to an end where a ramshackle low lying, windowless, corridor of a building housed the office.

Greeted by a man standing in the doorway who introduced himself as 'Rohm,' I was delivered from the
bright sunlight of the street into its grimy twilight
world. I no longer protested against invitations to take
a seat in such salubrious settings since to do so was
perceived as being rude and useless in any case. So
bidden, I selected a chair that had recently undergone
renovation by the looks of the hastily nailed on splints
between the seat and the back while the cars were
brought for my inspection. An elderly man with yel-
lowed grey hair and wispy beard was already installed
at the back of the office, and he peered at me through
thick, smoky lenses as I skimmed perspiration off my
forearms.

'Ayes!' He called out to a small boy twiddling with
the flex of a long redundant air conditioning unit in
the corner of the office.

'Etta Pepsi!'

In no time at all a bottle of cola was placed in front
of me which by the looks of things had had a healthy
swig taken out of it in transit. No sooner had my beverage arrived than the blue off side panel of a heavy
navy blue vehicle rolled into my view through the
doorway.

On the street a convoy of the three promised vehicles stood, arranged in varying degrees of dilapidation.
The blue: a tired example of a recent model; a beige
older version and a white old work horse on the doors
of which the heavy logo of an aid agency peeked
through a thin, touch-up job of white paint. However
futile I thought the exercise of acquiring three extra
vehicles with which to complicate the collection of our
visitors, there was no way we could use the white one.
I returned to my Pepsi with Rohm to let him down
gently and thrash out the bottom line.

I had, I thought, rashly taken Rohm at his word
that he could source a third more suitable vehicle.
Looking down on the car park from Brenda's office at
the front of the building I was relieved to see a maroon

vehicle lined up behind the other two at the appointed time. Matters had been complicated somewhat by our having to use Rohm's own drivers so Rana came down to the car park with me to brief the drivers on their duties before we headed off in convoy to the airport to meet our visitors.

I always enjoyed a drive down the open airport road an opportunity to get out of central Dhaka and its dreary skyline. Elevated to the status of the Pager riding classes my extra height gave me a new perspective on the sights I had passed so often. A parade of cane furniture shops the first landmark as we left the city reminded me of my morning and I shuddered to think about the size of the cane mite population within. A beached motor torpedo boat outside a Naval institution passed at eye level and while stopped at the railway level crossing by an entrance to the cantonment I found myself looking down the barrel of a cannon mounted on a long since redundant tank. Ahead of us two policemen wandered through the stationery traffic and coming to our blue Pager ahead of mine, spoke to the driver through the window. To my amazement both of them got into the back and the Pager drove off executing a U-turn before heading back in towards central Dhaka.

'What on earth!' I spluttered in amazement.

'Police requisition.' The unlikely explanation offered by my driver for the day.

The jewel in my crown taken from under my nose we pressed on to the airport there was little else we could do.

In this sort of situation I was lucky to be able to rely on Masum. I had sent him off to the Board of Investment to collect Mr Badruzzaman and bring him to the airport to help me with the VIP aspect of proceedings. Masum was standing placidly watching the comings and goings on the airport runway through the fence of the VIP car park as we arrived in our shortened convoy. Zaman Badruzzaman in contrast, was in a state of great excitement inside the building.

'Mr Mark, come, COME!' He blurted as I bumped into him the VIP lounge. 'She is here, the little aeroplane!'

I followed his overweight run through previously uncharted territory for me in the airport, down a thin corridor that effectively circumnavigated the entire arrivals area. Through the unmanned arch of a metal detector and a pair of double doors to be met by a blast of warm air as we arrived out on the tarmac.

'Look!' I followed the line of his pointed finger to a distant spot on the outskirts of the airport. There was indeed a tiny plane stationary in the distance.

'They can come no closer,' said Zaman.

'So how do we collect them from over there?' I asked wearily.

'Airport microbus!' He announced the delight of his being able to resolve the matter evident in his grinning face and he pointed out the most extraordinarily shambolic conveyance that had once been a small people carrying van painted in the livery of the national airline.

Mala would have had conniptions had she known that our precious visitors were being subjected to a squashed, bone shaking excursion in a filthy old bus but with no other option I urged him to go ahead.

'Sir, it is very difficult for me....I need tips.'

'Not now Zaman!' I snapped angrily. 'Get in that heap and get it over there!'

The stately progress of the microbus came to a halt at my feet and I was mortified that Zaman had managed to squeeze in five men, a woman, a driver, assorted luxurious luggage and himself. Hopefully they would see it as local colour I thought to myself stepping forward to take the proffered Louis Vuitton suit bag from the woman stepping out of the vehicle.

'Hi I'm Beth. I'm married to someone in there!' She made an airy wave in the direction of the interior.

Her husband, a tall, barrel-chested man introduced himself and his two identical colleagues leaving me wondering which one was Brad, Chuck or Dan. Finally, unfolding himself from the back seat the last occupant a neat, bespectacled young man with a razor sharp parting and slicked down hair introduced himself as 'Dwight Templeton'.

His youth belied his importance, with a hasty glance at my list I identified him as the CEO: and I inwardly winced that it had been him who had endured the worst of the crush. He appeared to have taken things in his stride, and with everything safely extracted from the bus, I made to lead the way into the airport building.

'One second please.' Interjected Zaman halting our progress by stepping in front of us, both hands raised like a policeman stopping traffic.

'Photograph please!' He produced a small, antiquated instamatic camera from his pocket and motioned for us to shuffle together as he framed his shot. The driver of the microbus was pressed into action and placed behind the camera. Zaman squeezed in amongst us and we all smiled inanely at the lens.

After this inauspicious start to the visit the smooth processing of all the passports restored my credibility and I was relieved not to have to subject our five star guests to any more of the local delights. Arranging them in the lobby of the VIP lounge I nipped out into the car park to orchestrate the manoeuvres of our remaining Pajeros. An elongated island separated the pick up point from the rest of the car park and the vehicles, with Masum bringing up the rear, lined up in a pleasing curve around it from right to left as they waited to receive their charges. No doubt relieved that a more sophisticated type of conveyance existed in Dhaka to the one they had just experienced, the party decanted themselves into the first two vehicles and expectantly waited the off. Having secured the rear door the driver of the first vehicle

219

leapt behind the wheel and attempted to start the engine.

For an anxious minute the starter motor laboured until the battery sapped of its charge refused to give any more. As I requested that our guests step down for a moment I was sure I detected a twitch in the face of the unflappable Mr Templeton and he swept passed. Enlisting the services of Zaman and the other drivers we unceremoniously pushed the stranded vehicle out into the open car park. Having got up ahead of speed the driver let out the clutch and the engine exploded into life in a cloud of black diesel smoke.

The woes of the previous day forgotten, I picked up Beth from the Lalbagh Hotel. Her mission on the visit was to reconnoitre the city for she and Brad with a view to setting up home in the event of their accepting a posting. It was a service that we could have well done with and I was happy of the excuse to get out of the office and impart some of my hard won knowledge.

Beth was a pleasant, if not very forthcoming, person. Her fleshy face, framed with an unnaturally tinted pageboy cut and precise appearance, suggested life in Houston Texas was comfortable. I wondered what her friends would make of the photographs she intended to take with the hi-tech apparatus resting in her lap on the creases of her khaki chinos beneath her folded hands with their red painted nails.

'That is some camera.' I remarked motioning towards what to my untrained eye was surely the choice of a professional.

'This?' She said holding the camera up to a critical eye. 'You, well I used to take photographs for a living before I married Brad.'

'How exciting.'

'Yes.' She replied thoughtfully. 'It's taken me all over the world Vietnam, China, Africa.'

'Well in that case we must try and find you something of interest to photograph here.'

My now well-worked tour of the delights of the expatriate area culminated in a trip to the American School. Here, I was able to assure her that the cricket teacher was to be highly recommended, since I had been drafted in on my day off to coach an energetic group. The sight of cosy classrooms of children being ministered to by faces from the expatriate community that I recognised, was reassuring for a parent considering the uprooting of her children. An amazing fully functioning American High School complete with facilities and sports ground cocooned in the midst of Dhaka by a twelve feet wall.

It is remarkable that within four miles of the American School, with its million dollar budget and tranquil Baridhara setting on the tree lined banks of Gulshan lake, lies the extraordinary chaos of Old Dhaka. If Beth wanted a photograph then the densely populated narrow lanes around the Sadarghat Boat Terminal on the Buriganga River was the place to visit. A combination of bustle and subsistence living squeezed into the confined space contained by decaying masonry of days gone by. An unplanned warren choked with rickshaws of shops, bazaars, workshops and impromptu warehouses full to bursting with coconuts and bunches of green bananas. The water front area with its comings and goings of tens of water borne craft. Substantial local ferryboats bound for destinations up river, cargo boats and the twenty foot long low slung dories, traditional riverboats operating as river crossing taxis. Their cargoes of sometimes as many as twenty-five standing passengers sinking them to depths where the waterline appeared to lap perilously close to their gunwales in danger of overwhelming them. It is the stuff of photojournalist's dreams.

For me the old city gave a glimpse of what I had perceived Dhaka to be like when first we had contemplated our move. Remnants of the European Mughal style incorporated into the contemporary landscape of concrete corrugated iron and hastily strung up telephone lines. I drew Beth's attention to a blue painted two storey building with a grand frontage now a police station.

'Shall we get out and have a closer look?' I asked.

She politely declined and peered intently at the passing scene preferring to take the odd shot through the closed car window. Old Dhaka is not designed for cars, however, and progress was slow as Masum edged us through a maze of streets. An opportunity to examine passers-by minutely and them us as the concept of personal space had not been well publicised in this remote corner. Perhaps in retrospect to someone who had not been in the old city before it was a threatening scene. People pressed up hard against the car eager to get where they were going regardless of us and the occasional scrape of a rickshaw mudguard on the bodywork, as its driver refused to give quarter and squeezed by.

'Well we should definitely get out and have a look at Ahsan Manzil.' I pointed to the imposing long pink building visible through wrought iron gates ahead of us. This was the former palace of the Nawab Abdul Ghani the interior of which was definitely worth the minuscule entry charge. An opportunity to visit twenty-three rooms restored in a slightly kitsch way to something approaching their former glory. Presumably Lord Curzon would not have approved of the paper doilies on the banqueting table but other rooms were virtually intact. The billiard room with its faded green baize table and hunting trophies my particular favourite. I urged Beth to join me but either she had misled me or I had over estimated her sense of adventure. There was no way she was getting out of the car.

In the light of this development, I thought it best to give another place of interest on my itinerary a miss. The residence of Sheikh Mujib Rahman the man who lead the Bangladeshi people through the 1971 war of liberation against Pakistan to the development of the nation. In 1975 Sheikh Mujib and his entire family, save one daughter, were murdered in this house and it is preserved as it was left on that fateful night. However fascinating the house might be as a time capsule the ferocity of the attack left its mark and the residual evidence, preserved on the walls and ceilings under perspex, is definitely not for the squeamish.

Having dropped Beth at the hotel, I returned to the office to find that Mala had issued an edict that all those members of staff of a certain level attend an event being organised by the Economic Section of the American Embassy that evening at the Sheraton Hotel. The complaints I fielded at this eleventh hour call to arms were more out of a sense of injustice than a reaction to pre arranged plans for the evening being interfered with. By their own admission the young people in the office had little to do in the evenings and preferred to work late rather than return home to the family abode. Even for the more upwardly mobile element social commitments amounted to a weekly rendezvous with the nomadic disco. So the argument that free food and drink, albeit in the company of Mala, had to be better than being stuck in the office was a fairly easy one to win.

I was surprised by the turnout at the reception and in the crowded ballroom of the hotel Brenda and I were able to keep a low profile and people watch. A dark-skinned waiter at the bar caught my eye and we discussed the possibilities of him being of Tamil descent or perhaps a member of some indigenous tribal people.

'Hang on a minute here's someone who might be able to tell us.' I had spotted Asif sauntering past with a can of beer the label obscured with a napkin in his hand. Calling him to us his eyes he looked at us through blood shot watery eyes and it was apparent that my advice regarding the hospitality hadn't been lost on him.

In a conspiratorial whisper I pointed out the waiter and asked if he knew whereabouts he hailed from.

'Sure,' slurred Asif.

'Thousands of years ago there was a massive earthquake and it shook up all the continents.'

It was fascinating stuff, he went on.

'With all this movement Africa swung round and it collided with India.'

It sounded unlikely.

'In the collision a number of Africans fell off Africa and ended up in India. There you go, they were his descendants!' He held his hand up as if to affirm his point and swung away in search of another beer.

His explanation owed something to the arguments put forward by palaeontologists as evidence of continental drift and I accepted his explanation, not fussed about the technical flaws it might contain.

The American connection had secured an invitation for the visiting oil men and Brad, Chuck and Dan spotted us and wandered over. They were friendly enough and we made polite conversation about their impressions of Dhaka and the likelihood of Chuck accepting his posting.

'If you don't mind me asking,' he said changing the subject. 'You see that guy over there.' He motioned over as subtly as he could to the waiter standing behind the bar.

'Is he from some kinda special tribe?'

'Ah yes I can actually, this is rather interesting!' And I launched into Asif's spiel.

Blank faces met mine as I triumphantly finished my explanation. Was there something they were missing or was this some strange quirk of the English sense of humour.

Chuck whose profession presumably had left him armed with more than a passing knowledge of plate tectonics spoke up.

'But, surely man wasn't around two hundred million years ago?'

I wished for the intervention of localised seismic activity so that the ground would open and swallow me up.

chapter twenty-five

Mala's strict implementation of a dress code in the office, that owed more to Wall Street than the activities of a satellite office in a steamy third world country, provided steady business for the local dry cleaning fraternity. It would be fair to say that dry cleaning is in its infancy in Bangladesh and we had had our fair share of disasters. It was more a case of when than if, and we had been warned of the consequences of committing our most treasured garments to this hit-and-miss service.

Brenda and I had got round this problem by duplicating our wardrobe at a local tailor, called "Ferdous", enabling us to subject our 'stunt double' clothing to the vagaries of the local dry cleaning process. The opening of a branch of an established Indian dry cleaning shop was an exciting development and we had started to drop our guard finding them to be more sophisticated in their procedure. Although as a concession to local convention they retained the services of that vital machine the button crusher and a tendency to fasten an identifying label to a prominent part of whatever the garment with a thread akin to parcel string. Should one be in a hurry in the morning unable to locate scissors to remove such a label sewn neatly through the bottom of ones tie it would take the strength of a thousand men to break said thread.

Even with the new regime, the warning signs were there which we failed to respond to. A number of my shirts went through the blast furnace of their laundry only to be returned shrunk to Masum's size, an occurrence which he appeared to be rather pleased about. A sweater of Brenda's that was returned bleached and stretched beyond recognition was more of a disaster. Since she had not wanted to convert her entire wardrobe to one that was suitable for a Muslim country, she had a number of outfits that served the purpose well. With no local option to replace these items, the loss of one of them had been badly received by her and a desire to chop whoever was responsible into very small pieces had taken a superhuman feat of restraint to overcome.

It was perhaps a sign that we were due a break from Dhaka, that common-sense having deserted me, I took my pride and joy, the navy blue suit I had bought in London before we set out, to the same establishment. Masum had collected it for me and on taking it from its polythene wrapper the resultant cry of anguish at the carnage inflicted upon the garment was no doubt heard many miles away. Its hue reduced from navy to a dusty royal blue and trousers that, as well as no longer fastening, flew at half-mast above my ankles.

There was no point in getting excited but a reasoned complaint supported by the evidence I thought was justified. After a telephone call with the polite and apologetic manager, Major Alam, at his behest I sent a letter accompanied by the offending garments to his office for his perusal and waited for a response.

Elsewhere my humour was not helped by more unwelcome contact with our local solicitor. In the early days I had rather more interaction with Mobarok Uddin than I would have liked when we were signing leases and agreements on a regular basis. 'Rocky' as he was affectionately known out of his earshot had been educated at Oxford in more than the ways of the law. Unusually tall for a Bangladeshi, he was an elegant man with a sallow complexion, long nose and a high forehead, from which he scraped back a bank of grey Brillo pad hair. This gave him the appearance of having a very long face, and since having affected the demeanour and accent of the British ruling classes, he appeared to be able to look down his nose at me from a very great height. The effect of which, I found not a little unnerving. There was no question that he was a more intelligent man than I, but the disdain with which he treated me had often rankled.

A renewal for the lease on Mala's apartment needed to be drawn up and my request for this matter to be expedited was met with a 'why do you bother me with this trivia' type response. Faxing through the details to his office I decided to go on the offensive and having typed out a letter to him I signed it the 'Hon MT'. This blatant falsehood was never alluded to, but the fact that our lease was delivered to our office in double quick time would suggest that it had the desired effect. I had met him in the lobby of the hotel some time afterwards.

'Mr Mark how nice to see you.' He had been the model of politeness. 'I noticed you signed your letter "The Honourable" the other day,' he observed in a reverent tone. 'That does mean that you are the son of a Lord.'

I beckoned him closer and he stooped towards me. Looking over my shoulder I whispered: 'I don't really like to mention it. You do understand.'

'Oh quite...quite. Yes of course absolutely!' he spluttered.

I wasn't sure if I preferred the old Rocky to the fawning toady I had created.

Brenda had been showing signs of stress as well but this was self inflicted rather than a reaction to the local environment. She having contrived through email, Federal Express and the surrender of her one day weekend to complete the course work for a professional exam. One of three people in Bangladesh sitting the exam overseen by an organisation based in the States. I had wondered at the wisdom of this August body when Brenda was notified of the venue for her exams. With a perfectly good US-funded, American school in the city complete with perfectly serviceable classrooms at their disposal, they had opted for an annexe of Dhaka University campus. Situated in an area with its own thin blue line of police toting shot guns I was not overjoyed at the prospect of Brenda having to spend six hours in the heart of the city's most potentially violent area.

A reconnoitre of the location had confirmed our worst fears with pockets of police camped out in a small tented settlement on the campus. Since the officers on duty were in full riot gear with knee protectors and hard hats, Dhaka students were either a rowdy bunch or more sinister forces were at work here. We had eventually located the room in which Brenda was to sit her exam high on the fifth floor of what appeared to be a deserted block of sixties vintage, the faculty of Business Administration. There was evidence that once there had been students in the building in that scraps of paper fluttered from redundant notice boards and scrawled graffiti on the plaster walls. Their last course work appeared to have been a practical session in the implementation of a scorched-earth policy. Barely a window in the building was intact and looking into the classrooms as we made our way along corridors open to the elements not a stick of furniture remained intact.

I was faintly amazed that, on the appointed day a University lecturer had turned up at the designated room, to invigilate over Brenda's exam. It was not a surprise to hear that, during the course of the exam, a little friend of his had turned up to while away the time in chatting and smoking. I had collected Brenda at teatime, drained and feeling the heat. Surely the hardship she endured was worth an extra ten percent and whatever letters she would be able to list after her name in the future bear the additional distinction of having passed under the most arduous circumstances.

We had dropped into the office on the way back from the University, and finding the building in the grip of a power cut, walked up the stairs to the seventh floor. Sitting on the stairs adjoining the lobby outside the office we were astonished to find Roger smoking a cigarette. It seemed the even the best prepared of expatriates had undergone a discernible metamorphosis in the Dhaka environment. Roger had arrived better prepared than the rest of us. His grasp of the language alone was a skill that could remove the silly, everyday stress one encountered. Trying to discover who it was ringing the doorbell or why the man who had just installed the mosquito net in the bedroom had removed a square foot of plaster from the ceiling were foolish things, at the end of a hard day that drove you to distraction. He had arrived in Dhaka a picture of health, slim, fit and of course teetotal. A bowl of apples refreshed daily on a desk a testament to a regime of healthy living. It was a spectacular spiral of descent.

In my office, a sticky note had been attached to the screen of my computer with a message from Major Alam at the dry cleaners. I gave him a quick call back and was given a firm assurance that the matter was in hand and he would come back to me. Putting down the telephone I became of aware of music in the office, and going to investigate tracked it down to Douglas's office.

Dhaka is a city where it is impossible to buy cheese or a pair of socks that will fit a fleshy western ankle without cutting off the blood supply. It is, however, possible to buy the most expensive hi-fi known to man, from a small office located in Gulshan that panders to the needs of wealthy Bangladeshi's. I found Douglas surrounded by empty boxes and miles of cabling not in the best of spirits listening to the demonstration CD provided with his brand new purchase. He had bought it as a form of compensation for the fact that Tabitha had decided that Dhaka was too much like hard work and was going back to England.

To be fair Douglas had been putting in very long days at the office and prolonged periods alone with no other distraction other than the planning and setting up of their apartment would test the mettle of the longest suffering of girlfriends. She was our first casualty, although expatriate folklore told of plenty of others who had not survived so long.

We arrived home that evening to find that the square of plaster from our ceiling that really had been removed during the installation of a new mosquito net had been replaced. The local man hired for the purpose had ensured that the mosquito net become a permanent feature of the house as he had plastered the top of it and the hook it hung from into the ceiling.

The upkeep and running of a house in Bangladesh is a much more complicated business than at home. We had contemplated life without a cook but it was not practical. The absence of labour-saving materials and devices could complicate the simplest of tasks. The need for vigilance against tropical insects, the energy required to shop for food, the increased amount of time required for food preparation, the demands of our jobs and the enervating effect of the climate. As employers by local standards we were far from demanding. Mina had two main functions to clean the apartment and cook an evening meal. Despite her diminutive stature, these were things that she should have been capable of, but sadly, was not. That evening a leathery chicken left standing in a thin grey gruel-like liquid decided us that it was time for Mina and us to part company.

Much to my relief it was Brenda's turn to be the bearer of bad news and Mina's departure the following morning was a sorry episode. The painful transfer of our collected rubbish to the lift, tears and a rather uncomfortable bout of being clung to marked the end of our association. As callous as this sounds, an unannounced severance eliminated the risk of souvenir taking and, armed with a months salary, we sought to make her sudden loss of employment as painless as possible.

By the end of the day ,Noel the cook upstairs had heard the news and was hard at work expounding the virtues of a lady he knew called 'Kampona.' Rashly we believed his sales pitch and we employed her for a period that was brief even by our standards. A light fingered trait was exposed by the fact that in a moment of complete boredom I had alphabetised our CD collection shortly after which most of the F section went missing. As well as stocking the shops at DIT 2 market with our belongings we received an unsigned sinister note which read as follows:

'Sir,

Your cook Kampona she bery bad lady.
She foking in your hous.'

It was not unheard of for other servants to wage a smear campaign on others to create employment opportunities. Alleged prostitution was ground that was not negotiable and her dismissal was one of the easier jobs I had undertaken in Dhaka. Knowing the game was up she went without a word.

They were depressing times and, whether or not it was a seasonal adjustment that had caused all the gloom, the local malaise finally took its toll on me. I had not heard from the dry cleaners for a while so I gave Major Alam a call.

'Major Alam is not here.' Came the terse response to my enquiry.

'Is he coming back?'

'No coming beck. He go away.'

'Is there a new manager?'

'I am manager Abdul Rob.'

I did my best to explain the purpose of my call and re-establish the ground I had made with his predecessor but it was too difficult over the telephone.

'You come to the shop.' He suggested and was gone.

Tip-Top Cleaners was situated on the first floor of a parade of commercial buildings in Mahakhali a small commercial district situated off the DIT 1 roundabout. An area thick with traffic, Masum had managed to drop me at the foot of a staircase leading from street level up to the shop before driving off to find somewhere suitable to park. Two security guards stood at the foot of the stairs, I walked between them, and up the concrete steps, which made a sharp left turn at the top presenting me with a panoramic view of the Tip-Top establishment.

Two half glass partitions formed a corridor between the shop on the left and the mechanics of the operation. This area was heavily populated with people engaged in various dry cleaning and laundering activities. A door leading to this area marked 'No Admittance' was manned by another security guard while opposite it a gap in the partition served as means of ingress to the shop. Round the walls rails of finished clothes sealed in polythene hung awaiting their owners. Two girls dressed in *shalwar kameez* served from behind a large L-shaped counter behind which large baskets awaited their next load of soiled clothing.

I politely enquired of them whether Mr Rob was available. Having established who I was and what I wanted, a request was made to the security guard to fetch him. In no time the guard was back and the three of us waited uncomfortably for ten minutes while Mr Rob remained behind the scenes. In due course a small man emerged from the door marked 'No Admittance' the trousers of my suit folded over a crooked arm.

'Mr Mark?' He enquired ignoring my outstretched hand and smoothing out my trousers on the counter in front of me.

'Yes, how do you do?' I said smiling determined to keep the whole exchange on as friendly a footing as possible.

'Here is your trouser. What eez problem?'

'Firstly...' I steeled myself to explain my gripe for the umpteenth time '...the colour has been bleached out of them.' I searched a seam to reveal the true colour,

'...and they have been shrunk.' This was simply demonstrated by holding the shortened trousers up against me.

'This is not possible dry cleaning not shrink.'

'Precisely! Therefore it seems that these have been washed.'

'Theez not possible.'

'Well explain to me how they have arrived at this state.'

'You did not bring trouser here!'

'No, no I brought the trousers here that is one point that we can be certain of. As I was saying to Major Alam...'

'Major Alam he go. He no good.' Rob interrupted.

'Major Alam...' I took a deep breath and pressed on, '...accepted that the suit had been damaged and he was going to come back to me with a solution.'

'You liar!' came his outrageous retort.

'Look you horrible little person.' Rage welling within me. 'Let me explain to you! I have brought my property to your shop and you have damaged it. Would you like that?'

'You not come this shop.'

Out of his breast pocket I spied his spectacles and deciding to demonstrate my point I plucked them from his person.

'Now these are your glasses. If I take your glasses and I put them on the floor and I stamp on them...' I placed the spectacles on the floor out of his line of vision and stamped loudly on the floor raising his eyebrows some way.

'Then you will not be happy. This is because I have taken something of yours and damaged it.'

I bent down to pick up the spectacles.

'Now you see I am a reasonable man and I have not damaged your property.' I held the intact spectacles out at arms length and as he reached for them lobbed them over his shoulder into the basket behind him. The two girls giggled sending him into a rage at his loss of face.

'YOU CRAZY STUPID MAN!' He shouted his cheeks reddening through his coffee coloured complexion, his explosion silencing the two girls.

'LOOK HERE YOU!' I prodded him on the chest with my finger. 'WHY CAN'T YOU JUST ADMIT FOR ONCE THAT YOU ARE WRONG!' Now we were both shouting.

'YOU MAD PERSON!' He ranted.

'YOU CAN KEEP THE BLOODY TROUSERS, I'VE HAD ENOUGH OF YOU!' I shouted turning on my heel.

As I strode from the shop a small electronic register caught my eye and inflamed by injustice and frustration as a parting shot I swept it from the counter. As it hit the floor the paper roll detached itself and played out across the floor and a pleasing number of pieces detached themselves from it.

'AYEEEEEEEEEEEEE!' The shrill scream of the two girls let all hell loose, shouting, whistles and the heavy manhandling of me by what I now presume to be the guard.

As for me I had lost control, the red mist had descended and my eyeballs begun to spin. Breaking free of my assailant, I charged from the shop and down the stairs. As I passed it a crowd of wailing dry cleaners burst through the door marked 'No Admittance' and gave chase.

I was well ahead, however, and although I reached the bottom of the stairs unchallenged my hopes of escape were dashed as a metal gate was drawn across the opening and padlocked shut by the guards on the street. Faced with this immovable object I mustered all my strength and gave the gate a yank. Convinced in my rage that is was no match for me I was dismayed to find that it would not budge. My way barred I turned to face my pursuers. Realising I was trapped they had waited at the top of the stairs. A gaggle of twenty or so sweaty faces peering down at this strange white wildman. Determined to go down fighting I let out a blood curdling roar and charged into their midst.

Having made a pretty good attempt to make myself as difficult to hold on to as possible with assorted can-can type kicks and karate chops I was eventually bundled through the 'No Admittance' door and into an office in which I was locked to await my fate.

Meanwhile downstairs, all Masum was aware of was that I had appeared at the gate fairly agitated and was now locked in the building. Unbeknown to me, he had shot off to the office to get Rana and Mutton to save me.

After half-an-hour, the door was unlocked and Mr Rob and a well dressed, solemn faced man carrying the damaged register entered the room. By now I was feeling rather foolish and not a little apprehensive about my fate. Taking a seat at the opposite side of the desk at which I had installed myself, the solemn man sat and contemplated me for some time before emitting a long drawn out.

'Tut, tut, tut.'

I daresay I deserved to be treated like a naughty child and I was subjected to a lengthy lecture on how one should and should not behave in polite Bangladeshi society. Reference was made to the police, which concentrated my mind wonderfully, and although Mr Kabir, the proprietor, was prepared to hear my side of the story, a settlement was reached that I pay for repairs to the register and that the matter be considered closed. This presented somewhat of a problem as I had no cash on me and Mr Kabir was not prepared to let me leave the building without settling up first. I helpfully suggested that Mr Rob accompany me to the bank in my car. Judging by the way that he backed away from me at this suggestion he did not trust me to spare his life if left alone with him.

Eventually I persuaded them to let me call Masum to bring me my briefcase, which contained my chequebook. Escorted down to the still tight padlocked gate, I was amazed that my calls to Masum bought not only him but also Rana and Mutton, all of them looking rather shell-shocked. The commotion on the stairs had attracted a sizeable crowd and obviously gossip about the mad *bideshi* was rife on the street. Thanking them all for their concern and prompt action, I did my best to allay their fears that the police would not be taking me away and that everything was sorted out. Before I went back into the building I solicited a sheepish grin from Masum by miming a punch on the nose.

'Dhannabad Masum, thank you.'

A week later, the very sound lesson learned that it was possible to overstep the mark in Bangladesh: a letter was delivered by hand to the apartment. It was a friendly note from Mr Kabir apologising for my trouble, returning my cheque and enclosing a card authorising a 15% discount for all future business I gave the Tip-Top Cleaners.

chapter
twenty-six

It is refreshing for one brought up in the south east of England to find an almost classless society. Whether it was viewed as such essentially, the expatriate in Dhaka whatever the pretensions of certain elements within the local foreign population, had one thing in common—from somewhere, someone else was picking up the bill. Through all strata of our kind, whether it be a PhD student on a hard-won grant or a civil servant with the complete 'package'. However well provided for, there was another common bond in that everyone felt tremendously hard done by at any shortfall they perceived there to be in their lot.

We were very well provided for but our lack of 'passbook status' was our great complaint. Our constant quest for a supply of alcohol turned Brenda and I into hoarders, accepting offers from friends of part of their allowance, and squirreling away more beer and wine than we could ever wish to drink. Also an inability to prepare any of the recipes in the *American Woman's Cookbook* a well put together tome each recipe accompanied by a Bangla translation. These all demanded vital ingredients stocked at the out of bounds American Commissary or Duty Free Warehouse that were impossible to get in the local market.

In truth we should have been ashamed of ourselves when we compared our lifestyle to the plight of some Canadian friends of ours working with the Salvation Army. When we had first met them they were living in an area of the city called 'Lamatia', an area beyond our office that we had never had cause to venture to, let alone live in. Here they endured an austere lifestyle free of air conditioning and for prolonged periods of the evening shortages of water and electricity. The latter had caused them to adopt a sleep pattern starting their nights at 7pm.

Their relocation to a tired building in Banani ended their diurnal existence providing a substantial boost to their quality of life, and easier access to the Canadian Club. One day on the squash court, well out of earshot the husband, Mark confided in me that he had discovered an enormous colony of cockroaches living in his new kitchen. This secret would remain between the two of us unless his wife discovered that their new kitchen sink could be rocked on its supporting brackets to reveal an unplumbed fall to the drain heavily populated with the insects.

With stories such as this we were happy to offer them the relative luxury of the loan of our flat while we travelled back to Canada for a friend's wedding. We had returned to find a thank you note atop a pile of accumulated mail on the coffee table in the living room. In it they admitted that due to the novelty of a television and video they had found it hard to venture out of the flat at all and extolled the virtues of our recommended regime of cranking the bedroom air conditioning to full and sleeping under a quilt. Neither of them had slept under little more than a sheet resembling a handkerchief during their entire posting.

Beneath their note and our letters lay a copy of the 'Maple Leaf Rag,' the monthly publication of the Canadian Club with its listings of services and activities in the city for the month. A card advertising the exhibition of a Calcutta-based artist of Bengali extraction had been enclosed and the cross section of paintings reproduced looked interesting. With the last day of the exhibition coinciding with the forthcoming Friday weekend we decided to pay it a visit.

Mukul Art Gallery was located above Rossi Ice Cream Parlour. We had visited the ice cream shop before as it was one of the things that were heartily recommended in the only guide to Dhaka we could find in London prior to our departure. It was memorable in as much as we found its produce to be finger licking mediocre and well worth giving a wide berth. A narrow alley ran down the side of the shop leading to a wooden staircase that was partially lit by a dirty and foliage incrusted window. On a small landing, a firmly closed door barred our entry to the exhibition and while we waited for an answer to our knock, we examined posters of past exhibitions that lined the walls.

The flicker of a neon strip suggested that there was life behind the door and after a fumbling of the lock we were invited in by a sleepy and dishevelled youthful Bangladeshi. The exhibition filled a large open room divided with flimsy partitions to maximise the hanging space. We very much liked the work and were disappointed that we had not been able to view it sooner as the proliferation of red dots on picture labels suggested that business had been good. As luck would have it, one picture that we had particularly liked from the pamphlet was dotless and Brenda and I discussed its merits with a view to buying it. It was by far the most expensive picture that either of us had ever contemplated buying, and it took us several more circuits of the room to come to a decision. I found the boy and declared our intention to purchase the picture. We were delighted to find that it being the last day of the show we could take the picture with us and we left him to wrap our purchase while we nipped up the road to the newly installed cash machine at our bank.

Back in the apartment we were truly delighted with our picture and spent some time rearranging other pictures and furniture so that we could display it to its best effect. Eventually satisfied that we had found the optimum point I secured a sturdy nail on which I hung the canvas. In our opinion it was perfect and satisfied with a good morning's business we set off for lunch at the Canadian Club.

The club was fairly empty and we were able to sit at the table beneath the porch in front of the restaurant. This position ensured that we would be able to spot anyone we knew arriving and should they visit the restaurant they could not miss us. A leaflet from the exhibition had been placed on the table and while we waited for our order Brenda and I poured over its contents to admire our purchase again.

A woman with a ruddy complexion and blonde bob, whom we knew by sight only, approached us.

'Have you been?' She enquired motioning towards the leaflet. 'It's jolly good.'

'Yes we have. In fact we bought a picture.' Brenda said proudly.

'Really! So did I. Is yours in the leaflet?' The common ground suddenly making her over friendly.

Brenda pointed out our picture and her face visibly clouded.

'I think you must be mistaken. I bought that picture on the first night.' She said icily.

'Well it's hanging on our wall at the moment.' We responded in unison sending her off to seek out the gallery owner.

When she returned later in the afternoon having sought out the support of her husband we were on the tennis court playing doubles. Her ruddy face peered through the fence behind me.

'I have the gallery owner on the telephone at the moment will you come and speak to her?'

Despite the fact that I thought it rather cheeky, if she wanted to come to an amicable solution to drag me off-court, mid-game I grudgingly followed her to the restaurant to use the telephone.

'How dare you take that picture from my gallery!' An angry American woman's voice came down the telephone.

'Excuse me Madam, but I think you'll find that your assistant sold it to me and has twenty thousand taka in cash to prove it.'

'Well obviously he doesn't know what's going on!' The voice snapped back.

'Well he seemed quite happy to part with it to me.'

Ignoring this rather obvious observation she continued.

'You have to bring it back. This is a small community you know and we don't need troublemakers like you stirring things up!'

Brenda and I had already decided that had we been in the same position we would be pretty aggrieved and although it was a wrench we would give up the picture. Having informed her of this decision, I politely but firmly informed her that if anyone was taking it anywhere then it was jolly well going to be her.

Later that afternoon the honk of a car horn down below us and the sound of the gate to the car park being drawn back on its metal runners signalled the arrival of the gallery owner. A fat brassy blonde woman appeared at our door and gruffly thrust a wad of taka towards me and I equally unceremoniously delivered the painting to her trust. Brenda was incensed by the injustice of her unreasonable approach and although our blank stretch of wall stood as gloomy testament to the day's events we determined to not let it spoil the rest of our day.

That evening's planned events saw the culmination of weeks of work behind closed doors throughout expatriate Dhaka. A large cross section of the community had been hard at work putting the services of countless local tailors to good use in the creation of costumes for the Australian Club glitter ball.

I was due a visit from Shakur, the barber, before we got ready and I convinced Brenda that she should have one of his magical head massages to relieve the stress of the day. Shakur was a lovely fellow who did a roaring trade in providing tonsorial services to the ex-

patriate heads of Dhaka. Indeed his service was so
successful; that despite having to support thirteen children; he was still able to run a motorcycle and a pager
which were riches indeed for a barber based in the far
distant Mirpur district of the city.

In Dhaka terms, he provided a revolutionary service. A call to his pager would be returned and having
arranged a convenient time arrives on his motorcycle
to carry out the haircut in the comfort of the client's
home. His head massage was said to be a wonderful
thing and one Indian gentleman employed his services
for a marathon two hour session each week which
would leave Shakur exhausted. It was by all accounts
having a marvellously stimulating effect on the now
thick and luxuriant hair of the Indian gentlemen but
being of an extremely ticklish disposition I was in no
position to buck the trend.

Suitably coifed and relaxed Brenda and I donned
our outfits. We were part of a team of ten Maharajahs
dressed in bespoke Nehru jackets from Ferdous, the
tailor, and the crowning glory of sparkling sequinned
turbans and bejewelled curly toed slippers. I had first
come across these items in the proliferation of wedding outfitters on Elephant Road and had been itching
for an excuse to be able to buy some.

So dressed we took a rickshaw through Baridhara
and over the small rickshaw bridge at the top of Gulshan lake a short cut over to the Gulshan side that
brought us up close to a large field behind the Australian Club. We had never seen such a concentration of
people at any event and it was gratifying to see that
we were by no means the only people who had gone to
the effort of dressing up. A gold tented corridor
marked the entrance to the field and we edged our way
through the melee of people being dropped by cars or
seeking out their companions. Deciding that there was
no way we were going to assemble all ten Maharajahs
for a group entrance, we made our way into the field.

I had not reckoned on the thick ankle length grass when I suggested the slippers, but a wooden dance floor erected to one side provided an area where we would be able to display them to their best advantage. Beneath a canopy of presumably the entire stock of Banani Decorator's lights strung between palm trees, dozens of round tables were laid out to accommodate the revellers. We spotted Peter and Sue and the other people in our group and, taking our seats amongst them, the Maharajahs were complete.

We were delighted by the spectacle and amazed at the trouble some groups had gone to in their outfits. A group of Dutch gilded bishops were by far the most outstanding complete with mitre hats and crooks although the Canadian, who made no secret of his homosexuality, in a blue and red sequinned Mountie outfit—presumably he always got his man—had to run them a close second. As the evening wore on there was considerable wear and tear on some of the more flimsy creations; the sparkling Santa's all lost their beards and on a visit to the conveniences, I found myself having to help a large baby with a moustache reassemble his star spangled nappy. The presentation of prizes for the best costumes released people from their preoccupation from keeping their outfits together, and the final winners, a group of wizards delighted the crowd by lighting sparklers lodged in the top of their cone hats.

It was hard to believe that we were still in Dhaka, its difficulties and annoyances hidden by the night and the increasing effect of the contents of the bar. A fleeting glimpse of Mala, who waved to us gaily from the American Ambassador's table, and even a brief encounter with the fat American woman, who we extravagantly stuck our tongues out at, failed to spoil our evening. We bumped into Asif, who was obviously feeling no pain, and some of his friends on the dance floor and there we remained until the small hours entertained by a local disc jockey, he of the nomadic disco.

We arrived at the office the following day at 2pm with heavy heads. Mala, having realised that we were just about the only group of expatriates putting in a six day week, had relaxed her regime a little allowing us to take an extra Saturday morning off once a month which was extremely timely. There was no sign of Asif and it was not until late afternoon that he eventually appeared.

'Are you okay?'

'Sure. I had to go to the dentist this morning.'

'The dentist?'

'Yeah after you guys left last night I guess I passed out on the dance floor. When I hit the ground I must have knocked my front teeth out.'

I winced at the imagined excruciating discomfort.

'God, that must have hurt like crazy.' I sympathised.

'Well actually I didn't realise at the time but I got a hell of a shock when I woke up and looked in the mirror this morning.'

chapter
twenty-seven

Lawrence Rosario we presumed to be of the same Portuguese stock as John Cruze. We had interviewed him in tandem with another prospective cook, who despite having an impressive list of previous employers, was so scruffy that one look was sufficient to rule him out. Lawrence, in comparison, was a model of how to sell oneself. Well presented, bright, cheer-ful, fairly fluent in English and seem- ingly determined to secure the position.  Brenda and I were taken in, and having laid out the house rules, embarked on a relationship that at its best was excellent and at times tried our patience to the limit, but nevertheless one that would see us through to the end of our time.

He was a good deal younger than any of our previous servants, and had not yet determined when his boundless enthusiasm over stepped the mark. He was also the master of the 'Please Sir don't mind' opening gambit to a conversation which was normally followed by a request for an advance on his salary. On one occasion, however, he had requested an audience to present a considered argument and supporting time and motion study on why we should finance a bicycle for him. Blinded by his sophisticated marketing approach, we had crumbled almost immediately and an old fashioned black bicycle of Chinese manufacture was purchased from the aptly named 'Bicycle Street.' 'Sir' had, of course had to try it out, which had rendered Lawrence speechless with mirth.

More often than not, these wearisome requests were made as soon as I had ventured out of the bedroom for breakfast, and my humour was not at its best. This particular morning Lawrence's appearance at the end of the table with a folded tea towel wrapped round his head already had me on my guard.

'What on earth have you got that on your head for?'

'Headache Sir.' He responded obviously suffering.

'Would you like an aspirin?'

'Yes sir.' He busied himself arranging the toast rack and bowls of fruit on the table.

'Don't mind Sir,' I shuddered.

'Mr Dvai he is leaving?'

In a city where the most intimate details of ones existence might be freely discussed amongst the domestic staff, the keeping of rather obvious secrets such as packing up to leave was a tricky business. If the truth were known, Catherine who was supposedly on a protracted stay in India had returned to her native Canada some weeks previously. Dvai, in order to honour his contract and maximise his financial return, had had to make it past a certain date before joining her. Having done so and banked his last cheque, he had summoned the services of Going Places Movers and was ready for a quick getaway.

In the office we were fascinated to see what the fall out would be at Dvai's announcement. He had been quite a favourite of Mala's, and surely his leaving before the end of his two year contract, would come as something of a blow. There had long been rumblings of discontent throughout the ranks at Mala's tyrannical rule and, although plenty had threatened to desert their posts and resign, so far nobody had actually gone through with it.

He appeared in the doorway of my office, a free man, to collect me for a post mortem in Brenda's office. Douglas and Roger were already in there eager to know Mala's reaction to the first cracks appearing in her empire. We were all laughing as Dvai described the enraged quivering lip that we all knew so well when Raihan, a sweaty, fleshy boy who had recently joined us, appeared at the glass door and knocked urgently.

'Have you seen the tanks?' He asked pointing over our heads in the direction of the road.

As implausible as it sounded we all got up and looked out of the window. There trailing into the distance towards Motijheel belching blue exhaust were indeed a pair of tanks. In the days preceding the non co-operation movement, it was sight that might easily have been explained away but the political situation having long since settled down it was an alarming development.

Douglas turned from the window his face distorted into a fanatical grin.

'Thank God the Army's here. I'm going out to see what's going on.' With that he left us calling for the long suffering Asif to join him.

Meanwhile the rest of the staff were obviously quite frightened, and after the situation was brought to the attention of Mala, leave was given for everyone to go home. This seemed a wise precaution in a country where the military had taken more than a passing interest in Government and one did not have to delve too deep in the history books to find the words 'Military Coup'.

Masum bought the car out of the car park under the building, and while I drove, Brenda called all the people we knew in nearby offices to pass on the news. A terrible traffic jam in front of the Lalbagh Hotel blocked our usual route home so I gambled on the alternative route past the cantonment. Despite the fact that we had all acted quite speedily, there seemed to be no undue panic on the streets and as we drove towards the cantonment tank tracks in the asphalt were the only evidence of what we had seen earlier. Just when we thought that perhaps we had all acted rather rashly, another tank hove into view followed by three others. This we felt confirmed that something was up and as the first of the convoy rumbled past us, churning the road in its path, Brenda got through to Peter.

'Yes! Tanks on the road there is one going past us right this minute!'

A little further on we encountered another tank stationery by the side of the road. Its camouflage clad occupants standing beside it. Brenda and I could see the humour in the situation, its commander an imaginary Sergeant Islam, being called to arms for his first military coup only for his tank to break down yards from its base. It was Bangladesh all over.

Whether there was any wisdom in heading home in such a situation I know not, but there was I suppose a perceived safety in numbers. In our few minor scares we had envisaged helicopters swooping down to pluck us from the embattled grounds of the British High Commission and presumably that would only do us any good if we were in the locale. The Americans would no doubt have argued that there was always the detachment of US Marines who everyone presumed were armed to the teeth behind the red walls of the American Embassy. I had only ever seen the Marines in action at the Gulshan Lake Regatta. Then they had failed to complete half a lap of the course, incapable of paddling a low slung local boat in any direction other than a circle. They had been comprehensively beaten into last place by seven others crewed by a mixture of men, women and children all of whom were in fancy dress. Based on that I would not liked to have relied on them for anything although it was hardly a test of their fighting mettle.

Having made it home unscathed, we turned on the local television channel for an update. Although delivered entirely in Bangla, we felt sure images of tanks would dominate the news but we saw none. We called Feroz who had heard about the military activity but he knew no more than we did and so we remained in ignorance our only option to sit it out and wait.

The next morning we awoke to find our apartment still intact and we joined the entire population of the city in going back to work as though nothing had happened. We drove to work on tank track rutted roads and read in the newspapers reports of the previous day's events. A disgruntled army officer, who having taken exception to being removed from his post on the orders of the President, had mobilised those forces loyal to him to head towards Dhaka from local districts. Whilst tanks loyal to the President had been deployed to the area surrounding the Presidential Palace in Motijheel. Confusion had reigned briefly when local commentators became unsure of just whose tanks were outside the Presidential Palace. But as quickly as the excitement had been created, it dissipated and for the local inhabitants, it was just another day in Dhaka.

True to form ,this was the sort of news that made its way straight to the world news pages in the papers in Britain. A short fax arrived from my father, issued secretly, stating that he had seen news of tanks on the streets in Dhaka, but managed to keep it out of sight of my Mother but that a call home would be appreciated. Another arrived from a Scottish stockbroker who had planned a visit to the city in order to witness at first hand a new local phenomenon. A steady climb in the fortunes of the local stock market had prompted some overseas interest. Although the returns would have to be good for even a canny Scot to risk life and limb against an armoured division of the local armed forces. As unlikely as it seemed we had managed to convince him the tank movements had been prompted by more a misunderstanding than any threatened political posturing and that under no circumstances was it cause to postpone a visit.

Despite the fact that Brenda and I had a vested interest in his arrival, having preyed on David Mcilroy's good nature to import a small Red Cross parcel on our behalf, our appraisal of the situation was sound. I had collected him from the mid-afternoon British Airways flight and steered him towards the foot high letters and oversized arrow that spelled out the VIP status I had conferred upon him. For someone arriving with the lowest of expectations, it was somewhat of a surprise. The goodwill this small diversion preserved in shielding Dhaka debutantes from the possible frustrations within the arrivals area, let alone those in the car park was immeasurable. Timing the location of one's luggage with an incoming flight of pilgrims from Mecca, each accompanied by several gallons of *jamjam* water in jerry cans or a plane load of homebound UN troops, might put an hour on the time taken to make it from immigration to the exit.

We were delighted at the prospect of a visitor. Here was someone who only hours before had been at home. We received him like a long lost friend, grateful of an opportunity to show off our level of comfort with our wild and woolly surroundings and the home that we had established. With barely sufficient time to get him into the hotel before dusk, I reasoned that despite his long journey dinner alone in the hotel would be very dull and that Masum would collect him should he wish to have dinner with us. We had however misjudged our guest's constitution and, having mentioned in passing that there was a squash court at the Canadian Club, it was seemingly a matter of minutes before he and I were on it ready to do battle in a pre-dinner match.

Peter, Mike, our American friend, and Mark from the Salvation Army made up a quartet who met on a Friday morning for a round robin of squash at the Canadian Club. With the extreme temperatures we endured in our sessions we were sure that the development of our ability must surely have taken us to the brink of World Champion standard. David's appearance on the scene provided a mere mortal on which to try out the finely tuned skills of one of the Canadian

Club squash Gods. The fact that he soundly beat me barely breaking into a sweat left me questioning myself on whether or not to broaden my horizon with regard to my playing partners.

David was, however, in the country ostensibly on a business trip. The following morning Asif, he and I drove to Motijheel to visit the Dhaka Stock Exchange. Perhaps a sharper initiation would have prepared him better for the daunting mass of people veiled in a mixture of exhaust and dust, thronging the main drag the aptly named 'Motijheel Road'. Local police were attempting to beat back a crowd already spilling over one lane of the road contained by a raised brick central reservation. It was obviously a busy day at the kerb market. In Dhaka, the local trading of stocks exists in an official and unofficial capacity side-by-side. The kerb market is the universally accepted marketplace for the activities of unlicensed brokers, which has established itself directly outside the entrance of the Stock Exchange proper. With a prolonged upward trend in the market business on the kerb had exploded beyond all recognition. Attracted by news of big profits to be made, a section of the population hitherto untouched by the goings on of capital markets were arriving in the city on a daily basis with their life savings determined not to miss out. The concept of the stock market going up as well as down had been lost on them, not to mention Brenda and I. Lured by conditions where greed outweighed fear, we had made a small investment in a local pharmaceutical company. As the market stood this appeared to have been a wise move.

We abandoned Masum some hundred yards short of the Exchange and let Asif lead us through the crowd doing our best to squeeze down the covered arcade the length of the pavement formed by the overhanging porches of the buildings lining Motijheel Road. The Stock Exchange was picked out by two security guards standing sentry at its entrance. Beyond them in a corridor their supervisor sat hunched behind a small scuffed desk better suited to use by kindergarten children than a grown man. Despite his constrained accommodation, he was able to nod his assent to our entry and we followed Asif down a corridor, one side half-glazed, that provided our first view of the Dhaka Exchange bourse.

The Dhaka Stock Exchange runs an open-cry system of trading stock, and transactions are documented on a large blackboard running the length of the bourse. The brokers, neatly seated at a square described by long desks, are ministered to by a caller who works his way down the list of stocks offering one opportunity to trade any given stock on that day. In short for a fund manager used to the computerised screens of a London Trading desk, the prehistoric surroundings were something of an eye opener. Asif was well known at the Exchange, and having got us into the bourse, we watched as brokers called out bids to each other as particular stocks came up in the order of the day's business. As all the proceedings were held in Bangla, David and I were blissfully unaware of the announcement that currently the Exchange was being laid siege to by an element of the kerb market. An unpredicted fall in one particular share price had been mirrored on the kerb and the resultant loss incurred was not an eventuality that many of the punters inexperienced casual investors were prepared for.

Asif broke the news to us his manner as relaxed as ever. As interesting as the Exchange is, there is a limit to its appeal, and the prospect of an afternoon camped inside it was not an attractive one. David shot a glance at me that voiced this sentiment eloquently and I asked Asif if there was a back door through which we might affect an escape. This comparatively simple requirement, it appeared remained the preserve of the chairman of Exchange—it being in his office and since he was by all accounts in Chittagong, short of breaking down the door, we were marooned. Asif, however, seemed unperturbed by our predicament and urged us to follow him back out to the corridor.

I had not noticed a small lift that we had passed on our way in which he directed us to and unquestioningly we awaited its arrival the call button depressed by Asif with a careless slap. The lift arrived promptly its dull metal doors drawing back to reveal a minute cubicle which improbably already contained a lift attendant. The four of us squashed in and were transported to the fifth floor of the building, intimately pressed together. After an uncomfortable thirty seconds, we arrived at our destination and erupted out of the lift into the fifth floor lobby. To our left a staircase led still further skywards at the top of which ,the opening of a door that might well have concealed a cupboard, gave us access to the roof of the building.

'See! There is a good view of the Presidential Palace.' Asif directed our gaze over the Dhaka skyline determined to make our detour as interesting as possible. Content that we had studied the view in all directions he stepped over a low dividing wall between the Stock Exchange and the attached neighbouring structure, which was a building undergoing major refurbishment. We picked our way past nonplussed, dust-coated labourers, three men in suits that had seemingly appeared from nowhere.

Our escape route brought us out in a small dead end street. I recognised it from a previous episode, which had required me to make an unofficial withdrawal from the Motijheel branch of our bank, having missed its closing time by minutes. I had been directed round to the back door after a conversation with a bank employee through the letterbox at the front of the building. My tentative knock had been answered by a junior manager who invited me in, cashed my cheque and handed me fresh bundles of notes direct from the safe. Everything it seemed in Dhaka was possible whilst at the same time being impossible.

Having extracted us from the Exchange, Asif left us and I suggested that if David hadn't already seen more local colour than he had bargained for we nip down to the boat terminal in the old city. I had been to this area a number of times but never yet made it onto a boat. If David, who had started his working week in the Square Mile of London, thought the juxtaposition of the Stock Exchange bizarre then to find himself bobbing around on a native boat on the river would take this phenomenon to a new extreme.

Having negotiated the maze of streets into the old city, Masum was pressed into service as our tour guide. He obliging lead us to the seething, covered area at road level that served as the ticket office for the Sadarghat Boat Terminal where we were relieved of two taka each. This nominal fee gave us access to a small muddy beach area which, one reached having negotiated five or so well worn rustic stone steps worn smooth with the passage of countless pairs of leathery feet. At the waters edge, the captains cum oarsmen of traditional river-boats were landing their craft depositing numerous passengers and accompanying baggage. Masum rather gruffly accosted one of these pilots and I got the impression that he was told to take us rather than being given the opportunity to negotiate a fare.

Preferring to stay on land, Masum left us to our own devices and David I attempted to board our boat. Other boats continued to land all the while and we were well advised by our pilot in a mixture of Bangla and sign language to keep our fingers away from the rim of the boat. Once we were both on board and seated on the uncomfortable woven bamboo covering the deck, our boat was edged out into the river. Shaped much the same as a sliver of melon that has had the flesh eaten from it, we were neither of us that confident in the sea worthiness of our craft. We seemed precariously balanced on her until we cleared the congested river bank and our man hit his rhythm with the single oar protruding from the back of the boat.

For the occupants of the varied passing traffic we were clearly as fascinating to them as they to us. A mixture of small boats like our own past by some with the luxury of a curved bamboo open cabin. Cargo boats loaded with bunches of green bananas and sacks of I know not what. Their crews shouting questions to our helmsman, no doubt enquiring how much cash he had managed to extract from his two *bideshi's* for their tour of the river. Rather foolishly he had failed to negotiate a fee prior to our departure, but as we approached the opposite bank and looked back at our point of embarkation and an excellent view of Ahsan Manzil, the pink palace, he could have named his price.

Although the stretch of water we had crossed was barely quarter of a mile wide, our proximity to the waterline gave the impression that we might be overwhelmed at any time. We had made it to the other bank and admired at close quarters the beached hulks of sturdy vessels, propped precariously being broken for scrap by men with little more than hammers. We had returned the waves of those trying to catch a ride across the river and taken photographs of each other pretending to make important telephone calls on the mobile sat beside the helmsman. Rather than tempt fate by prolonging our trip, I shamelessly ignored the nautical conventions of port and starboard and asked the helmsman to 'drive left'. This manoeuvre took us back out to the centre of the river and the choppy water stirred up by the comings and goings of fast packet boats, small motor-powered dinghies ,and the stately progress of the inappropriately named 'Rocket ferries'. Those we inspected, when brought uncomfortably near to their bows by our helmsman, were tired, heavily rusted and spartan. Stripped of all amenities and not a safety feature in sight, their crew indulging in assorted activities to ensure that their craft was sound. The only place it was possible to imagine them rocketing to was the bottom of whatever waterway they were plying.

Disembarking from our boat was considerably easier to the hurried and uncertain way in which we had boarded. Our helmsman ploughed the bow of his boat into the beach for us and we stepped neatly from it our brogues squelching into the mud and receiving a band of thick brown goo. I paid our helmsman exactly double the going rate ensuring a minimum of fuss in taking our leave and no doubt bumping up the rate for those few foreigners foolish enough to follow in our footsteps.

One more delight lay in store for David before he took his leave of us. We felt honour bound to draw his attention to that most loathsome of creatures, the Englishman abroad with a visit to the British Administration Guesthouse Association or BAGHA Club. When we had first arrived in the city and found that we did not have the necessary qualifications for any of the clubs, a helpful soul had suggested that we try the BAGHA, a less stuffy version of the British High Commission Club to cater for British Nationals on short term contracts. Strictly speaking, we were not eligible for membership, but had paid it a visit one evening and been signed in by a member who was leaving as we arrived. This we took to be a good sign although it was apparent that our sponsor, despite the relatively early hour, was plainly intoxicated.

We had been thoroughly dismayed, having made it through its hallowed portals, to discover that the sum total of the BAGHA's facilities was a dingy bar complete with horse brasses, dartboard and a hard core of career dipsomaniacs who were hard at work drinking away their postings.

Since then we had divested ourselves of our high hats and although we had wangled our BHC membership would exercise our reciprocal membership at the BAGHA to enjoy its lush, palm tree lined gardens and tropical outdoor bar which we had failed to spot on our first visit. Here one might indulge oneself in spectacular examples of English culinary excellence that involved the use of baked beans, fish fingers and sausages washed down with imported bitter all vital foodstuffs acquired from the off limits commissary.

Of course David, as a Scot, could distance himself from this aberration. Had he wished to immerse himself in a culture more in keeping with his own then we could have probably arranged for a spot of Highland dancing with the local Caledonian Society. Although I had heard it said that the society was not what it had been since the last Chieftain was posted to tool up a biscuit factory in Delhi.

chapter twenty-eight

'...and here the tree of the mango.'

Brenda and I gazed wearily from the doorway in which we were propped at the speckled image being played on a portable screen.

I am reminded of the lines of the poet Tagore:

> '*Your mango groves make me wild with joy*
> *Ah the thrill*
> *The Mango our gift from God...blah, blah...*'

It was punishing stuff. An exercise in endurance at the home of the editor of a local magazine in which we were treated to an evening of poetry and photographs of Bangladesh presented to a mix of polite Dhaka society by the learned Professor Jahangir.

At social outings we had attended in Dhaka went it was a shocker. We had been the second guests to arrive and had spent an uncomfortable half hour with the outgoing Australian High Commissioner whom, although a personable man, did not have limitless capacity for small talk. Silently I cursed the local convention of being one and a half hours late for social events that despite many opportunities to cultivate this trait we had failed to adopt. Slowly our fellow guests had filtered in and the subtle osmosis of women to one end of the room and men the other had taken place.

Our host elegantly clad in the finest Messrs Marks and Spencer has to offer and the bench mark for style amongst the Dhaka elite flitted from group to group. A generous man he urged his guests to partake in a sumptuous although uninviting buffet comprising various flavours of the standard fare, bone laced biriani. No expense, however, had been spared on the alcoholic quota for the soiree, and as the evening wore on, it was evident that Mr Sarker was dividing his time evenly between his guests and his drinks cabinet.

When after an agonising wait for a polite break in the *son et lumiere*, Brenda and I had attempted to slip away undetected but we bumped into him in the corridor. Polyester cravat lolling from his blazer alarmingly askew, he had subjected us to a rambling farewell before releasing us into Gulshan's humming, chirruping darkness to locate our car, which had been rendered indistinguishable amongst a lengthy line of neatly parked identical models.

At the other end of the social scale, we had endured similarly painful evenings in a variety of settings. Always keen to cultivate our local contacts and cement friendships, we had found it difficult to refuse invitations. These, however well meaning, rarely constituted a 'good time'.

All too often the demon drink was the deciding factor. Its absence in awkward social situations highlighted those social inadequacies that one or two 'sharpeners' might have camouflaged. There were, of course, exceptions. An invite to the residence of a very earnest junior bank official, for which we might have justifiably put in for some sort of bravery award for accepting, unexpectedly yielded several illicitly obtained beers. The fact that our host had flouted the conventions of his religion so spectacularly had been taken as a lead by his servant to do the same. I had experienced a mixture of amusement and revulsion as his servant, clearly visible behind a frosted panel dividing the sitting room from the kitchen, had paused to sample each drink prior to serving it. The evidence silhouetted behind his master and visible only to the guests.

Hemanto is a season of rebirth in Bangladesh. The rains subside and the land emerges with fresh deposits of super productive silt from its three major rivers the Jamuna, Padma and Meghna. *Hemanto* also marks the start of the wedding season which, squeezed into December, provides a month of excess as a precursor to the abstinence of the month of Ramadan. For us it provided a minefield in the social calendar and more than one wedding scenario through which to negotiate it.

The intimate home-based function to which we were welcomed as part of an extended family reunion: or the 'universal invite' wedding at which all those with the most tenuous of links to the bride and groom within a hundred miles radius might be expected. Within this second category one encountered the charmless free-for-all of the downmarket, though presumably not cheap variety and the upmarket universal invite which, depending of the status of the protagonists, might produce an attendance of which organisers of an open air pop festival might be proud.

All three provided me with an opportunity to indulge my childhood passion of dressing up and I had three outfits to correspond to each wedding type. There was the Englishman abroad look of linen jacket, establishment tie and grey flannels which I favoured for the more intimate occasions. At these it was apparent that we had been invited to be shown off and there was no point in disappointing the punters. If holed up in a private room to be presented to and photographed with a procession of friends and relations the last thing that was desired was a *bideshi* who had 'gone native'.

An unwritten law appeared to dictate that those weddings that fell into the downmarket universal invite category be held at the depressing multi-storied

Rafiqul Islam Memorial Community Centre or some similarly depressing municipal building. Four floors of tawdry celebration peopled with a heaving cross-section of the local populace welcomed on the flimsiest of pretexts. Many of those present, had they searched out either bride or groom, would have only recognised them by dint of their being located under gaudily decorated canopies, one situated above the other in a sandwich of the sexes segregated by floor. Common ground lay in the filling, the communal dining area, in which all comers from guest's drivers to *bideshi* hangers-on were treated to *biriani* washed down with the revolting yoghurt drink *lassi*.

At one such wedding Brenda had attended the bride and her entourage as a bridesmaid; consequently we had acquired the most expensive *shalwar kameez* this side of Calcutta for the occasion. Determined to get as much wear out of it as possible, it was a given that it should be given an airing at any suitable event. In sympathy, I would attempt an unsuccessful Imran Khan impersonation in billowing cotton *kurta* pyjamas and curly toed Indian slippers. For all our efforts and excited compliments about our appearance, I had yet to encounter a foreigner of either sex who actually looked good in traditional local dress. Those ladies who resorted to day to day wearing of *shalwar kameez*, doubtless out of a lack of suitable alternative, appeared too buxom for the flowing lines more suitable to a slight Asian frame. Instead pink glowing complexions topped garments, seams bursting against well-fed western hides, making the occupants appear ungainly throwbacks from the sixties.

For us the upmarket universal invite was easily the softest option. At these events the wedding guests were far too preoccupied with the ostentatious display of their own status and scrutiny of their peers to attach any novelty to the appearance of a *bideshi* couple. In fact a combination of the cosmopolitan and sprawling nature of these affairs meant that we could wander

freely **together** unnoticed and, indeed, unacknow-
ledged. The anonymity we enjoyed at such gatherings
enabled Brenda to wear her *shalwar* less self con-
sciously and gave me an opportunity to wear a magnificent but totally impractical *Nehru* jacket that in a
moment of weakness Mr Ferdous, the tailor, had
talked me into having made.

Local weddings for those without close family
links or direct involvement in the ceremonial side had
as much charm as some of the social events I had a
hand in. Somewhere in my contract, although I had
yet to find its reference in print, I had been appointed
the company social convenor. As such with the complete armoury of Dhaka's high spots at my disposal, I
had contrived to entertain a sizeable chunk of the
business community in the name of corporate hospitality.

Mala was a zealous taskmaster and I had long ago
come to the realisation that mine was not to reason
why at her assorted preposterous requests. Consequently we booked the entire ballroom of the Lalbagh
Hotel, a venue suitable for four hundred people, at
which to introduce the visiting Chairman of our company to an unsuspecting Bangladeshi public. An up-
beat speech by our glorious leader was delivered to a
motley assortment of pressmen, a handful of businessmen and the entire staff of the office who, pressed
into duty, enabled us to bring the headcount to three
figures.

Lavish parties were arranged at her residence, the
planning of which depended on my working through a
lengthy checklist and placing my faith in up to half a
dozen local contractors, each of which might fail to
deliver. Messrs Sajna, the southern Indian restaurateurs to do the catering. Gulshan Decorators to provide the crockery, and the Canadian Club for extra
waiting staff. Asif's mate who could provide a *tannoy*
system with which to page the guest's drivers when
leaving a function, and of course Colonel Latif's secu-

rity boys to save us from invasion. It was not difficult to set this line of dominos up, but the knocking of the first one over so ensuring a neat knock on effect through to a the culmination of the event that was the tricky part. Ensuring that Mala had sufficient wine and beer to serve her guests might have been the hardest part of all.

The prospect of two dry years in my new home had galvanised me into searching out every possible avenue through which to obtain illicit alcohol. Having complained long and hard of our plight to just about everyone we met we now had an embarrassment of riches. We were able to purloin several chunks of friend's passbook allowances, an 'in' through Mike to the American Commissary and, if all else failed, the paint and hardware merchant at DIT 2 market. This unlikely supplier, if given enough warning, could be called upon to produce the odd dusty can of Heineken or murky bottle of wine of dubious pedigree.

Such was my success in this department that it long ceased to be an issue as far as Mala was concerned. Indeed I quite enjoyed my reputation for resourcefulness in the face of the considerable odds stacked against me by some of her more outlandish requests. My duties as far as she was concerned had long since passed from office manager to those of surrogate husband. Although I was happy to hacksaw keyless padlocks off 'servant proof' cupboards or collect astonishing heaps of cash from the bank on her behalf, a request to inspect an 'original' Raphael painting languishing undiscovered in a corner of Saju Art Gallery at DIT 2 had me in a quandary. Surely to concede to such a demand would leave me questioning my own sanity since the sub-continental journeys of the sixteenth century artist are not well documented!

It was clear that this dependence would need to be reigned in when one evening at a dinner party, a call on my mobile interrupted my tucking into one of our friend Lu's extravagant buffets.

'Mauuurk!' Her plaintive north American tones emanated from the cursed mobile telephone.

'The American Ambassador and some of the movers and shakers in Dhaka have come to dinner at my house and I just realised that I have no wine to serve them. Could you...?'

I resisted the temptation to point out that at 8pm in the evening on my one day off a week whilst attempting my own 'moving and shaking' it was perhaps not the best time to call. However the fallout of not responding to such a request outweighed the inconvenience factor. I made my apologies to my disbelieving fellow guests and wearily set off to select the filthiest bottle of wine in our collection in the name of the common good.

In this respect she was a good ambassador for the company, rarely letting an opportunity to entertain in the name of business pass her by. The opening of a new Korean Restaurant at DIT 1, which coincided with a visit from the head of the Bombay office, proved an irresistible combination. A three-line whip was duly issued to all the senior members of the staff, who assembled at the appointed place, having grudgingly cancelled various extra curricular activities.

What might have been an uncomfortable evening of stilted conversation was eased by the fact that Sebastian Kent was an unashamed party animal. On discovering that the proprietor of the restaurant before departing Seoul had remembered to pack his Karaoke machine, he insisted that the whole party adjourn for some impromptu crooning. A universal feeling of dread was soon assuaged as Sebastian and his accompanist for the evening, Douglas, got us off to an uncompromising start with their way of singing 'My Way'. Not wishing to disappoint a public who were positively baying for a contribution, Mala joined me in a touching rendition of 'Unchained Melody'. My declaration that 'I need your lurve' proved too much for Mala, even in the name of business, and I was left to finish alone whilst she blushed profusely and the assembled fell about in fits of the giggles.

Despite her embarrassment, the evening had mentally registered as a hit. When early in 1997 we were running through the venues for a belated staff 'end of year party', it was her first choice. For me, the party was the culmination of three days hectic activity, the Bangladesh office's contribution to a regional tour of the group Chairman and his attendant acolytes. The product of months of planning and fine detail lavished upon a trip involving private planes, tight schedules and assorted destinations throughout the subcontinent.

My involvement in the project had been initiated with a short email which advised:

'Mr Pose has heard that it is possible to shoot wild boar whilst riding elephants in Bangladesh. Please arrange this and revert.'

Tentative official enquiries of the Ministries of Tourism and Forestry seemed to suggest that anyone venturing into the open spaces of Bangladesh with a view to decimating local wildlife would be deported pretty smartly. Unofficial sources suggested that if he had to shoot things he might take a few pot-shots at birds in the tea estates, but that it was unlikely to involve elephants. Some helpful types even went so far as to put forward names of friends and relations who might help me out. I questioned the wisdom of placing the chairman's sport in the hands of someone's 'Uncle Raffique', who may or may not show at the appointed time and, therefore, I decided that scotching the whole idea was a better tack to take.

Within the ranks news of the chairman's visit was overshadowed by the excitement generated by the announcement of the staff party. A further edict issued from Mala's office was that everyone should come up with a sketch or similar to provide entertainment split the camp into two factions. There were those content to let apathy take over and a hard core who revealed hitherto undisclosed talents. Janet, the tabla playing receptionist, and Jasmin, Mala's secretary who threatened to accompany her in song. Momin, the magician, and Mutton, his grinning loon of an assistant, who ventured that if Momin's magical prowess proved insufficient to satiate the baying crowd then he would be able to step in to recount one of 'a great many amusing tales'. I somehow doubted that Mutton's quality control in the joke telling stakes matched mine, but nevertheless, I suggested that he make the unflappable Asif, the designated entertainment co-ordinator for the evening, aware of his talent.

On the evening of the party, Brenda and I stepped out of our car to be greeted by an assembly of the company's entire stable of drivers, who unbeknownst to me, had been pressed into overtime by the party going staff. The row of shiny, chestnut coloured faces that beamed toothy smiles, lit in the darkness by a mixture of headlights and the porch lights of the restaurant, suggested that the prospect of a reasonable tip and some supper if they were lucky, would be sufficient recompense. This, however, would do nothing to assuage my guilt at their working into the small hours and it was with some relief that we extricated ourselves from their presence, finding our way round to the garden at the back of the restaurant.

We had arrived well ahead of Mala and the chairman's entourage, which gave us an opportunity to greet our colleagues and their partners. The entire gathering had descended on a cluster of circular tables where they perched uncomfortably presumably awaiting instructions on how to go about having a good time. The tables were laid out in a crescent round a raised stone platform, a product of the landscape gardeners art that would serve as a rustic stage for the evening's entertainment. For the moment ,Asif was its sole occupant tinkering expertly with a microphone and stand. Here was our master of ceremonies, hair coifed to one side in an oily pile, shirt collar splayed ala seventies over his suit jacket lapels. His self confidence in marked contrast to those members of the local staff, apparently rooted to the spot, for which a foray to the promised land of Gulshan was a mite intimidating.

Through the well-behaved ranks of startled-looking Sunday School children that seemingly peopled our office, Momin raised a glass to me. It contained what appeared to be that 'small drop of whisky' he had quantified in my office earlier in the day by holding his hands several inches apart against his stomach. By the scale that he had used it would take several tankards of whisky to fill the space he had indicated and by the looks of the impressive, and totally illegal bar our Korean host had laid on, such a feat was eminently possible.

A scraping of chairs on stone heralded the entrance of our illustrious chairman, stopping what chatter there had been. Mala, in attendance, fussed around as he picked his way between the tables as twenty or so pairs of eyeballs scrutinised this small man who for many was just a name and photograph in the corporate propaganda. As the principal sit-upon was lowered into a chair, the rest followed suit and the initial ordeal over, all parties concerned breathed a concerted inaudible sigh of relief.

Dick and Sam, two English senior managers who had the dubious honour of being included on the tour, excused themselves immediately from the inner sanctum and furnished themselves with drinks from the bar. Brenda and I joined them and we were all, it seemed, pleased to have an opportunity to indulge in a little corporate bitching. We had met both of them before and we chatted easily and animatedly, our bond made all the stronger by trying circumstances and conditions.

Dinner was served under the stars, their effect dampened by strings of coloured lights playing in the gentle evening breeze above our heads. Any cultural anomalies in Bengali's being served east Asian cuisine were ignored until the drivers trooped in to fill their plates. Their expressions revealing a thinly veiled disgust at being duped into extra curricular services for foreign food.

A gentle 'boum' blown into the microphone by Asif as a test focused the attention of those assembled on the stage. He effortlessly delivered his patter graciously, thanking Mala for organising the party, and welcoming the Chairman to Dhaka. Having accepted an invitation to speak, he reciprocated with a speech unsuited to the social setting regarding the spectacular growth of his organisation. In my short career with the company, I had heard this speech least half a dozen times.

The polite applause, that sent him back to his seat, gathered momentum as Momin replaced him on the stage ably supported by his assistant ,Mutton. Their well oiled routine was the product of a good deal of preparation both in and out of office hours. I had become quite used to the sight of Momin producing a small red, crumpled handkerchief from the clenched fist of a previously empty hand with a flourish and the words 'Abracadabra bin galle galle'. It was good trick. although its beauty lay in the simplicity of the mechanism with which it was performed. I was apprised of its cunning, having vowed not to divulge the secret.

The finale of the act had, however, been kept from me and the shredding, on stage, of copious amounts of paper was a new departure for me. The fragments were pressed into a metal bowl and passed among the audience for examination. Mutton, taking his duties very seriously, was at pains to ensure that a final ripping was made by our chairman before returning to the stage. Although I had long ceased to be surprised by Momin's antics, the sight of him consuming several handfuls of fragmented paper gripped my attention. Replete, he treated us to a theatrical regurgitation of his papyraceous feast, the initial output being deftly plucked from his lips by his assistant. A six inch long strip of paper soon became a foot, then three before finally being stretched across the breadth of the stage to reveal the legend 'The Dhaka office welcomes our chairman to Bangladesh'. It was touching stuff.

There followed a quiz, presided over by Asif, to establish which couple amongst the married contingent of the office knew each other the best. This succeeded in soliciting the information that Brenda and I knew barely anything about each other. That Rana modestly wore a 'sleeping suit', whatever that was, in bed and that embarrassingly few of the husbands concerned came up with the desired answer when asked to reveal the identity of their dream date.

Entering into the spirit of things as the office 'bahadur' and 'begum' had been crowned, Sam responded to a request for a contribution from the top table by taking to the stage to deliver a joke, that whilst erring on the risqué side, was well received. Taking a lead from this, the unkempt Raihan thrust his hand into the air and was duly invited to make his contribution.

'Well my story is not so much a joke as a funny story. In my last office in the bathrooms there were western toilets. One man in the office had not encountered these before and so when he went to the lavatory he would squat whilst actually standing on the bowl. One day there was a terrific bang from the bathroom and the man had broken the toilet!'

Whilst barely constituting a funny story it was entirely inappropriate and he left the stage to a polite titter. Asif, restoring some semblance of decorum thanked Raihan for his story. He then acknowledged the eager signal of the usually meek and unexcitable, Qamrul, who was a relatively new addition to our number. Much to my horror the uncensored part of our evening continued. His inhibition relaxed he delivered his opening gambit.

'One man asks his friend, "Hey, Shafiq, why do you have such a big backside?"'

I winced.

The punch line was worse, and Asif, having seemingly struck a rich vein of talent amongst the staff. No sooner had we lost Qamrul when his place was taken by Mutton. Surely the bashful Mutton could not further sully the proceedings.

Mutton's six monthly appraisal had required him to put some time into improving his English, and although he had worked hard at this, he was still sometimes hard to understand.

'There are two men in the desert with no water and a terrible thirst. They meet a merchant who is travelling with a horse and cart and a large supply of fruit. "Please can we have some of your fruit?" the men ask. The merchant replies "If you want my fruit then first I must put one pineapple up your beck..."'

'...up your beck?' I thought to myself, what on earth does he mean. Then it dawned on me 'up your beck...back...backside', another bottom joke.

There was nothing for it, other than to restore some semblance of order, and as Mutton regained his seat, I was found myself looking down from behind the microphone on the panorama of the evening.

Brenda and I left the party with our colleagues energetically 'strutting their stuff' on the dance floor in a mixture of styles that drew upon both cultural styles and definite seventies influence. Waving our goodbyes to the drivers, we set off to pass by Douglas's apartment to check out what it was that had caused his unforeseen absence form the evening's events.

chapter twenty-nine

Masum and I were on a vital mission to replace the dead goldfish that I had plucked from the surface of the office tank that morning. For Mala to discover such an incident was unthinkable. The tank had been purchased in keeping with the company policy of adhering to all things lucky in the ways of the Chinese, its installation timed to coincide with the visit of our superstitious group chairman.

When first I had set out to buy a goldfish and tank, my misgivings at the likelihood of there being anything approaching a pet shop in Dhaka were unfounded. A mile or so up the very street on which the office was situated a linear market ran up one side neatly broken up into sections of vegetables, meat, fish and finally animals. From one of half-a-dozen fish salesman, I had bought a tank complete with an overly ornate wooden stand which, after amendments to the design, was deemed suitable to grace the office reception.

Although it was probably quicker to walk, I summoned Masum from the car park and, having paused long enough for me to jump in, we shot out from between the gates to the office compound into a tiny gap in the assorted traffic. A sharp right hand turn and a deft foot on the brake brought us up sharply and we assumed the more sedate speed of the vehicles squeezed around us as they edged their way in the in the direction of the market.

Idling rickshaw *wallahs* looking for business blocked the inside lane in front of the assorted shops and stalls. Having overshot the market in circumnavigating them, Masum eased the car out of the traffic, mounted the kerb, and brought us to a standstill, the offside of the car hard up against the concrete wall of a Dhaka municipal refuse collection point. Stepping from the gently listing car, I was struck simultaneously on both shoulders, the head, and a glancing blow to the chest by what, on first sensation, I took to be water. This water was of a more solid and clinging variety than I had encountered before, and as I pulled my shirt out in front of me to inspect it, there was no mistaking the bluish splash on my shirt. Unwittingly I had stepped into the line of fire of a row of crows, waiting, patiently on a telephone line above the rubbish, for some tasty morsel. Had someone emptied a bucket of the stuff over my head I could not have been more comprehensibly splattered. But, having made it to the market, I braved the curious glances of passers by as I chose my fish, before asking Masum to take me home to bathe and change.

Accompanied by the latest addition to the staff, who seemed unperturbed by his transition from tank to plastic bag, I sat back and ruminated on the probability of being struck by two birds at once let alone five or six, as Masum drove the well worn route home. My messy baptism was in keeping with a sequence of events that marked a downturn in our fortunes. A series of disruptions to the order in our lives that we had worked so hard to establish.

One of these had being the reason behind Douglas's absence from the staff party. The slight dogleg to his apartment on our route home from the restaurant had taken us no time at all on the deserted night time streets. We had turned off the main road and down a track to his brand new apartment building. The gleaming, white-painted concrete block stood adjacent to a still yet, to-be developed piece of waste ground, which had been colonised by a group of the city's more colourful and less fortunate inhabitants. Normally at that hour of the night, any self respecting slum dweller would be sound asleep. However, on this particular night, it was clear by the amount of people milling around and camp fires still lit that something fairly momentous was taking place.

Part of the appeal of the apartment to Douglas had been the large plate glass windows which gave the impression of space and afforded an excellent view of the nearby Banani Lake. He had never actually got round to installing blinds or curtains and, as a result, the fully lit second floor of the building set against an inky backdrop was quite a landmark. As we approached, a dark object silhouetted against the bright interior spiralled out through a window and fluttered to the ground, precipitating a struggle amongst the people below, each of them eager to stake a claim on it: Douglas was moving out.

A combination of disenchantment with his surroundings and the toll they had taken on his private life, had led him to make the decision to leave Bangladesh, after having only worked a little over six months of his contract. His unorthodox moving strategy ensured a liberal redistribution of wealth in the community from which we, too, had benefited with the addition of a small sofa of Indian extraction to our collection of sub-continental furniture. Our own careful assimilation of souvenirs could not have been in more contrast to the careless way with which he dispensed with his material life, delighting at the thought of rickshaw *wallahs* and their spouses mincing around in his girlfriend's designer clothing.

We had been sad to see him go and Brenda and I had made a point of going to the airport to see him off. It had not been a stress free send-off, the security guards on the gate to the check in area following their instructions to the letter and barring the entry of anyone not in possession of a ticket. We left him fighting with a heavily laden trolley, a number of pairs of *bak-*

sheesh hunting, helping hands and barking orders at the local officialdom.

No sooner had we dispatched Douglas, than the news broke that our friend, Kim, had accepted a post in Cambodia. Images of past events flooded my memory at the thought of such a core member of our social group hanging up his Bangladeshi boots. His unorthodox, but exuberant displays for the illustrious Canadian Club tennis team. The sight of his thunderous calves pounding the roads in preparation for a notional marathon. Epicurean delights served at his well-appointed home, painstakingly prepared with the help of his devoted housekeeper, Choidy. His unflappable demeanour and good natured approach to all things. Only once had I seen him rattled, incensed by a flagrant display of queue jumping in a crowded travel agent in Calcutta. His uncompromising handling of the two dopey offenders had made me feel considerably better about my own past explosions in the face of sub-continental adversity.

As was befitting for one whose time clocked up in Dhaka had spanned the best part of four years, a number of events were staged to give him an appropriate send-off. All too soon, however, it seemed that we were back at the airport only this time accompanied by Peter and Sue, all of us having taken the precaution of arming ourselves with used airline tickets with which to thwart the over zealous doormen.

We bade him a tearful farewell, the scene made all the more poignant by the pathetic contents of a large oblong wooden packing case that the three men in the party had struggled with to get into the building. Polo, Kim's globe trotting hound, a South African Ridgeback Great Dane cross, having been heavily sedated had been incarcerated in what, with its metal grill looked like some medieval instrument of torture for the journey to Cambodia. The last we saw of him he was a pitiful sight unable to stand, with lolling tongue and half-closed eyes. Although in the first message we received from Kim a few days later, he recounted how Polo had apparently perked up on being stowed in the hold his barking clearly audible from the bowels of the aircraft. By the time the plane had touched down in Bangkok, he had broken out of his box and was last seen cavorting over piles of cargo, Kim having been summoned from the passenger cabin in hot pursuit.

Peter and Sue's household during this period had seen wholesale change. Their long serving cook, Mukul, had been sacked on suspicion of being in cahoots with a team of painters, the culmination of whose work at the house had coincided with the disappearance of Sue's jewellery. Having been secreted in the master bedroom, its theft suggested an inside job, rather than the product of a quick rummage around by some light fingered opportunist. The things that were stolen were irreplaceable including, amongst other things Sue's engagement ring and as such it was determined that the police be contacted.

This option would not necessarily be the one that first sprung to mind based upon the effectiveness of those police one observed on a daily basis. The ones marshalling the traffic at various points throughout the city wielded little power, which when exercised, had little effect on most of the population. Sadly the rickshaw *wallahs*, the slowest moving targets, bore the brunt of their vindictive frustrations, being harassed for small amounts of *baksheesh* or provided with a puncture from a practiced stab of a screwdriver into the top of their rear tyre as they passed by. It seemed unlikely that such a force was likely to be over stocked with super sleuths.

The job had, however, been made easier for them as the man who had undertaken the decorating commission had rounded up his unreliable workforce and assembled them in Peter and Sue's garden. There he had proceeded to beat each of them with a three feet long metal candlestick he had found on the porch until they divulged the whereabouts of the loot. Peter had returned from work just in time to halt the rough justice being meted out before anyone was killed and the candlestick bent beyond recognition.

This dramatic development only served to upset Sue further and, since the consensus of opinion was that the jewellery was long gone, the matter was placed in the hands of the police and the suspects taken away. Peter was required to file a report at the nearby ramshackle Gulshan police station and I went with him for moral support. We were afforded the luxury of an interview with the most senior officer, although not his undivided attention. Throughout the interview he continued a disjointed conversation with one of his minions, who would intermittently poke his chubby, sweaty face around the side of the door. Peter patiently recounted the events leading up to the discovery of the missing items and the officer took notes in an abstracted way. It was clear from his demeanour that we were wasting his, and our own time. From the frequency and increasing urgency of the interruptions, it was clear that he had other things on his mind.

Our visit had coincided with the arrival of a recently departed baby taxi driver, doubtless the victim of some airport road madness. On leaving the compound, Peter had utilised his six feet three inches to look over the heads of a gaggle of onlookers gathered around the back of a police pick-up truck.

'Uggh, there's a dead guy in there,' he reported. It had amazed me he needed to look.

We passed the police station, situated on the main artery through the centre of Gulshan, everyday. We had never really seen any great evidence of activity within the compound walls. Outside, however, was a different matter and the pile of twisted modes of transport deposited beyond the perimeter wall underwent constant change. One dreaded to think of the state of the occupants of some of the mangled vehicles which varied in size from flimsy baby taxis to buses, their rectangular shape bent to form a rhombus. I did not have to wait long to find out what injuries might be sustained nor to pay another visit to the police station.

Driving past the British High Commission Club one day, I was waved to by Abul, a small boy who had cornered the market in overseeing the parked cars outside the club. His remarkable grasp of English and tender years was a winning combination. For a small fee, he would provide his services as a *chowkidar* making an elaborate show of opening doors and polishing wing mirrors before sloping off to the nearest tea stall to await the arrival of his next commission. When I first encountered him, he had a horribly septic abrasion on his chin, which with the aid of our first aid kit I had cleaned up and dressed. He had made a speedy recovery and on subsequent visits had made a big show of greeting Brenda and I.

This day there was a strange urgency in his gestures and as I slowed and wound down the window his earnest face met mine through the open window.

'Saar, you docktor, you come!' He implored.

Cursing Messrs Boots, whose antiseptic cream had worked such wonders, as to turn me into a fully-fledged doctor, I parked the car and went to see what the matter was.

Abul ran ahead of me and slithered into a gully running along the side of the road that served as a storm drain. He was apparently undaunted by the fact that there appeared to be a dead man by his side an urged me to join him. Stifling an initial revulsion, I steeled myself and lent forward for a closer lock. Abul gently lifted the hem of the crumpled man's *lungi* and at the first sight of dried blood I bade him stop.

'Policeman need Abul.' I ventured and having assured him that I would be back in double quick time jumped into the car and sped of in the direction of the police station.

Much to my silent jubilation my visit was taken seriously by the local force and I was ably dealt with by a large man, with sergeant's stripes and a modicum of thickly-accented English. Relishing his contact with a foreigner he took every opportunity to manhandle me, shaking me warmly by the hand repeatedly ,and resting a friendly and heavy arm across my shoulders. So entwined, he led me out of the police station, rallying a group of subordinates idling on a bench to accompany us as we made our way out of the police station.

I felt distinctly uneasy at his request to travel with me as like the entire expatriate population I had never formalised my Bangladeshi driving qualifications. Consequently I set off at a very sedate pace, the lead vehicle in a small international convoy threading its way through Gulshan bound for the aptly named 'United Nations Road' in Baridhara.

Abul had not left his post and came skipping up to the car as I brought it to a standstill.

'Man not sleeping!' He announced which, was indeed, good news.

My new best friend, the sergeant, deployed his men to rescue the casualty, pausing briefly to send poor Abul on his way with a torrent of gruff Bangla. It was evident that he viewed the self-appointed British High Commission Club *chowkidar* through rather less sentimental eyes than I. This difference in our attitudes highlighted, I decided it was time that I take my leave. My mind suddenly filled with expat folklore horror stories of blame being apportioned to unwitting foreigners by dint of being in the wrong place at the wrong time at the scene of accidents.

That evening we were invited to the house of the man of the 'thirty chickens' fame and at dinner I recounted my story.

'I really was pleasantly surprised by how helpful the police were.'

'Haa! How long have you been in Bangladesh?' Came the scornful response. 'As soon as you went away they will have taken any money the man had and thrown him in a ditch somewhere.' He concluded with a grin.

I could make no claims to be the world's leading expert on local culture and had always regretted my failure to get to grips with the language; which was surely the key to greater insight. Instead I was a *bideshi* who had a comfort level in existing despite the chaotic system. Could the outlook for those who lived within it really be so bleak?

chapter thirty

Way back in Bombay, Brenda's counterpart had likened working for a company whose approach might have at times been dubbed 'cowboy', but nevertheless whose growth in Asia was unprecedented, to working for a friend. It had been exciting and we had gone with the flow. We had arrived with no money and contracts left deliberately ambiguous but we were, as in the words of an enlightened employee 'Pioneers'.

Under the original brief, our job had been complete for some months. The office was fully functioning, and we had peopled it with an interesting mix of people drawn from the local labour pool. With our two year horizon approaching, our appetite for life at the cutting edge of third world business development was on the wane. Although we had no definite departure date set in stone, subconsciously we were on the home straight with our minds set on the prospective return to London and its associated creature comforts.

I had made some tentative enquiries regarding employment in the UK and, although job-hunting from four thousand miles away isn't to be recommended. I had got an offer from an ex-wine trade colleague. A combination of the urgency with which I was required in London. and a souring of relations with Mala. who for some reason had taken it upon herself to withhold a payment to which we were contractually obliged, saw our plans gain momentum. I had tendered my resignation after a great deal of soul searching since to do so at this time would require

Brenda being marooned in Dhaka. For her to honour her contract, she would have to stay an extra six weeks beyond my notional departure date so securing the position promised at the group's London office as part of the deal at the outset.

The neat dovetailing of my jobs was too good an opportunity to pass over. If the truth be known, I had in fact racked up ten more weeks in Dhaka than Brenda if one totalled all her overseas business trips. Pointing this out was little consolation to her and although she would have a ready made roommate in Mike, whose wife had returned to the States, the prospect of being a single in Dhaka was a dire one. A plan was thrashed out that we pack up our life together and that Brenda return to the UK with me in order to lay the groundwork for her transition to the London office. Having safely bedded me in, she would then return to the sub-continent to enjoy the spoils of Mike's bachelor life and concentrate her energies on studying for her next bout of professional exams.

As far as preparing for our departure, the most pressing thing on my mind was that our visas were going to run out. Each of us tantalisingly thirteen days short of our target date.

'How long?' I responded incredulously to poor Rana who had returned from the Passport & Immigration office with the gloomy news that extensions of our business might take anything up to three months. It seemed ridiculous and extremely unlikely.

'The problem, Mark, is that for persons who have been resident in Bangladesh for more than three months there is some delay and maybe even then you will not get it.'

'Can we pay some *baksheesh?*'

The response came hesitatingly in the affirmative, but I knew Rana too well by this stage. It was the reply he gave when he intended to do nothing about a problem in the hope that it would eventually go away. Two weeks later, I would be asking how the application was going; fully believing the expedited version underway only to find out a month later that we were still very much at the bottom of a weighty pile of other hopeful submissions.

The simple solution would have been to move everything forward. However, we had plenty to do and Brenda and I had commitments. In a perverse way although I had had my dark days in this place, now that the end was in sight, I wanted to take my leave on my own terms and not in a great rush. The answer lay within the confines of Zia Airport. A day trip to Calcutta would enable us to re-enter Bangladesh and acquire a fourteen day tourist visa from the small booth situated just before passport control, in the innermost core of the terminal building. I viewed this option with scepticism mainly as it involved two avoidable flights, somehow there had to be a better way.

The initial excitement that had coursed through me on coming up with an alternative strategy was now starting to be replaced by feelings of trepidation. Masum hunched over the wheel was steering a path to the main terminal building at the airport. In the back seat, one hand resting protectively on a plastic wallet on my knee that contained a counterfeit Board of Investment VIP document, I ran through the finer points of my plan in my head.

I consulted my watch, 11.55am, I was on schedule for the arrival of the 12.15 Thai flight from Bangkok but with little margin for unforeseen delays.

'VIP Saar?' Masum asked his eyes fixed on the road.

'Na, e-straight.' I intoned in my best Banglish pointing a finger past his left ear and into his line of vision. Past the large concrete arrow directing us to the VIP entrance we drove and mounted the ramp that led up and round to the front of the terminal building. We went past a couple of baby taxis depositing their loads of people and exotically packed belongings before coming to a stop in a designated no parking area directly outside the entrance. With the car barely stationary, Masum had his door open and placed one foot out on the tarmac. With the well-practised technique of stretching back to grab the handle of the back door he heaved himself out of the car and opened my door in one fluent motion. I pressed a five taka note into his hand for the car park and with no luggage to retrieve he was back in the car and heading off down towards the car park before a policeman, moving cars on, could turn his attention to him. From my plastic wallet I retrieved a used airline ticket cover, which worked its magic when waved under the nose of the security guard, and I walked unchallenged through the doors into the departures area.

There was really very little of Zia Airport that I didn't know my way around. In moments of panic when official VIP collections were not going to plan, I had sprinted up to the offices of airport manager in the gods of the building, searching a warren of offices for anyone who would see reason. Waiting for delayed flights, I had investigated every corner and even had a nodding acquaintanceship with various characters within the building, in particular the teller at the Bureau de Change who would totally illegally exchange Bangladeshi taka for dollars after a furtive glance around the horizon. As such I knew that one could freely descend the staircase situated just to the right of the entrance, which according to a flimsy sign on a hastily constructed post, was declared off limits to passengers. At the foot of these stairs lay a goldfish bowl that gave on to a vista of the entire 'arrivals' area, from baggage carousels to the distant desks of passport control at the end of the great corridor of a room. This glass encased area was set aside for a privileged few, sanctioned by security to watch for their arrivals, although, as I had demonstrated, was by no means off limits to those of a slightly more determined nature.

At the foot of the stairs, encased by more glass, lay the key to my success. A small cubicle housing two security men who, if taken in by my bogus official note, had the power to issue me a security pass that would literally give me the run of the place.

'*Asalaam alaikhum.*' I opened authoritatively 'VIP, Board of Investment, I am this man.' I ran my finger under my name on the paper and pushed an official looking laminated identity card complete with photo—and also made by me—under the glass to accompany the paperwork.

The surly individual, behind the glass, retrieved the day's ledger from a shelf below the counter and, noisily sucking his teeth, searched the entries for my name and my document's reference number.

'Na. is not here.'

Well of course it isn't: I resisted the temptation to respond.

'Maybe there was a problem with the fax from the Board of Investment.' I endeavoured to shed some light on the mystery.

The man consulted with his colleague. This was the make or break part and I had been turned away at this point before; even when in an official capacity. After an agonising wait the ledger was turned round to face me and swiftly I entered my details and signed the entry before receiving my clip-on badge that would give me access to the 'arrivals' area.

Checking the one dusty monitor slung from the ceiling, I noted that the Thai flight was thankfully on schedule. I wandered over to the three passport control desks, each manned by two officials, that formed a bottle neck in the corridor leading from the arrival gates to the main vestibule and, walking as far beyond them as was permitted, I leant casually against the wall and waited. Ahead of me, nestled in the corner my ultimate goal, the visa issuing kiosk. I was in position, I had our passports, I had the dollars, now all I needed were some passengers. The first feet appeared on the stairs at the end of the corridor. The first trickle of business class not nearly enough to provide cover.

Now that I had got this far I felt it was unlikely that I would be challenged, but I preferred to wait for at least one other visa-less person.

At last he arrived and I dodged between his fellow passengers, my progress to join my fellow 'traveller' hampered slightly by being the only person going against, rather than with, the flow.

'Now you take the pass-i-port to pass-i-port con-tro-lll.' The rolled ending of the word offered in advice sent shivers through me. Passport control? I hadn't really reckoned on that. Nevertheless it was my turn and I pushed the two passports through to the official and the prescribed amount of US cash. In theory I would be all right. I had collected visas in this way for visiting business people and then gone on to get them stamped by immigration.

'Thwack, Thwack', two stamps went into our passports and with a nod of thanks I gathered them together and joined the queue of the incoming passengers as though I, too, had just arrived from Thailand.

As the queue shuffled forward, all those things that should have perhaps occurred to me earlier rather unhelpfully occurred to me then. Would they notice that I had an entry stamp in my passport, yet no evidence that I had left the country? No, surely I had so many stamps in my passport by now that one errant entry would go unnoticed. What if I was to be found out? I started to concoct a feeble defence, '*Well if the system wasn't so ridiculous, I wouldn't have had to resort to this!*' That would not go down too well. I began to sweat. I began to sweat a lot.

'BAD IDEA, BAD IDEA' thundered between my ears as the queue worked its way past the official. '*OH GOD, OH GOD!*'

Then with a rush the sounds of the real world broke through and, with a feeble smile, I found myself handing over our documents. A squat individual clad in combat gear, which did little to calm my nerves, shot a glance at the badge clipped to my lapel and then turned his attention to thumbing through the two passports. Laboriously he flicked back and forth between the pages pausing eventually to break the back of each in turn, to ensure they remained open at the correct place so that he might endorse our newly purchased visas.

Thankfully I gathered them from the desk and resisting the temptation to break into a run set off for the exit.

'HEY!'

I stopped dead in my tracks and turned to meet my fate. With a careless nod of the head my official indicated that his partner, seated at a console behind him like the co-pilot in a bi-plane, had his part to play. Cautiously I eyed the computer terminal would this be my undoing. As Mr and Mrs Mark were typed into the database would every bell and whistle erupt in the building. Thankfully not. This time successfully taking my leave from passport control, I made for the goldfish bowl and made my exit out into the midday sun still a free man, resisting the temptation to punch the air and cry 'Yesssssss!' until we were a mile or so away from the airport.

The visa situation remedied, we were able to concentrate on taking our leave of our surrogate home, and as such our energies were concentrated on two areas of activity. The conclusion of all aspects of our personal life and my departure from the corporate microcosm we had helped to create.

We had accumulated all manner of paraphernalia associated with living in the sub-continent that, when it came to living in London SW12, were surplus to requirements. The cyclical nature of expatriate postings provide a ready market for the purchase of household effects and the club notice boards always seemed to have one or more lists of items for sale. Moreover these lists provided considerable entertainment and fuel for gossip for those not in the market since the lengths to which some people would go in attempts to plumb the depths of meanness were indeed extraordinary. In making our inventory we had thought better of including half used bottles of shampoo and restricted our hand me downs to the more standard fare of cane furniture, electrical transformers and our peculiar plastic washing machine. We had pinned our notice hopefully to the Canadian Club notice board and with a mixture of delight, relief and dread soon afterwards received our first enquiry. Jalal, the Canadian Club tennis professional, was the caller and having paid us a visit to assess the goods made us an outrageous offer for the entire list which we gratefully accepted so ridding ourselves of one potential headache.

This still left us with the small matter of the hundred and eight items we had shipped from the UK, not to mention several newly acquired bulky items of furniture. Having been warned that we might encounter a slight shortfall in performance of local contractors, compared to the whirlwind efficiency of the packers who had dispatched us, we decided to go for a dry run. At the front of the flat we had a room full of things that had sat idle for approximately two years. Rather than find homes for these belongings of varying degrees of uselessness, that we had brought with us out of sheer laziness and since they were things we could plainly do without, we thought this a good place to start.

Our movers had been selected for us, singled out on cost rather than reputation. The relief that our company had honoured Brenda's contract in this respect quickly abated when a slightly shell-shocked looking, ramshackle group of vest and *lungi* wearing packers had been deposited at our front door. The tools of their trade a heap of flat second hand cartons and a football sized ball of string.

We had failed to consider the fact that, if one's own possessions are limited, it might be hard to conceive that any individual who has more than his fair share of apparently useless objects can value them highly, if at all. Foolishly we had left the packers to their own devices and really should not have been surprised at the consequences of this rash decision. When we had popped in to see how they were getting on, the most visible violation of our belongings had been committed against a Norwegian sweater and acoustic guitar. We found the instrument propped against a wall, the neck protruding through the neck of the sweater, the arms of which having each been stretched one complete revolution had been neatly secured with a tight knot. Had this not been intensely annoying it might have been deemed an extremely sophisticated combination of items with similar attributes to minimise on space. Further aberrations met our eyes, mainly involving the folding of items not intended to be folded to squeeze them into the tiniest of gaps. An investigation of one of the packed boxes had disclosed a number of L-shaped shoes and a layer of loose glass and ceramic items wedged into place with paperback books. These were innovations that we could do without, and it was soon apparent from our initial experiment that packing to go home would be a lengthy process and one that would require close supervision.

While we selfishly fussed about the dismantling of our Dhaka home, there were two individuals for whom to witness this must have concentrated the mind. Lawrence was very vocal about his distress at the news of our departure. Whether this was on account of the fact that he was unlikely ever again to find a pair of employers who were such a soft touch or genuine anguish at his impending unemployed status was hard to tell. The enhancement of his wardrobe provided some consolation and we were treated for several days in succession to passable impersonations of Brenda as he alternated various permutations of her hand me downs. While if all else failed, he could comfort himself as he was apt to blurt out, apropos of nothing at all.

'My bicycle always remember me you!'

Masum, in contrast, had been reticent to the point of indifference. Together we had toured the city paying farewell visits to all my usual haunts. During this time I had attempted to discuss his future with him and he accepted my pep talks, delivered over his shoulder, with an occasional solemn and considered 'Yes Saar' but there was no body language to suggest that I was making an impression.

We addressed the updating of his CV, wrote letters of introduction to the American Ladies Servants Registry and potential new employers. We had been together to the branch of a local bank to open an account in his name and bought new shoes in Elephant Road. These were all feeble attempts to expunge my guilt at abandoning him and as if to make me pay all the more not a hint of emotion would he let go.

There was a suitable wailing and gnashing of teeth amongst my more junior colleagues at the office and, in order to give me a fitting send off, they insisted upon a party to commemorate the occasion. On the premise that they had missed our wedding in Canada, a Bengali version was staged. In the presence of the entire staff, down to contracted cleaners and lift attendants, Brenda and I were dressed, painted, garlanded and bestowed with a range of touching if not altogether useful gifts. The highlight being a presentation by Asad, Selim and Monir, the *peons*, who had saved and clubbed together to buy a garishly framed print of the Mona Lisa. Photographs were taken of the four of us together with me looking suitably delighted. Photographs were taken until seemingly every permutation of combined personnel and pose had been exhausted. We left them all dancing like whirling dervishes to the strains of Asif's ghetto blaster.

On the drive home, still in full costume, the cold air of the air conditioning chilled us. In the excitement of the end of day events neither of us realised that the garlands about our necks were soaking wet. As we struggled in the confines of the back of the car to extricate each other from our flowery necklaces Masum broke his silence.

'Saar?' He ventured. 'You, Madam, come my houch?'

Here was proof that the English lessons, the super camp Shanti, a local affiliate of the British Council, had been paid to impart had had some effect. Masum had uttered possibly the longest sentence I had heard him use. I caught his expectant eye in the rear view mirror. How could we refuse?

chapter
thirty-one

A driver-less Brenda and I peered through the early evening half light looking for a landmark as I slowly drove the length of New Eskaton Road. Approximately two years before that well-used phrase in our 'Masum speak', 'hotel backside', had been coined by him in response to my enquiry about the exact location of his home. It had worried me initially since one of the most populous and least fragrant slums lay just behind the hotel, but now that my knowledge of  the locale was considerably more developed, I had been roughly able to pinpoint our destination.

Although Masadur Rahman, to give him his full name, was nominally assigned to Brenda, my aversion to being desk-bound meant that I would seize any opportunity to venture out of the office and press him into service. As a result of the many official and assorted more spontaneous missions we had embarked upon, we had spent many hours together. We had discovered parts of the city that the mere thought of would have made the ears pop and noses bleed of that strange breed of expatriate for whom Dhaka was only one mile big and called 'Gulshan.' Unquestioningly he had taken me wherever I had wanted to go, whether it be on fruitless searches for imagined items that took my fancy in the most foul, stinking and inaccessible market or to drive blindly at official areas clearly signposted as inaccessible to mere mortals such as us. During this time I had gained an intimate knowledge of the back of his head, but little insight into his background.

Rana had ventured with his customary reserve that he was a 'good man' when pressed for his opinion which, was reassuring but largely uninformative.

Indeed, neither Brenda nor I knew any more about his private life than when we had first met him in the lobby of the Lalbagh Hotel. This fact might be considered all the more extraordinary since at the time we were entrusting our safety on that maelstrom of the roads of Dhaka to this quiet, woolly haired, Bangladeshi twenty-something.

Masum had sensibly stationed himself at the entrance to his street and had spotted us long before we acknowledged his energetic waving. I followed his signal and turned off the main road into a debris-strewn side street.

On the corner stood the inappropriately named 'Majid Mansion'. A brooding, overused, discoloured five storey block, set in trees enclosed by a high wall, blackened with mould cultivated by the open drain running its length. In contrast Masum was scrubbed and his clothes neatly pressed. I was pleased to note, as he opened the passenger door for Brenda, that he was wearing a *kurta* made of local Grameen check that I had given him. One could never quite be sure what became of gifts such as this in a land where just about anything might be traded for cash.

Despite its run-down appearance, the building had a pleasing symmetry, and as we were led through a gap in the wall that would once have housed a gate, our attention was drawn to the lower of two balconies set in the middle of the facing wall.

'Here my father have.' Masum made the introduction with an outstretched hand pointed skywards. A wizened Masum look-alike, who up until then had been contentedly watching the world go by, raised a hand in acknowledgement before turning his attention to some distant point on the horizon.

We left him to his vigil and followed our host down a heavily overgrown narrow path that circumnavigated the building. Ever since I had encountered a slim brown snake that slithered from beneath a bush outside a post office near the University, I had been somewhat wary of the local undergrowth. As thick leaves brushed our ankles I shuddered to think what creepy crawlies they contained. The odd cockroach in the flat was an occupational hazard and geckos quite acceptable. Playing tennis under lights after dark, we had encountered some fearsome beasties that would scuttle inadvisably across the court only to be dispatched by a ball boys' *plimsoll*. Now with a time span left in the country that could be literally measured in hours, I felt strangely vulnerable. However, I kept this to myself and unscathed we reached a paved area at the back of the building.

It appeared that the entire central section of the rear building was festooned with assorted garments placed hopefully in the humid night air to dry. This faded and bedraggled evidence that, in addition to the Rahmans, several other families were squirreled away inside the building. Masum indicated our goal, the second of a succession of landings, accessed by an external concrete staircase. With a steadying hand on a rudimentary concrete skimmed banister, the rounded top of which was worn smooth and greasy with the passage of time, and a great many hands, we followed Masum upwards.

On reaching his floor we encountered two young women standing stiffly to attention, heads bowed. The small enclosed landing where they stood appeared to be communal washing up area, and a bevy of galvanised pots pans, stacked in a small trough surmounted by a single brass tap, suggested they had been busy. Despite their obvious coy demeanour, they were excited that we had come. Brenda and I made fleeting eye contact, and exchanged toothy grins, before they scuttled away into what appeared to be the kitchen.

Meanwhile we were ushered into the adjacent dimly lit room.

A single table lamp illuminated an ostensibly brown room, which, at first glance appeared to contain only a double bed with an immaculately ironed white sheet stretched over it. Admittedly there was little room for anything else, but we had definitely had to squeeze between the bed and a glass fronted cabinet the only other item of furniture to gain access. Both feeling rather large and awkward in the enclosed space, when asked to sit down, we did as we were bidden and each took a corner of the foot of the bed. With that Masum disappeared giving us an opportunity to examine our surroundings more closely.

We had been in plenty of wealthy Bangladeshi's homes where a mixture of the best that money could buy locally, western influence and perceived taste made for an uneasy marriage. At the other end of the social scale the profusion of less formal dwellings by the side of any road, where people existed rather than lived, showed how unsophisticated human requirements can be when stripped down to items of necessity. This middle ground, in which we now sat was not how I had imagined it would be, and the austere conditions we found ourselves in I found as shocking as anything we had seen in Bangladesh. So many perceptions shattered in one blow. Masum's neat appearance suggested more than this. The casual way with which our hand me downs had been accepted, as though they might be tossed away. Here they all were. Last years Haq's Bay calendar and some postcards we had sent from London—the only pictures on the walls. The baseball cap we had brought him back from Canada attached to a nail by the door. Neat piles of our clothes, towels, glasses, crockery stacked in the one other piece of furniture, a long glass fronted cabinet no more than a foot from the bed. Even the sheet on which we now sat had come from us. Had he collected all that we had given him together to display for the evening or was this how they lived, all these people in one room, protected from the outside world by a single grubby curtain and surrounded by incongruous bedroom items?

The clink of plates announced Masum's reappearance and he paused in the doorway holding a small metal tray. I swung my legs to one side so that he could squeeze in to lay the tray between us. Bangladeshi goodies were neither Brenda's nor my forte, but these were exceptional circumstances and I steeled myself for the worst. Neatly laid out was Masum's approximation of what delicate *bideshis* might enjoy and he had obtained two of everything accordingly. Two apples side by side, two bowls of a rice pudding type preparation and two Heiniken beers in tin cans.

'But, Masum what about you?' We enquired in unison.

'Masum no eat, this my Saar and Madam.' He returned to the doorway and watched as we uncomfortably helped ourselves to his food and drunk his hundred taka a tin beer.

'My sister rice make!' He announced and she was duly summoned so that she might witness us consuming it.

After what seemed an eternity we both finished our rations, the tray was cleared away, and again we were left to our own devices. No sooner had we started to quietly discuss what the odds were that the rice pudding would make us both ill then Masum returned with a plastic bag. Unceremoniously he handed it to me as he had purchased it, the niceties of presentation dispensed with.

'What's this?' I enquired of him playfully. Shifting uncomfortably, he grinned and hid behind his hand.

Dividing the spoils, four packages rolled in newspaper, Brenda and I unwrapped his gifts. A brass ashtray with an aeroplane motif, a brass bell, a brass lady with two candle holders bolted to her hands and a stylised brass animal. It would seem that Masum had been to the brass object emporium. We both expressed our delight and I'm sure both inwardly determined to make sure to top up his *baksheesh* to reflect the outlay he had made on our behalf.

For such an undemonstrative individual this was, indeed, quite a demonstration of affection and we were both deeply affected by it. I, perhaps being slightly less in control of my emotions than my wife, found that I had tears in my eyes as we drove away from Majid Mansions, Masum, a waving silhouette in the rear view mirror.

Owing to the weight of brass gifts we were glad that part of our shipment had yet to leave. Divided into two parts the bulk of our possessions had been loaded into what we had thought was a sealed container a few days before. Three months later when I was reunited with this object in London, it was apparent that this was not the case.

'That's a vented container, mate!' The delivery driver had cheerily told me.

The fine white coating of mildew over just about everything, the result of the contents of our home being effectively lashed to the deck of a ship open to the elements for several weeks.

A small consignment of things vital to my existence in London were to be sent by air, and seeing these last five boxes off the premises was the last task before closing the door on 'Apartment 401' forever. Thankfully, since our departure was turning out to be something of an emotional roller coaster, Lawrence had left us without too much fuss, full of smiles asking that he be remembered in our prayers. A final look around to make sure that there was nothing we had missed revealed that we had done a thorough job. The beauty of the third world at your doorstep, whatever it is, someone somewhere will take it off your hands. Surveying the whitewashed, featureless space that was left, only the faint marks from where Banani Decorators had fixed the Christmas lights and our mosquito net still firmly plastered into the master bedroom ceiling, suggested we had ever been there at all.

So we left our Baridhara home with one last port of call before the trip out to the airport and a final opportunity to enjoy 'the finest place in Dhaka' as someone had once jokingly referred to the British Airways departure lounge. Lawrence had hung around with the guards at the gate of the building and enthusiastically waved a last goodbye as we set off down the bumpy unmade Road 6 to meet up with and take our leave of our expatiate friends.

Why the Salvation Army office had been chosen for this last reunion escapes me now and matters not. I found it to be almost a goodbye too far, too premeditated for any spontaneous displays of affection and more uncomfortable than anything else. I was teased mercilessly, despite my protestations, for consigning my poor wife to a potential further six weeks in the country, which added some levity to the situation. Peter with a captive audience couldn't resist an opportunity to ham things up and, when the time came to leave, melodramatically lay in front of the wheels of the car to halt our progress. Brenda would be back shortly to re-unite the group. Against a run of form that suggested that there were times when I could have quite happily packed up and gone home prematurely, perversely I found myself envying her this. London's central position globally between Asia and north America and our own regular trips to Canada would ensure that before too long we would all be re-united again but, notwithstanding, it was with a considerable lump in the throat that we struck off for the airport road.

Half a mile from the airport, a succession of signposts depict in a style, only slightly more sophisticated than the gaudy rickshaw artwork, views of tourist icons around the world. 'Biman Bangladesh Airlines invites you to New York, Rome, London, Paris' the world tantalisingly laid at your feet. When incarcerated in the city on my way out to the airport to collect some lucky person from the outside world, I had viewed these signs with something approaching envy. Now I would be the first to admit that somewhere in the last week I had acquired an extremely large and thick pair of rose tinted spectacles with regards to living in Bangladesh. Here we were on our way back to the so-called first world, with what had seemed a big step in going to live in the sub-continent appearing to be a considerably larger one in reverse.

Allowing ourselves the final treat of someone to carry our bags, we gave into the pestering 'official' luggage handlers who swarmed around the entrance to the airport departures area. Masum and I emptied our numerous bags from the boot of the car and Brenda confirmed the date of return with him so he might be there to meet her. With that she was gone, leaving me to press some *baksheesh* on Masum and give him a brief hug.

'I miss you,' he said gruffly in my ear.

'I'll miss you too, Masum.'

As I glanced back to give him a final salute, a restraining hand on my chest halted my progress.

'Ticket! Ticket!' demanded the security guard at the entrance to the departures area.

Brenda had gone ahead with both of the tickets, leaving me to protest at this last piece of Bangladeshi officialdom. Taking out the stress of my emotion-filled day on the hapless guard, I picked up my hand luggage and bellowed:

'LOOK YOU IDIOT I'M GOING HOME!'

July 1997 -15 November 1998 - Bombay, London, Cairo

Printed in the United States
75698LV00002B/254

9 781846 670015